STRAIGHT GUY
in the
QUEER SKIES

Brian Easley

STRAIGHT GUY
in the
QUEER SKIES

Brian Easley

Gatsby's Light Publications
Austin, Texas

Copyright © 2012 by Brian Easley
www.BrianEasley.net

Published by
Gatsby's Light Publications, LLC
Austin, Texas
www.GatsbysLight.com

First Edition

All rights reserved. No part of this publication may be reproduced or transmitted in any form or by any means, electronic or mechanical, including photocopying, recording, or any information storage and retrieval system without proper written permission from the publisher.

978-0-9829895-5-5

Edited by Christine LePorte

Cover & Author Photograph by
Brian Easley
www.BrianEasleyPhotography.com

Interior Design by Colin Shanafelt
www.ColinShanafelt.com

A very special Thank You to Amanda Pleva, Bobby Nelson, Colin Shanafelt, Colleen Kane, Dondra Nichelle, Heather Poole, Lon Monreal, Malin Nilsson, Niklas Pivic, Nina Lidder, Rob Cuyugan, Sarah Steegar-Delaney, Sharon Miller,

and of course, Mom and Dad.

Table of Contents

Part 1: Welcome Aboard
Now go abroad! 1

Part 2: Flight Attendant Training
Welcome to the Dollhouse. 10

Part 3: A Flight Attendant Overview
It's about to get real. 23

Part 4: Welcome to New York City
Breathe through your mouth.
Don't make eye contact. 57

Part 5: Getting to the Airport
By far the worst part of your day. 81

Part 6: Pilots and Air Marshals
A love/hate story. 98

Part 7: The Flight Attendants
Us vs. the world, and each other. 113

Part 8: Passengers
Without you, I am nothing! 141

Part 9: Inflight
It's business time! 173

Part 10: Celebrities
    A short chapter. 186

Part 11: Final Descent & Ride to the Hotel
    Buh bye!. 199

Part 12: Layover Hotels
    Your home away from home. 210

Part 13: Out and About on Layovers
    Bring a camera and a credit card. 229

Part 14: What I've Learned from Gay Coworkers
    From docking to donkey punches. 246

Part 14: Non-Revving & Commuting
    Marry me, fly standby!. 254

Part 16: Ill Effects
    What the small print says. 273

Part 17: Call to Duty
    Get out there and make us proud,
    "Straight" boy!. 278

Part 1: Welcome Aboard

Now go abroad!

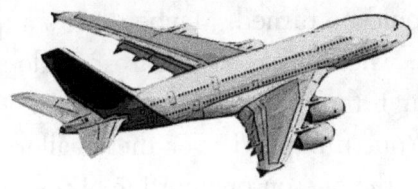

Chapter 1

You're a man, you think you're straight, and you've just landed a coveted flight attendant job. Congratulations! You've made a great decision, and I'm here to guide you through the complexities of your journey. You've just discovered a wonderful loophole in society that allows you to have a socially acceptable job that pays all your bills, gives you medical and travel benefits, and allows you the flexibility to drop everything you're doing for a few weeks and live like a stupid, carefree kid for as long as you want. You can make your parents proud and still do whatever the hell you like.

You said, "I'll cut my hair and go anywhere." You somehow managed to break through the walls that keep most straight boys out of this profession. Maybe your interviewer had a crush on you. Maybe he thought you could be turned. Maybe there's a quota. Maybe it's affirmative action, who knows? Who cares? It doesn't matter now. You made it through the mass cattle call interview and subsequent personality test. You triumphed over the smaller group interview, and finally through the one-on-one portion of the process.

Sometime very soon, as long as you pass that pesky drug test, you'll be heading to training for several weeks, the length depending on which savvy airline procured your services and how many aircrafts you'll be trained on. Some airlines only fly one or two types of aircraft, but others have six or seven! At the time of my hiring we had the McDonnell Douglas DC-10, McDonnell Douglas Super 80, Fokker 100, and Airbus 300, as well as the Boeing 727, 757, and 767.

I am going to tell you everything you need to know to make it in this crazy, unpredictable business and what to expect from everyone involved in your work life. You'll soon be wearing many hats: babysitter, nurse, therapist, mediator, translator, teacher, judge, supermodel, psychic, waiter, bartender, travel agent, whipping boy, punching bag, prostitute, track star, chef, mechanic, busboy, garbage man, fireman, and security officer—all rolled up in cheap blue polyester-blend fabric imported from Poland's finest sweatshops. The job description might have read something like, "Flight attendants' primary responsibility is to make sure safety regulations on airplanes are followed. They also do what they can to make sure passengers are comfortable during their flights," but you'll be doing so much more. You are the modern Renaissance Man.

Airplanes will be your cabs around the world, and oftentimes taking a cab to the airport will cost more than the flight to wherever you want to go. The world just opened up for you in ways you cannot yet imagine. Even if your airline doesn't fly to that many places, because of airline alliances and the ZED (Zonal Employee Discount) fares, you'll still be able to reach any corner of the planet for under $400. Round trip! Ignore for now that it's all standby, because flying standby is absolutely horrible, and I don't want to ruin this moment. Let's focus on the positive.

You'll be able to talk to anyone from anywhere about anything. You'll be able to agree with Californians about how the In-N-Out burger is the best hamburger in the world. You'll know that! You'll be able to complain with a Londoner about the cluster fuck at Covent Garden on a Saturday night. You'll sigh and lament with the Italians about how Rome turns into a scorching ghost town in August. You'll know all about the Coliseo Gallistico cockfighting arena at 6600 Isla Verde Avenue in San Juan, Puerto Rico.

When someone talks about their favorite pizza spot in New York City you will be able to confidently express your opinion and explain why their place is crap. Fuhgettaboutit! You'll know about the secret side door at Ajax stadium in Amsterdam that you can use to sneak into the stadium. You'll be able to weigh in on the best beach to spend Australia Day in Sydney on January 26th. You can dazzle an audience with your tales of how a testosterone-fueled bar fight in Austria is settled. Surprisingly, very often it's resolved by open-palmed slaps to the face, no real punches. A world traveler such as yourself will know all about it!

You'll sound so debonair when you praise the Japanese for their value of respect because you've seen the charming way the airline ground staff lines up and bows to your plane as you pull away from the gate in Narita, wishing you a safe journey. You'll know when the Ice Hotel is open in Sweden or where the best place to see the Great Wall of China is. You'll learn the rules of cricket. You'll be able to tell the difference between a Kiwi and an Aussie accent. You'll be able to quickly convert Celsius into Fahrenheit and back again without even consciously thinking about it. You'll know the exchange rate for seventeen different currencies at any given time. You'll learn little secrets like how staying on the top floor of a hotel may give you the better view, but sometimes it's not worth sacrificing the loss of water pressure. You'll learn all the clever flight attendant jokes like "the best ways to spread gossip: telephone, telegram, or tell a flight attendant" or "the best way to keep a secret from a flight crew, announce it over the PA."

You'll always be able to quote duty-free prices on liquor all over the world and know where to find the cheapest deals for each variety of liquor. Hint: they're all in the Caribbean. You'll also know the best deals on pills all over the world at the pharmacies and which places will give you what. You'll also know that the Big Pharmacy and Perfumeria at 615 Paraguay Street in Buenos Aires will deliver to the hotel! You'll quickly become an expert on sleeping pills because we all use them and talk about them. Just a pointer: the best way to mule pills across the border or through customs short of inserting them into your anus is to wear tightie whities and keep them down there.

There will be so many opportunities for fun for you, ones you haven't even considered. There are parties and festivals going on all over the world right this second! Any time one of your crew mates is going anywhere on a layover, if you don't already have plans, go with them! Especially if they're the foreign language speaker and you're in a random country where no one speaks English. Tokyo is okay by yourself, but life changing if you have the Japanese girl from coach as your tour guide.

    This job has allowed me to visit six continents, go to the World Cup in Germany, Wimbledon, and music festivals in England and Australia, as well as soccer games in Brazil, Holland, Italy, and England. I've hit parties like Mardi Gras; Carnivale; a random but endearing festival in Narita, Japan; Zwiebelfest (Onion Festival) in Griesheim, Germany; and Oktoberfest in Munich. I've seen the overly hyped Stonehenge, had brunch on Lake Como, floated on the Dead Sea, burned my eyes in the Dead Sea, gotten wasted on rooftop bars in Madrid and Sydney, sung karaoke in Tokyo, gotten a sunburn on Christmas Day at Copacabana Beach in Rio, gone to the Beatles festival in Liverpool, and seen a Chinese Beatles tribute band. I've seen The Last Supper in Milan as well as beautiful art at the Uffizi, Louvre, Van Gogh, and Riks museums, Tate modern, and Hermitage in St. Petersburg. Not to mention the wonders of the Erotic and Torture museums in Amsterdam. It's all there for you. It's sitting there waiting right this second! You can do and see whatever you want; you just need to do it. Nothing is stopping you now that you have this job!

    You'll sound like a prick when you mention the pâté you're serving at your party is from Paris, the olive oil is from this little place on the outskirts of Athens, and the Parmesan cheese is from a mom-and-pop shop somewhere in Tuscany, maybe Siena, you really don't remember. Oh, and that wonderful sangria you serve at your parties back home? It's just from a grocery store in Barcelona, three euros a carton. You can be that pretentious asshole! If you want to be.

    You'll want to apologize when your friends ask you about where you're flying next month and you sigh and complain that you have four trips to Hawaii and two to Zurich, but they're such a pain because it's so expensive there! They won't get it. They just hear that you'll be on Waikiki or hiking in the Alps when they're in their cubicles. Be mindful that even though a place may get mundane to you, it may be a dream destination for whomever you're talking to. When you speak about the job it's natural to downplay how awesome it is for all those people that have shit jobs, but let them know you're excited about it and don't take it for granted. Nothing is worse than someone who doesn't appreciate what they have.

Chapter 2

Because this wonderful new job, long-distance relationships are now possible. You've just expanded your dating area/hunting ground by five thousand miles in any direction. You can go to those places where they rarely see Americans and they actually like the accent and attitude. I've found that saying I'm from Texas rather than New York works out much better, even though I don't have an accent at all. For some reason people outside America are fascinated by Texas, not so much by New York City; they've all seen Friends and know what it's about. If you choose, you can turn into the complete stereotype and have a girl in every port. Most flight attendants don't have lovers in every city, but they may have a friend or two to hang out with in all the places they fly. It makes sense and after a while you will meet people in every city you go to.

You will see the grandeur of all that's good on this planet and beyond. Nothing is as beautiful as a spewing volcano at night from seven miles above. Even massive forest fires are breathtakingly gorgeous. The world looks peaceful from above, even in its violent fury. You'll see and fully appreciate the majesty of the Grand Canyon, powerful glaciers, the haunting Aurora Borealis, and amazing thunderstorms that offer towering thunderheads and lightning storms that will scare and thrill you. You'll see them so often, yet never get desensitized. It never gets blasé. If I ever get tired of looking down at the Grand Canyon, I'll know that I'm no longer a properly functioning human being.

Before you get started in your new career, and yes, these days it is a career and not just a phase, go to the store and buy the essentials. You're going to need an international electrical adapter, pocket-sized camera, and a change purse for all your foreign coins. Those are imperative—never leave home without them. Before those, though, buy a journal. Start it immediately if not sooner. I don't have many regrets in this life, but not starting a journal sooner is a massive one. Even if what you're experiencing and writing down seems ho-hum, trust me, in a few years you'll be so happy you had these times documented.

The way it works is very simple. You will not be taken seriously as a "straight" male flight attendant until you pass a series of tests. First and foremost, if you can go your first year without touching another man's penis, then your friends, family, and colleagues MIGHT stop making air quotes when they talk about their "straight" male flight attendant friend/son/coworker/neighbor/lover.

Most definitely you'll be met with disbelief and skepticism. You are guilty until proven innocent. You are gay until proven straight, but don't overtly flaunt your straightness; it'll seem like you doth protest too much. You'll hear phrases such as "closet case" and "in denial." That's fine, just let them roll off your back. Let's face it, you are a minority, and people will let you know that every day of your working life. Learn to love the gays. They are a lovely people. You're on their island and they can make your life miserable or wonderful. If you play your cards right, you'll have the best wingmen a single straight boy could ask for. Having a good-looking, stylish gay man on your side when you walk into any bar in the world will only help your cause. They don't give a shit about impressing girls so they'll be confident and completely at ease with even the hottest, most unobtainable girl. You can just take the backseat and let your new best friend do all the work. At the end of the night he's not going to be an option for her, so there ya go!

For the first few months your same-sex oriented coworkers will hit on you—don't think they won't—even though your airline might have strict rules about saying and doing inappropriate things on the job. Please, no one follows those rules. That's why we all got into the business of International Man of Mystery in the first place, right? Be flattered and appreciative, no doubt, but also be polite and unwavering in your declination. After a while you'll be down with the gay boys, and not a "closet case" or "in denial." They'll accept you as their token straight friend and all will be right with the world. Within the job you'll be stripped of your air quotes but you'll still have to work on the general public's opinion of you, and honestly, you'll never win them over. Just don't go touching any penises unless that's who you are. Don't do it just to fit in with the rest of your crew. Be above the influence.

Part 2: Flight Attendant Training

Welcome to the Dollhouse.

Chapter 3

Before you start your adventure of a lifetime, for a lifetime, you have to jump through all the hoops and get qualified by the Federal Aviation Administration. The FAA is something to be feared, just as most three-letter acronyms are: the IRS, DMV, CIA, FBI, CNN, etc.

You'll have to prove to your airline that you're fit to be put in front of passengers and perform basic customer service tasks. You'll also have to prove that you'll be useful in emergency situations. Your training will be torture, but not because it's difficult. You'll find that some people take it way too seriously and others just haven't been in school in forty years so the thought of having a test every week scares the shit out of them. They freak out and try to bring the rest of the class down with them.

Some people will cry on the first day of class when they show you the company's propaganda films and every commercial your airline has put out in the last thirty years. You'll look at these people in slack-jawed disbelief, but at the same time it makes you think that maybe you've really stumbled upon something special. People don't get teary-eyed when they think of their upcoming promotion to middle management, right?

Some of your classmates will be convinced that the company is trying to weed them out and trick them with the material. Don't believe it! It costs a lot of money to fly people in for the interview, drug test them, and then pay for their training/meals/boarding. It's in their best interest that you pass and go on to have a forty-year career up in the sky.

I know what you're thinking; forty years is ridiculous, you just want to do it for a year or two, until you figure out what you really want to do when you grow up. Everyone who's ever had an airline job, no matter how old and frail, has uttered those exact words. It's a cliché. It's a joke. It's on par with how everyone at Shawshank is innocent. When you try to tell that to your crew mates on the plane, they'll laugh and roll their eyes. Even if you have every intention of quitting after you get a little adventure and excitement under your belt, you won't be able to cut the cord and give it up. I said those words after I got hired less than a month after my college graduation. It's now fourteen years later and I'm still trying to figure out what kind of job would be great enough for me to give this all up. The job of a fight attendant is too easy, flexible, and fun. The sooner you realize that you're now a career trolly dolly, the better. Get used to the names too: stewardess, flight attendant, air hostess, air whore, sky slut. You'll hear them all, so embrace them. Most of the people who make fun of our profession are just envious.

Basically, the three things you'll be learning in these weeks at your training center are 1) Emergency Procedures, 2) The Food/Beverage Service, and 3) Medical Situations. The ones that are most important are the ones that you'll rarely need to even think about. You don't even need to pay attention to how they want you to do the food/beverage service. Once you get "on the line" you'll find out that the flight attendants do things their own way and will yell at you if you turn into Brainy Smurf and say, "That's not what the manual says" or "Well, they taught us in training specifically NOT to do that." Just go with the flow and adapt to how it's really done. It's usually easier to do it their way anyhow.

Your safety manual will be like your Bible. It has all the answers to everything you need to know. Much like the Bible, everyone has one, but few people have taken the time to read it from start to finish. You have to carry it with you all the time, though, and it's annoying because it takes up valuable real estate in your suitcase, as well as weighs it down.

The Emergency Procedures portion of your training is basically how to crash comfortably and how to get off the plane if there's need for an evacuation, both on land and in the water. It's important to know, but will probably never come up. They keep changing the crash position so we have to keep learning all these random positions. If you looked at all the different Brace positions over the years, it'd look something like the Kama Sutra. It's ridiculous; none of it matters. If you fall out of the sky from 35,000 feet and hit land or water, it really isn't going to matter if you have your head resting on your hands which are crossed just-so on the seat back in front of you, or if you're grabbing your ankles with your face in your junk. It really won't matter and that's fine. As long as we have a plan on what to do in these situations, passengers will feel a little better, a little safer. Deep down they know they're going to die, but we can all cling to that allusion of control and preparedness. I just don't see why they keep changing the positions. How do they test which position really is the safest if you splash down in the Potomac? Isn't it all hearsay and conjecture?

They want you to learn the commands verbatim, but every year they change what the commands are. I think the person in charge of all these changes is trying awfully hard to come up with new procedures in order to justify why his or her job position is necessary at all. No matter the wording, the commands all basically say the same thing: "Unfasten your seat belts and don't take anything with you." Your instructors will go on to say that if you're really in an emergency situation, afterwards no one is going to fault you for saying the wrong thing, as long as you get the people safely off the plane. I'm sure in real life, swearing would be mandatory. "Don't take anything with you" doesn't have the same effect as "Leave that fucking bag and get your ass off the Goddamn plane! NOW!" So, while it's really pointless to learn this stuff for real-life situations, you do need to know these commands in order to graduate from flight attendant training, so play the part, act like it's important, and just do it. Be a good little trained monkey!

There will always be someone in your class who will ask why it's done this way or that way and offer suggestions to make the evacuation process better, but just ignore that old lady (it's always an older lady). There's one in every class and you throwing a shoe at her every time she says "What if…" or "Why is it…" will only get you in trouble, so just go to that special place in your mind where the palm trees sway and the sun graciously coats you with tropical goodness as you sip the frosty beverage of your choice.

You'll learn about ditching in the water and it'll be scary because until very recently there has never been a 100 percent successful ditching. Someone always dies. Someone always inflates their life vest inside the plane as water fills up the cabin and they get trapped and drown. Just don't be that idiot. The best part about an evacuation is that you're allowed to do whatever it takes to get someone down the slide or out onto the raft. You can kick them, push them, toss them out bouncer-style by their ear. You can give everyone a nice slap on the ass if you want to. You can abuse the people and at the end of the day, you'll be seen as a hero.

You have to learn evacuations and drill commands for every plane you're going to be flying. They are almost the same from aircraft to aircraft but sometimes there are subtle differences. Sometimes the slide will have two lanes so that people can and should go two at a time, side by side. The commands you use for a single or double lane slide are different, not that it matters whatsoever in an actual emergency. Just drink the Kool-Aid and play the game. Nod and smile through clinched teeth. You're still just playing the role of a doe-eyed child and the instructors will be playing the part of kindergarten teachers.

Chapter 4

The next part of the training is Food Service. This is very simple, but for some reason you have to go over it for every single aircraft. If your airline has eight different planes, you'll have to learn eight times that you need to get those beverage carts out into the aisle eight to ten minutes after takeoff. No one ever does this. It's insane to go out so quickly unless you're flying from Dallas to Austin and the flying time is thirty minutes. You're still climbing and it's dangerous. Oftentimes, common sense wins out over what procedure says. Laziness wins out quite often too.

You'll learn how to use the ovens and the coffee makers eight times even though they are exactly the same. They'll try to teach you how to do a mid-movie water service and the proper way to pick up trash with a coffee/tea/juice accompaniment, but no worries, the line flight attendants will show you how they really do it—no water service and no coffee/tea/juice accompaniment. The line motto is, "If they need something they'll come back to the galley and ask." That line is used almost as often as, "That passenger didn't really mean to hit their flight attendant call light. I'm sure they're just trying to turn on their reading light."

The final part of training consists of Medical Situations. This is incredibly important, though you won't face these very often. They can range from air sickness to heart attack and everything in between. We've had pregnant women delivering inflight, cuts, seizures, fainting, food poisoning, hypoxia, vaginal bleeding (from a bite), burns, and people getting knocked unconscious after hitting their heads on overhead bins. You'll be taught CPR and rescue breathing and every year you'll get a refresher. There's a defibrillator on every plane and you'll be taught how to handle that. There's a medical kit that anyone can use and an Advanced Medical Kit that only an M.D. or D.O. can use. We're not there to diagnose what's going on, just to treat the symptoms.

As long as you're not working for an obscenely low-fare, no-frills airline, there's a great chance that a doctor will be flying on your plane as a passenger. If anything ever happens, page immediately for a doctor but make sure you say, "Is there a doctor onboard that will volunteer their services?" If you don't say "volunteer" the prick might try to bill the airline for putting the stethoscope to the person's chest and then simply saying, "Give him some water." You will never be so happy to hear a passenger's call light chime than when it happens two seconds after you make the paging-a-physician PA.

The most important thing to remember is to get the hell away if you see something happening, as long as someone else is closer to the ailing person. One of your most used lines will be, "I maintained service. I was not involved." That's all you'll need to say in the Accident and Incident report while the flight attendants actually dealing with the problem have a heap of paperwork to do. Sometimes you won't be able to avoid it though. Someone may be walking back to the bathrooms by the galley in the back of the plane because they're feeling lightheaded and they'll just collapse into your arms. It's yours then, and there's nothing you can do about it. That's when the training kicks in. The obvious solution to that situation, though, is if you see someone walking toward you at any time, run away as fast as you can!

The test on the Medical information is one of the most difficult parts of your training. Learn it. Know it. Live it. Unlike the emergency evacuation bullshit, you'll need to know this stuff. The emergency evacuation hoopla is just as effective if you improv. It's jazz. Dealing with illness is an exact science and you have to know what's going on. You really can save a life.

When it comes to New Hire training, just keep your head down and stay focused. It's easy. It really is. The older people will freak out and create this air of impossibility, but just ignore that noise. Your instructors want you to do well. They want to be seen as good instructors and keep their positions, so they want you to pass.

Just like in college you'll see that it's very easy to balance studying enough to get by and having lots of fun. If you're lucky you'll be staying at a hotel that has a bar and dance floor. My class had about twenty students under the age of twenty-five so we were at the bar every night. The DJ would let us play whatever music we wanted. We owned that place.

Flight attendant trainee hotels are very interesting places because all the locals know there are cute little stewardesses partying there, so they're there every night too. One creepy guy got arrested for pretending to be part of our airline training program. He told some girl that he was a former navy SEAL but now was with the airline and was going to play a terrorist in some security exercise in Week 4 of our training. Of course, she believed him and he took advantage of her willingness to get along with everyone company related. Luckily, the bartender noticed when he slipped a pill in her drink while she was dancing.

During training you can be sent home for any reason, so make sure you're nowhere near anything controversial. If you get halfway accused of something, deny, deny, deny! Admitting to anything will get you kicked out so you might as well make them prove that you did whatever they say you did. That'd just be a slightly more embarrassing situation but it doesn't matter. Once you get kicked out of training you might as well be dead to your classmates. They will never give you another thought and will forget your name within weeks.

Every straight boy in my class hooked up with at least two other girls from our class except for the married man who was my roommate and the weird guy who ended up getting kicked out at the end. It really is like a continuation of college. You're having fun, the gay boys are having fun, it's just the older ones who are stressing in hell. It's fantastic. For me, the fun started the very first night of training when we were given our Safety Demo equipment. We were supposed to partner up and practice making the PAs while the other one demonstrated how to put on the seat belt, showed off the briefing card, donned the life vest, and put on the oxygen mask. Alcohol was involved and it turned into a truth or dare game where we both did the demo in our underwear, half serious/half striptease/all hot. I knew then that this might just be the job for me.

Chapter 5

Since airline classes start every week, there's a good chance that classes ahead of you are staying in your hotel or training center. Find them and ask them what to expect week to week. They'll tell you what's what and most likely give you the answers to the tests. They won't care, they'll be too caught up in themselves and how they're senior to you and everyone knows that seniority is EVERYTHING. It is. Nothing else matters. They'll want you to pass so you'll be under them, plus they just like sounding like smarty-pants.

Before training starts, the airline will give you a list of hundreds of airports and their three-letter code. You're supposed to have these memorized by the first day and they act like you'll be tested on it. You won't be, so don't sweat it. Don't even waste your time.

During the course of training you'll learn top secret methods of what to do if terrorists try to take over your plane. You'll be taught and you'll be tested. You'll know exactly what to do and what not to do, but you won't be able to tell anyone. When you receive updates on these measures and tactics, you'll be instructed to destroy the communication immediately and not to just casually throw the paper away in a bin. No, it says to Destroy After Reading, like you're a spy who's just been given classified information. For all practical purposes you are, and that should make you feel a little bit important. It should also shed some light on how dangerous this job can potentially be. Never mind that you're bouncing along at six hundred miles per hour, seven miles above the ground, getting exposed to insane amounts of radiation, and if anything happened you're certain to die. No, in addition to that glaring reality you also have to worry about one of your passengers doing something to expedite the plane being brought down.

The first time you go through security and witness the high-quality people TSA hires to protect the airlines, you'll be scared shitless. Just don't think too deeply on it and never, EVER, talk back to TSA. Yes, add TSA to the evil three-letter anagrams to be fearful of. No matter how ridiculous they are, they are the authority and can make your life hell. They may also throw coffee on you. Just smile and nod when they miss the infant going through the X-ray machine because they're too busy texting or checking out the underaged Dominican girl wearing next to nothing, bending over to take off her shoes.

In training they teach you that a great all-purpose tool is your wings. Pretty much anything that may need to be unstuck, freed up, popped, pierced, slowed down, or punctured can be done by the sharp part of your pin-on wings. If the oxygen masks fail to drop in the event of a decompression, you poke the manual drop button with the point of your wings and they release. If your inflatable life vest inflates too much and cuts off your breathing, you pop the vest with your wings. If a hijacker needs to be slowed down and you only have the items on your body, those wings right into the eye is the way to go. Can't get the milk open? Stab it with your wings. Need to put holes in the OJ to get air flow and a smooth pour? Use your wings. Someone gets a splinter? Dab the point of the wings into the vodka to sterilize and then dig out the splinter. Gum stuck where the headphones need to plug in? Clear out the area with your wings. Your passengers and/or crew members grating on your last nerve? Dig your wings into your palm and focus on the pain. Anytime you face a problem that doesn't have an obvious solution, first ask yourself, can my wings get me out of this? Chances are the answer will be a resounding yes!

One of the most exciting parts of training is when you get to do a work trip. We had two of them—one was a turnaround where we flew to a city and came straight back; the other was an overnight. For me that meant a night in San Diego on July 4th with my best friend from high school, who drove down from LA to see me. After several weeks in the classroom, it really is an eye-opener when you see how theory makes way to reality. The best part about the overnight work trip is meeting up at the bar when you get back to the training center and sharing your stories with your classmates. Everyone had something terrible or wonderful happen and we couldn't get enough of all the recaps.

Toward the end of your training, people will start to flip out mentally. Eventually it gets to everyone: the tests, the classroom lectures, and the erratic hours, which often means waking up before the sun comes up. Some people go mental after week three, some in the last few days. Hopefully, your breaking point won't be until a week after graduation day.

I didn't have a problem until our class, or what was left of it, had to come up with our class song. Every class during their last week will go into the classrooms of the people behind them and serenade them with some cheesy song they came up with, usually a popular song with airline lyrics replacing the originals words. Our class got along great until we started our rehearsals, when it all fell apart. There were arguments on which songs to do, the choreography, the arrangement of the song. It brought people to tears and almost to blows.

This like this will invariably happen to every class. By the time graduation day comes, you won't even enjoy it. You'll just have this huge feeling of relief and you'll never want to see your classmates again, even your best friends, even the girl you tied up with the seat belt extension in your room the night before. You'll probably want to forget the stuff you had to do in order to make it through training, just like a prisoner must forget what he had to endure during his sentence.

Beginning with training, and during your flight attendant career, you will never know the days of the week again. You'll only know dates. Your weekend may be Tuesday-Wednesday or you may not have a weekend for two weeks. Then again, you may have a six-day weekend; it's whatever you want it to be. But forget the word "weekend" because you'll never need that word again. You can usually figure out if it's a weekend, though, based on traffic patterns during rush hour and ambulance sirens at night. If you're looking to pick up an extra trip somewhere in the month and you see that the fifteenth has a ton of trips available; it's probably a weekend. Most flight attendants try to avoid working weekends. They have husbands with normal jobs and kids in school. Some people, on the other hand, prefer to work weekends because it means they're in a fun place on a fun night. Also, everything will be in terms of hours. You will never have a "two-day" Moscow layover. It's a "forty-eight-hour" Moscow layover.

Part 3: A Flight Attendant Overview

It's about to get real.

Chapter 6

Before you start your career as a flight attendant, you must first watch every season of Lost. That way you can truly appreciate why you should be freaked the fuck out if you have all the actors that played the "Oceanic Six" onboard your flight. I can't think of anything more terrifying than sticking my head out in the cabin and seeing those six people sitting in first class. If I were them I'd just fly around together all the time to mess with people. Capturing the reactions on video would be as popular of a television show as Lost ever was. By watching the show you'll also learn some basic survival skills for when you crash-land on a fairly deserted island that moves through time and is patrolled by a smoke monster. Consider it an extension of your training.

When you start with the airlines you're going to give up a part of your soul, at least a little bit. You will definitely break some of the Ten Commandments, some immediately, others later on. It's not a job for the pure of heart, and if you have a generally optimistic outlook on society and where we're at in this year of our Lord, you won't in two years' time. You're going to see human beings at their absolute worst and it will affect you, but try to remember that airline travel is a nonstop hassle for almost everyone.

It begins when they start packing and continues when they're trying to get to the airport. Checking in is a pain in the ass and going through security is a nightmare for even the saintliest of people. I've seen a priest in his garb mutter "for Christ's sake" while dealing with TSA. Those poor passengers may have been poked, prodded, and violated six ways to Sunday before they even get to you. Cut them some slack and don't take it personally when they snap at you. Just turn the other cheek and remember that you're a brand new flight attendant and most likely on probation. The airline is test-driving you to make sure you're fit to be placed in front of customers as the face of your airline.

Every major airline has a probationary period that starts after you complete your training, when you get "on the line." During this hellish time (usually a few months) you can be fired for absolutely anything without an explanation or apology. One day you'll be working, the next day you'll be back wherever you came from. During Probation you will be scared shitless any time anything goes remotely wrong, no matter how ridiculous or insignificant. Any time you have to tell a passenger that you've run out of their first meal choice or that they won't make their connecting flight, you'll say it with unspeakable dread. Any disagreement with a fellow crew member is reason to toss and turn all night long. It's best if you just hold your tongue no matter what people say to you or how horribly they treat you. Like a slave, you just turn the other cheek and take whatever is thrown at you. Thank you, sir, may I have another?! You'll feel like you have no soul or backbone. In your mind you have all your witty comebacks and know exactly how you're going to tell the passengers off, but just file those away for a while. You'll have plenty of time to be a jerk right back to the passengers later on, but for now, you have to play ball.

You may find yourself allowing three hours' travel time to get to the airport when it normally takes forty-five minutes. You cannot be too careful. That day when you get off of probation is circled in red on your calendar. The skies will open up and your life will change that day, especially if you work for an airline that has a union. Once the union covers you then it's damn near impossible to get fired, no matter how hard you try. Feel free to use all the witty retorts and give all the attitude you wish after you make it off of probation.

Just in case you think you may get fired, though, here are some Must Dos that you need to accomplish ASAP. Once you've completed this list then you've pretty much done the best things you can do as a flight attendant and you can hold your head up high as you're being fired for gross incompetence or whatever they say you did or did not do. You'll also have the staple photographs and scars that prove that you were at one time, albeit briefly, a flight attendant. The flight attendant must-do list goes like this:

- Have your picture taken sitting in the captain's seat inflight
- Have your picture taken standing in an engine (not inflight)
- Have your picture taken lying inside an overhead bin
- Join the Mile High Club
- Stay out all night on a layover and show up for pickup without sleep or a shower
- Hook up on a layover with a local
- Show up to the airport on your days off and fly somewhere random, just because you can
- Sit in the cockpit for either takeoff or landing (amazing)
- Hook up on a layover with another crew member
- When you ferry a flight (no passengers, just crew) sit on a plastic tray at the front of the aircraft in the aisle and "aisle surf" during takeoff. Hopefully, you'll be on a wide body aircraft with two aisles and you can race a friend. Gambling will occur, not only on who wins the race but also on who bleeds the most. Fun times for everyone.
- Upgrade someone just for the hell of it. Let them feel the strong hand of fate reveal itself through you.
- Get an oven rack burn/scar. No one will believe you were a flight attendant until you have scar lines on your forearms. In fact, burn off all your fingerprints as well, just like a real flight attendant.

As a new hire you'll probably be subjected to a series of hazing rituals. We've all been traumatized by them. One is getting shoved into an overhead bin—see, you're working on that to-do list already! Another is when the captain calls back and asks you to get an "air sample." You'll be instructed to get two vomit bags and catch some of the air in the front and back of the cabin so the pilots can run a test and make sure everything is ship-shape. Don't fall for it, it's like a snipe hunt! The passengers will be entertained, at least.

Another classic is when the lead flight attendant asks you to check on the pilots because they've "been awfully quiet" for the last hour. When you go up there they'll pretend to be asleep, or worse, murdered. They really need to have a camera on for that one!

A favorite for the immature is to take the used coffee grinds and place them in saran wrap. They'll roll it up like a Cuban cigar so that it looks like a big piece of shit, then leave it on the floor in the lavatory or on the toilet seat itself. You'll be told to go take a look and deal with it. A good rule of thumb is to never do anything a flight attendant tells you to do that they could easily do themselves.

One of the best tricks ever is the fake drug test. Right before landing all the flight attendants will pour watered-down apple juice into a cup and tell you that you got a message in the cockpit saying that the entire crew is getting a drug test. To save time on the ground everyone went ahead and peed in a cup and you should do the same. When you come back with your cup of piss, the crew will be in stitches. If they're a truly hardcore crew, they'll take it a step further and take their own urine sample and drink it down while you stand there and stare in horror. Everyone will laugh their asses off at you. That one never gets old!

Chapter 7

After a few years you might think the flight attendant job isn't anything to brag about, but others will be fascinated by the job and lifestyle, so when asked, act excited, even if you're over it. Flight attendants will understand when you bitch and moan about having to fly to Paris yet again and how you're so bored of the same old thing, but think for just a second about how that sounds to a non-airline person. You'll sound like the biggest prick in the world so be mindful of who you're talking to. It may be your sixth trip to Rio this month, but maybe the person you're talking to has been waiting their whole life to go Rio just one time.

Every non-airline person has always wanted to know certain things about the flight attendant job. This can work for you in some rare cases, but usually it'll lead to annoyance. When meeting someone for the first time and the subject of employment comes up, pray that you're not the first flight attendant they've ever met. If you are, they'll take their big opportunity to ask all the questions they've ever wanted to know and they'll shoot them off at you like an AK47.

The script goes something like this… Stranger in bar asks you, the aloof drunk muttering to himself, your name. They don't understand what you say, they just nod and smile followed by, "What do you do for a living?" You cringe and mumble, "Flight attendant." Their ears perk up. At this point you know you're either going to hear them bitch about how their last flight went horribly wrong, or you're getting the dreaded Flight Attendant Interview. You pray for a lost luggage story. The stranger's eyes widen and without a moment's hesitation, out comes:

- What's your route?
- Are you gay?
- Do you get to fly all over the world for free?
- What airline do you work for?
- How long do you get to stay at the city you fly to?

- Do they put you up at a hotel?
- Do they pay for your meals when you're away?
- Do you hook up with all the stewardesses?
- Are you sure you're not gay?
- Can you hook me up with a stewardess?
- Can you get her to wear the uniform?
- So are you like called a steward or a flight attendant or what?
- How does your schedule work?
- Do you have a boy/girl in every city?
- How long have you done the job?
- Where are you stationed? (yeah right, it's like the military)
- Did you have to do some kind of training or schooling?
- What's the worst thing that's happened?
- Have you ever had really bad turbulence?
- Have you almost crashed and died a gruesome death?
- Seriously, you're not gay?
- Have you had any violent passengers?
- Have you had any celebrities?
- Do you see many people trying to join the Mile High Club?
- Have you joined the Mile High Club?
- How might I join the Mile High Club?
- Do you have Buddy Passes?
- Can I have a Buddy Pass?
- What was your major before you failed out of community college?

After going through that song and dance a few times you'll just stop asking people what they do because you don't want the question returned. When someone asks you, just say you're unemployed, it's easier for everyone.

Chapter 8

Now you might be asking yourself, "What could be worse than the Flight Attendant Interview?" Well, what's worse is sitting on a bus leaving the airport in between two people when one is giving the other the Flight Attendant Interview. In once such case I knew from the second I sat down that the young blonde was a flight attendant. I could tell by the luggage but it was confirmed when I saw a bidsheet sticking out of her bag.

There was only one empty seat on the M60 bus leaving La Guardia and it was right between this girl and this older guy. He was probably only thirty-something, but still a lot older than this girl. I guess they were already talking before I got on, so immediately I was right in the middle of their conversation. I tried to ignore it, but that was just impossible since they were both leaning in toward each other, right in my lap. I wanted to pass the time talking on the phone but it was in my front pocket and I couldn't get to it because the guy was all up in my bidness. They chatted for ten minutes about where they were from and where they've lived and finally, inevitably, it came out that for the last five glorious months she'd been a flight attendant for Delta Airlines. Then the questions came like an avalanche. What is your route? How long do you get to stay at the city you fly to? Do they put you up at a hotel? Do you get to fly for free? Have you ever almost crashed? Do you see many people trying to join the Mile High Club? Blah blah blah. I've heard it all before and can seriously answer the questions in my sleep even before the person asks them.

I really felt for the girl. It pains me to hear someone go through that, but the terrible part was that she was so new, young, and cheery that she actually enjoyed answering all these questions. I was horrified! I give one-word answers but she was expanding on hers. The whole interview should have taken seven minutes and forty-three seconds if she did it right.

To make it even worse, she didn't even answer the questions

correctly! She'd give an answer of what was glorious or horrible about the job and it wouldn't even be true. It might be randomly true one time but if you've been flying for more than five months, you'd know that it's completely, totally untrue over the course of a career.

I wanted to jump in and correct her on certain things but I knew it wasn't any of my business. Actually, that wasn't really what stopped me. I had no problem butting into that conversation. What stopped me was that I could tell the guy was really into the girl by the way he nervously and uncomfortably tried to ask more and more questions to keep the conversation going. He seemed like a nice guy and me butting in might have disrupted the little thing they had going. She was obviously into their exchange so why did I need to get involved? He might have seen me jumping in as some kind of cock-blocking and I didn't want to do that. She, being a sweet as pie girl from South Carolina, probably would've included me in the conversation and might even have started asking me a bunch of questions and ignoring him.

No, I did the right thing by not saying a word, but I would've given anything for an iPod to suddenly materialize on my head. The more interest he showed, the more cocky she got. I thought she was getting kinda boastful when she talked about how cool it was to have a morning macchiato at the Trevi Fountain and then dinner on a rooftop in Manhattan in the same day. Of course it is! Everyone in the world knows that would be brilliant, but you don't need to sound so proud of yourself. I've been guilty of thinking how bad-ass it is to see a soccer game in Milan and the very next day catching US Open tennis in New York. I catch myself in these thoughts but would never in a million years say them out loud. I don't want to be that guy.

Still, though, he was totally into everything she was saying and completely validating her superiority. What annoyed me the most, even more than the airline lies, was when she started dissing New York City because it's not acceptable to go out in scrubby clothes like it is in Charleston. I couldn't believe I was able to hold my tongue! She thought it was just the coolest thing in the world that you can go to the beach all day and then go to a bar in your flip-flops and no one would say a word. She didn't understand why New York wasn't like that and that everyone spends at least four hours getting ready for a night out, even to the local bar, dressed to the nines. Where the fuck was this girl hanging out? Had she never set foot downtown? Or in Brooklyn? I defy you to find someone at Max Fish who doesn't look like they woke up in a gutter and then dragged themselves to the bar.

Yeah, she was new to New York City, but I think after Week Two I'd found some low-key, hometown dives. You can walk into a bar in flip-flops and a ratty T-shirt in every single US city I can think of. That's not exclusive to Charleston, South Carolina. The guy (who was born in Jersey, moved to Pennsylvania, then Arizona, and now New York) kept his mouth shut and didn't even challenge this notion at all. I was sweating and squirming in my seat. He must have really wanted to screw her. Even if I really, REALLY wanted to win over a hot young stewardess on a bus, I still would've corrected her on this outlandish misconception. Enough is enough!

I mean, just by throwing out the names of a couple of neighborhoods or bars that are slack like that, he might have bought himself several dates with this girl.

"Oh, you need to go down to the East Village, Lower East Side, or even out to Brooklyn then. I could show you a ton of amazing places where the people are real and down to earth, and wearing flip-flops with unwashed hair. My favorite place is [insert specific bar here, preferably somewhere obscure that she couldn't find on her own and would need him as an escort]."

"Oh wow, that would be brilliant! I'd love to check out some places like that. Places just like in Charleston, South Carolina."

Boom! Just like that they have plans and you know she'll be excited about it. It doesn't even have to come off like a date, just a local showing a nice transplant where to have a good time. I really hope that all went down after I got off the bus. I seriously doubt it by the way he just kept letting her talk and talk and talk but who knows, maybe he grew a pair and popped the question.

Chapter 9

Everyone loves and expects an emergency story, so have a good one and know how to tell it. This is your moment to shine. All eyes will be on you, and your audience will hang onto every word. Every time you tell it, pretend like it just happened the day before. You'll be a hit at any party. I don't have a great one but this is what I got for the time being. I hope I never get to upgrade this story.

    We got on our Airbus (Scarebus) scheduled to fly to Santo Domingo, boarded the passengers, and then sat for about an hour. We were told different things: they were loading bags, the mechanics were looking at something, there was ice that needed to be cleared off the tarmac. Typical stuff. Once we finally pushed back and made our way to the runway, the captain came over the PA and said, "Ladies and gentlemen, before we take off we need to make a quick pit stop at the gate to fix a minor problem. It'll just take fifteen to twenty minutes and then we'll be on our way to the sunny Dominican Republic!"

    We got back to the gate and waited an hour for the mechanics to show up and then thirty minutes later we left again. We were told that whatever was broken was what enabled us to turn the aircraft inflight. If that thing stayed broken, we could only fly in a straight line. It sounded like an important thing so I was glad we got it fixed. The passengers were pretty understanding too. Only one guy was a problem. Obviously he didn't fly that often. Before we took off he started acting up so we gave him a rum and OJ and that shut him up for a while. Then he got thirsty again and went back to the galley and helped himself to a handful of minis. Ex-Goth and delightfully gay attendant Rondee caught him and made him put it all back. There was a brief argument but that ended once we told the guy we could throw him off the plane if we wanted. After that he sat down and we didn't   hear a peep out of him the rest of the time he was on the plane.

Everyone else was cool as cucumbers, which was amazing considering we were already three hours late and had a plane full of outspoken Dominicans. Usually a riot breaks out after a ten-minute delay, but actually having them on the plane and not sitting in the terminal helped. We taxied out to the end of the runway and I took my jump seat in the middle of the plane and stared out the window. We were supposed to take off at 1:55 p.m. but it was now nearly 5 p.m. and the sun was setting, as it does in February. Not that you can see the sun; it was overcast and gray and very, very cold. The wind chill was below zero and there was snow everywhere and it had been there for over a week. It would be weeks before it all melted away. There was an old Dominican man sitting right across from me. Our legs touched if we both sat forward so we both angled our legs away from each other.

The engines started up and we thrust forward. We were over the frozen bay still climbing when things started happening. First, the back of the plane dropped drastically. I've been on a plane when the entire plane lost altitude suddenly but this was just the tail. It felt like we were straight up and down in the air. Then the engines shut off and everything went quiet. From where I was sitting I could see Rondee in the back doing his Hail Marys. I looked over to the other side of the plane to Charles. Charles had been flying for a long time and was also a Flight Service manager. He was always calm and even-keeled. Not this time. He was still in his seat but he was also somewhat standing and holding on to the side of the plane. His face offered no reassurance to me or to the passengers.

The Dominican passengers were freaking out, though it was so quiet you could have heard a pin drop. The guys right around me were all looking at me so they could gauge how freaked out they should be. I was numb. I didn't look scared. I didn't need to be scared. As I looked down at the icy water I knew for a fact that we were going down and I could only pray that I died on impact. The plane took a vicious turn to the left as we continued to lose altitude.

From the window by my seat I could see straight down into the water at the little icebergs. I hoped to Jesus that they fixed whatever it was that allowed us to turn in flight. The last plane that went down around Kennedy had the same problem and something snapped completely off. Everyone died, even random unlucky people on the ground, right below where we were now.

The captain came on the PA and said in a restrained panic, "Flight attendants, prepare for landing." The engines came back on but we dropped again. We slowly started to turn back toward the airport. The plane kept violently shaking. Once we got faced back to the airport things settled down somewhat. The plane was still making weird noises but there wasn't as much shaking. I kept looking out the window for dangling parts hanging off the plane or things on fire. Everything looked normal outside but inside everyone was petrified.

We touched down and started coming to a stop. The airport had been cleared of all other planes on the runways and taxiways. There were several ambulances, fire trucks, and airport emergency vehicles following beside us as we came to a stop. Their response time was unbelievable. Once we stopped, all the emergency vehicles surrounded us. The pilots didn't say anything about what we should do. We were all ready to evacuate the airplane, but hopefully it wouldn't come to that. These pilots sucked about keeping us abreast about what was going on. We just had a fucking emergency landing and we didn't even know it until we saw the fire trucks.

After a minute all the vehicles turned around and went back to wherever they came from. We started driving back to the gate. Once we got there we had to wait fifteen minutes before the ramp people came over and directed us in. The pilots made a PA apologizing for the delay getting back to the gate. Nobody gave a fuck about why we had to wait to get back to the gate; we all wanted to know why we nearly ended up in the ocean.

The flight attendants wanted to know what went wrong.

We never got that answer. The agent came on the plane and told the passengers that the plane next door was going to Santo Domingo and there was room for everyone. They all left and the flight attendants got sent home. We hung around for fifteen minutes and talked about happened and tried to chill ourselves out. We were mainly waiting for the pilots to come out of the cockpit so we could find out what the hell happened.

Finally we opened the cockpit door and discovered that they were not even there. Somehow they slipped out before the passengers did while the flight attendant by the door was gathering up some paperwork. With them gone there was no way we would ever know what happened unless we ran into them again. We were so fucking pissed. We called them pussies, and assholes, and every other name in the book. After a while we realized that there was nothing else to do but just go home.

That day was the first day since my first week of flying that I thought the plane was going down. I wasn't the only one. I know every sound on that plane and I knew there was a big fuck up. All seven of the flight attendants knew it. We all thought we were going to die and it was really interesting to hear about what everyone was thinking during our three-minute flight. Most centered around the water being damn cold and hoping to die on impact. Most of the passengers had no idea how dire the situation was and how close they came to dying. When we landed, we just smiled and shook our heads, like we were annoyed that we were wasting more time getting to Santo Domingo. I joked with one guy that I thought the Dominican Republic would have much less snow than this. He didn't get it, didn't understand a word. He just smiled and nodded at me. Ignorance really is bliss.

Chapter 10

What I was not expecting or even warned about when I started on this journey was all the plane crash dreams I'd have. They started almost immediately. I think my first one came during the first week of flight attendant training.

When all you hear all day and all night for seven weeks is about mechanicals, crashes, evacuations, medical emergencies, emergency equipment locations, terrorists, hijackers, and general airplane safety, it really is no wonder your brain keeps it going even while you're in repose.

I had several dreams a week during training and I prayed that once I was on the line and had a life again, it'd calm down. I thought getting out of the airline bubble and exposing myself to non-airline things would do me a world of good. The frequency of the dreams did calm down, but never went away, even after fourteen years.

For my first few years of flying I'd have plane crash dreams once a week. Then it slowed to once a month. Fourteen years ago today I was in flight attendant training and I can say that now I still have these dreams at least once a month. I have more dreams about planes crashing than about sex, which is a damn shame. Can we at least mix the two? Please?

It took me awhile to mention this to my other classmates during training, but once the topic was on the table, we were all in agreement. I wasn't the only one suffering from this nocturnal hell. My classmates and I even noticed several prominent, repeating themes in these dreams. One was a recurring dream where we'd be flying over water at a very low altitude, so low that the tops of waves would lick the bottom of the plane. Eventually, a big wave would come over and drag the plane down into the murky depths.

Another universal theme was flying under things like power lines or bridges, sometimes through tunnels as well. I'd say at least half of my plane crash dreams have to do with power lines or bridges.

We usually make it under but our wings would clip something and we'd go down.

I wasn't really that shocked when I learned that other flight attendants had plane crash dreams, but I was fascinated by the fact that dreams of skimming the ocean and flying under things were shared by most of my colleagues. Even some flight attendants from airlines in other continents have said the same thing. I'd really like someone to explain that one to me! So be ready for these dreams; it's your destiny.

I've had many dreams of plane crashes. I've wasted so many virginal white canvases of possible nocturnal perfection on those damn dreams. They used to scare me; now they don't even faze me. When I was going through the seven weeks of flight attendant training, I'd have them nightly and intensely. I've had a million of them. I'd say I've had more dreams of plane crashes than sexual adventures. What a shame. Sometimes I'm on the plane; sometimes I'm even flying the plane. Sometimes I'm watching from the ground, and once I was watching from a control tower in Pennsylvania. The plane ran right into that tower I was in. It doesn't matter where I am; I can't escape the point of impact.

I've crashed a Cessna into the Chicago River, hit the Los Angeles Bonaventure Hotel with the wing of a 767, plowed through a forest, and overrun the runway in San Francisco and ended up in the bay. I have seen planes impact in downtown Austin, skid off into hangars in Kansas City, and have midair collisions over Manhattan. Every time, though, I live through it. Sometimes many survive, but I'm usually the only one. In fact, the passengers never survive, just me and sometimes the other flight attendants and pilots. I walk away with minor scratches and minimal bruising. I'm almost looking forward to an accident now because I've lived through them so many times and I know I'll turn out okay. I'll be a hero or at least some kind of super freak that defies impossible odds. Either way, I'm getting my picture in the paper.

My last dream was one of the scariest, though, due to the

intensely graphic nature and the fact that it lasted twice as long as a normal one. My bad-dream defense mechanism was on the fritz, I guess. It all happened in super slow motion. We were trying to land at La Guardia when a big gust of wind began throwing us around. When we were about five hundred feet from the ground, making that final big turn by Shea Stadium, the plane turned all the way upside down and did a nose-dive into the water. In a matter of seconds we went from flying in the air to plunging into the bay. We dove straight down into the depths of the water, but the plane remained intact. I was in the last row so I opened up some door in the back (that may or may not exist) and floated up to the top. Not only did I escape unscathed, but I also managed to bring my backpack, and the water didn't hurt my camera. Luckily for me the water's never cold in these dreams. It's usually a relatively enjoyable swim back to shore in bathwater temperatures, even in lakes in the mountains.

I've accepted the fact that I'll die in a plane crash. I know this. I believe it will happen during the daytime, mid-morning, and I think it will be on one of the smaller planes. I see it happening in Texas too. I'll go out the same way I came in. Yeah, I'm calling my shot.

Even though I've accepted this fate of mine, I know that when the moment comes, I won't be ready for it. When I heard about a recent accident involving my airline, it made me feel a little safer. There hadn't been a domestic accident in nearly twenty years. Now with that one out of the way, statistically, there shouldn't be another for twenty more. But still, the dreams continue.

Sometimes we go through some really bad turbulence—and I'm talking real life, not in my dreams—and I start to wonder if this is it. I mean really bad turbulence, where people end up getting concussions from smacking their heads on the top of the plane. Passengers will start gasping, not screaming, and looking at the flight attendants for reassurance. During these times of severe turbulence, the flight attendants look more scared than the passengers. I used to be like that. My thoughts would immediately go to my family and to a certain ex-girlfriend whom I never stopped loving, and I'd feel guilty about never saying the things I wished I had. I'd promise to say those things if and when I got out of the catastrophe, though I never did. It wouldn't sound sincere.

Now, during these episodes of severe turbulence I just sit there like a stone statue and watch the scene, trying not to yawn or laugh. I could not care less if we crashed or not. Me getting hysterical isn't going to change fate, right? There are a lot worse ways to go. This wouldn't even be painful, just surrealistically fun, like an amusement park ride.

Someone once told me that if you die in your dreams, you would die in real life, right there in your bed. I believed that for a long time, until I was twelve and had a dream about a skeleton of a skyscraper. It was a steel frame of a twenty-story building way out in the desert, surrounded by sand dunes. It looked like something that would come from a post-apocalyptic wasteland. It looked like they started building this structure, then perhaps realized nobody lived within one hundred miles of it and would ever use it, then abandoned the project. For some reason I was on top of that building and I fell off when a big gust of wind knocked me off balance. I felt myself falling for the longest time, picking up speed every second. I knew I'd be killed instantly when I hit the ground; the formula for acceleration kept going through my head and it didn't look good.

Sure enough, when I impacted my soul immediately left my body. My corpse was badly broken, every bone shattered, but there was no blood. After a few minutes of staring at the blowing sand piling up on top of me, I got bored of the dream, awoke, and that was it. So I died and lived to tell about it. There goes that dying-in-your-dream theory. Also, how the hell do you ask a dead person what they were dreaming while they were dying in their sleep? Then again, according to William S. Burroughs in Naked Lunch, there's something called Bang-utot, where you die in the midst of a nightmare. One "survivor" said a "little man" was sitting on his chest and strangling him. It's a Southeast Asian thing, I guess, but several people a year are said to die of that in Thailand. I got all this info from Burroughs and never bothered to do more research on the subject. I like that story too much to find out the truth.

I experienced an interesting twist on the usual ho-hum plane crash dream recently. For the very first time, I had one of these dreams while I was sleeping on the plane inflight. I was flying up to New York from Austin to work a trip the next morning. That was real, not the dream.

In my dream we had just taken off from LGA and after a couple of minutes the captain made a frantic announcement as the plane started struggling and flying erratically. Unfortunately, the PA system was really bad and I couldn't understand a word he said; it sounded like on the subway, or Charlie Brown's teacher, or Kenny from South Park.

I could tell we were going down but also turning around, trying to make it back to LGA. It was exactly like my near-death flight from JFK-Santo Domingo a few years ago. I didn't care. I didn't even look out the window to see what was going on; I just knew it wasn't going to end well. People were screaming and we kept going down and turning sharply. I just stared forward and tried to go to sleep.

Eventually, I looked out the window right when we were about ten feet from the water, though we were also right by land. You could tell the pilot was trying to go down in the water, but close enough where you wouldn't have to swim very far to get to shore. That made a lot of sense to me. He did a great job with the dying aircraft and splashed it down with minimal damage on the edge of the bay. The top of the aircraft was blown off, but that only made it easier to get out.

When the plane settled, no one moved. I didn't understand why, so I jumped up from my seat, climbed out the gaping hole, ran down the wing toward the shore, and jumped out into the shallow water. I knew we weren't supposed to bring anything with us but I also knew no one was going to run me down and stop me so I grabbed all my stuff.

When I finally got off the plane and to safety, I looked back and saw that the wreck was actually worse than I thought. There was a very good chance the people in the front may have been badly hurt or killed. My photojournalism training kicked in and I started taking pictures of this 'spot news.' Funny how my need to help the other people didn't really enter into it. The entire plane exploded and the debris came raining down. I'm pretty sure after that I was the only one that managed to survive.

I woke up right about then, right when our plane started its descent for landing at La Guardia. I woke up in a fright; I mean it really fucked with me. Was it just one of those things or was this some kind of premonition? I can't explain how different it was having a plane crash dream while flying, but it definitely added an extra layer of terror. I guess because the best part of a nightmare is that you wake up and realize you're safe at home and so far removed from whatever you were experiencing, but this time I woke up and I was in the exact situation as in my nightmare.

Even though stress brings on these nightmares, your favorite part about going to your annual Recurrent Training will be Accidents and Incidents. That's when your instructors go over all the major drama, near disasters, and crashes that occurred in the last year. It's weird, but you'll be fascinated it; you just can't get enough.

Chapter 11

When you first get on the line you'll feel overwhelmed by all the stuff going on. There's so much to do and everyone seems really busy doing random things. You'll think that you cannot possibly get it all down, but that's okay. Everyone finds their niche. Some people like to work in the galley and ignore the passengers altogether, while others like to be out in the aisle and get to know everyone. Some people like to take care of the prima donnas in business class while others like to stick with their own kind in coach. It's more people but less of a service.

Some like to pass out the meals while others like to be in charge of drinks. It gets even more specific than that. Some people working on the cart like to "moon" (have their asses face the passengers) while others like to "shine" (their lovely smiles shining at the people). Some like to work the red-eye while others like daytime flying. Some like to just do one flight and then lay over, whereas others like to do several flights in one day and really get their hours in.

Some like to back up their trips so that they do three in a row in one stretch while others do one at a time and then take a day or two off. Some like to do trips that keep them away for six days and lay over in four different cities, while others prefer one-day trips that just fly to a city and back. It's totally possible for a mother to have a normal life with kids by just working these same-day trips. They can send their kids off to school, go to the airport, fly to Houston and back, then be at home waiting for the kids when they get home. You'll try all of these trips out and find out what works for you. I prefer to work three three-day trips in a row, then be off for a week. So that's nine days working and then six or seven off. I prefer night flying to day flying; it's so much easier because everyone is asleep. I also prefer one flight a day and then layover. Nothing is worse than having to work four legs and then only having ten hours to sleep in Omaha. Some people like that, though. Trips like that where they work you as a slave pay well in the end. One girl I flew with recently said her favorite trips are "one leg over, two legs up, one leg back." That means she gets laid on her layovers. Yeah, those are good trips. I just wish a sixty-five-year-old woman wasn't the one telling me that.

One of the first things you need to learn is how we feel about delays. Delays at the gate are horrible, but delays on the runway are wonderful. Why, you ask? Well, if you're attached to the jet bridge and you have to sit there for three hours because of a weather delay or maintenance problem, those three hours will be the worst in your life. You deal with the passengers at their most irate and understandably so. It sucks being all dressed up and nowhere to go. What makes it so bad for you is not the delay itself, but that you're not getting paid for it at all. Sometimes in those situations you have to work harder than any other time and you're not earning a damn penny. As long as the brakes are set on the plane, you're technically not on the plane. Your pilot might put in some fancy code to get some kind of minimal compensation, but it's not at all worth what you have to deal with from the passengers.

On the flip side, if you've pushed back and you're sitting on the tarmac when a thunderstorm rolls in and they close the runway, those are the best hours of your life. You're getting paid full flight hours and you're not having to do anything. The passengers are instructed to stay in their seats so you don't have to do anything but sit in your jump seat and watch the money come in. One late afternoon storm in June earned me over $300. Once, a Chicago snowstorm paid off to the tune of nearly $400 because we're equally thrilled when we have to drive over to the de-icing facility to get the ice dissolved off of our wings. On delays like that you've usually spent the money before you've even taken off. If I know I'm going to be getting several hundred dollars more in my paycheck, I start thinking of how to treat myself.

So if you've ever wondered why sometimes the flight attendants seem just as upset as the passengers during a delay, it was probably because you were still parked at the gate. If they were trying to conceal smiles when they pretended to care about passengers' missed connections, they were probably in heaven on the tarmac.

Sometimes delays and cancellations suck more for the crew than the passengers, though. If you have big plans to go out on a layover, that flight will be delayed or cancelled. It's Murphy's Law. Never buy a ticket for something and expect to make it in on time. It won't happen. If you have tickets for a concert in Los Angeles, you'll be delayed so that you only catch the last song of the encore. Yeah, that happened to me. If you make plans to hang out with your buddies in Denver, you'll divert to Albuquerque and never see them. If you have plans, never tell anyone else on the crew. That's the kiss of death.

It got to the point where I stopped telling my friends and family when I'd get trips that had layovers at home. It was just easier not to say anything and IF I made it in, I'd call them at the last second to let them know I was down the street. On the other hand, you can work it to where you force layovers in places you weren't supposed to go to. One time this incredibly self-centered guy and his equally selfish girlfriend were working a trip that went through DFW. It looked like they were barely going to make their connection to work the flight to some random town in North Carolina. They'd have to hurry to make it and even if they ran, it wasn't for sure that they'd get there in time. Her house was in Dallas so they decided to take it slow and not rush it. They stopped by Chili's for a snack and made sure they each went to the restroom, washing their hands better and longer than they ever had before. They dragged their feet as much as they could, but once the gate was in sight, they ran as if they had been running the entire time, wiping the incriminating salsa off of their mouths.

Of course, they could see that their plane had already pushed back and there was no way they'd come back for them. They put on Oscar-worthy performances for the gate agent's benefit, pretending to be upset that they didn't make the flight and would be missing out on a good time in wherever the hell they were going. If you're going to try that you need to get all crew members on the same page. You can't have one girl make it to the gate on time while the others seem to be rushing but don't make it. How do you explain that?

No worries about screwing over the passengers, though; the airline had called reserve flight attendants to work the flight and the couple got to stay in Dallas and just pick up the trip when they passed through Dallas again the next afternoon.

Personally, I would never attempt something so ballsy and wrong. You're potentially inconveniencing over a hundred people for your own petty self-interest. But then again, they were in a base airport and there were standby flight attendants in the terminal so no one was screwed over.

If the pilots would've been as impetuous, then the flight probably would've been cancelled. Airlines don't really have a good replacement system in order for pilots. They don't have to suffer through airport standby quite like the flight attendants do. It's scary to think that if a pilot just up and decides he doesn't want to go to work at the last second, hundreds of people don't get to where they want to go.

Crew members are very self-centered and rarely think about such things like causing passengers to miss appointments, meetings, weddings, funerals, cruises, etc. It's all about us and what we have going on. It becomes so common that you completely forget what you're doing to other people. One lady missed her son's funeral because a first officer dragged his feet driving from Pennsylvania to New York's JFK airport when he got called out on reserve. Without pilots we don't go anywhere, so that flight had to cancel and it was the only one of the day. The pilot said he was on his way and then got caught in traffic, but we all knew he never bothered to leave his house, much less put on pants.

Chapter 12

Women love a man in uniform. That is, unless it's a flight attendant uniform. Then it changes to "Women laugh at a man in uniform." It's not stylish. It doesn't flatter. It doesn't demand respect. It doesn't make women want to rip off their clothes. Other men in uniform just have to put on their rags, stand on a street corner, and girls will swoon: policemen, firemen, pilots, military men, athletes. We don't have that power, not at all, not even a little bit. In fact, we have to work extra hard to compensate for the layers of cheap Polish polyester blend we drape ourselves in. I hate wearing the uniform. I feel like I don't have a personality in it. The type of girl who gets wet by looking at a guy in a flight attendant uniform is probably not the type of girl you want to know.

There is a plus side to the uniform, though, if you're extremely good at rationalizing things. It's this: You will never look worse than you do in your uniform. That's rock bottom. If you can impress a passenger while wearing that ridiculous thing then you'll really like your odds for when she sees you in something a little more comfortable, a little more you. It can only improve from that first impression. This is true with your coworkers as well. We all look the same on the plane but when everyone meets at the hotel bar for drinks later, you get to see who people really are. If you do have a personality, or a little bit of style, then that will go a long way. First, though, you need to set up that second meeting. It doesn't matter how cool you look or how charming you are over dinner if you can't take the relationship off the plane.

Interestingly enough, the opposite is true of the pilots. They look cool as hell in their uniforms, but get them in their casuals and the ladies go from hot to meh. For every well-dressed pilot there's a woman that needs to be thanked.

When it comes to meeting girls, the biggest weapon you have being a flight attendant is that you must talk to everyone. It's your job and you have to do it. It's really the only advantage we have over the pilots—access to the cute passengers—since they're locked up in the cockpit for their safety. You really don't need an opening line; you can say or ask anything you want and they pretty much have to answer you. I think it's a federal violation if they don't. Use that to your advantage. Threaten that the police will meet the flight if they don't answer you when you ask their sign. Show them the flex cuffs. Wink when you do so.

There's no rush in talking to a cute passenger. They're stuck with you for a predetermined period of time, so you can come up with a plan of attack. It's not like seeing someone at a bar and not knowing how long they're going to be there. Time is on your side. A word of warning, though. If you sit on your jump seat and there's a potential target right in front of you while you're getting ready for takeoff, there's a ratio between the amount of time you wait before you say something and the quality the comment needs to be.

Just like anywhere else, even if you say something boring right off the bat, it's much better than if you sit there uncomfortably for a few minutes and then say the same lame thing. If you wait a little too long, then it's obvious that you've been thinking of what to say so it'd better be gold. You need to come off as the type of person who talks to anyone and everyone. When in doubt, just ask the person if they're going home or away from home. It's normal and harmless and starts a conversation, plus you get to find out where the person lives.

Many flight attendants will tell you that the ability to give out amenities is the most important thing we have. "Free Drinks" is a classic tactic and will never go out of style. It costs you nothing. It's not like at a bar where you have to part with your hard-earned cash. Let the airline pay for your social experiment. You're not supposed to give out drinks but you are allowed to reward passengers for being helpful. Come up with a reason to why you deemed her "helpful."

Upgrading someone to first class is a bold move when it comes to impressing a cute passenger, but usually reeks of desperation. If the girl is traveling with a friend or a small group and you can upgrade all of them, then that's a different story. They'll all be thrilled and you can just sit back while they all praise you to no end. You can single-handedly get their big trip off to an epic start and they will never forget it.

If you're lucky, the passenger you like will come to the back of the plane so you can do your flirting in private. While they're waiting for the occupied bathroom is the absolute best time to talk to someone. They're stuck. Even if the bathroom is vacant, lock it when you see her heading back. That will give you a few minutes before you "figure out" that there really isn't anyone in the "occupied" lavatory. If they stick around after they use the facilities instead of going straight back to their seat then that's a big indicator that she's keen.

Next to that, pray that she's on the aisle so you can kneel beside her and have a conversation without disturbing anyone else. You don't want anyone to listen to you openly flirt; that can get awkward. The worst situation is when they're sitting at the window and you have to talk over two strangers. You have to really want to ask her out if you're going to put yourself through that hellish public spectacle. If you're talking to someone at the window then it's not just her row that will be able to hear you. The row in front and behind will also be listening and watching the whole scene play out. That is your last resort and usually happens after the captain has told the flight attendants to "prepare for landing." No more chances of her going to the bathroom; it's now or never.

Your female coworkers are in that lucky position where the job and uniform add up to a universal male sexual fantasy. Just being there live and in person makes them desirable. Only deviants fantasize about straight male flight attendants. It won't be as easy for you, but you'll still get plenty of chances to meet people from all over the world. Just play it cool and remember that you'll fail more than you succeed, and that's okay. If a girl shoots you down, then just wait a few hours and you'll get a whole new batch of passengers stuck in a small space with you for hours at a time. Eventually, you'll charm one enough to give you her phone number.

You know what... Now I'm thinking it may be a good thing to ask out a passenger in front of a crowd. Who would break someone's heart in public like that? It's kinda like how the girl always acts like she's going to say yes when she's proposed to via jumbotron. Even if the answer is a resounding NO, the girl is usually kind enough to wait until all eyes are off of them before she breaks his heart.

Chapter 13

I would suggest that you change into your uniform only after you get to work if you take public transportation. Actually, even if you drive to the airport, don't wear your uniform unless your airline has kick-ass uniforms. Most of us have crap uniforms. You do not want to have an awkward scene like when Judge Reinhold's character in Fast Times at Ridgemont High gets laughed at by the hot girl when he's spotted wearing his pirate outfit from Captain Hook Fish and Chips while they're both stopped at a red light. That girl will not be checking you out if that scene replays itself while you're driving to work. Pretend you're on your way to a costume party or something.

At the end of your work trip, get out of the uniform before going out in public. Some flight attendants have been known to be half-changed in the aft galley by the time the last passenger exits the aircraft. Once you have on normal clothes you'll feel like you have a personality again. You'll be ready to once again face the world and take on whatever it throws at you.

The first person I dated seriously in New York City I met coming home from work after I'd been flying for about a year. I was twenty-four years old. Thank God I had already changed clothes. I wonder how my life would be different if I'd stayed in that damn blue polyester blend with the short-sleeved white shirt with costumey epaulets.

> We met underground, the first person I have ever met underground. I just love saying that. It sounds like a fairy tale, like she was a troll or something. The whole subterranean encounter was guided by the Fates. She never took the F train out of Queens, I never took the F train from La Guardia to the East Village, but there we were, the only two people in the car as I get on the Manhattan-bound F train at Roosevelt Avenue. I saw her dressed like a glam angel, velvet pants and glitter all over. I sat across from

her and then became shy, thinking it was too obvious. I could have sat anywhere in the empty car, but I went out of my way to drag all my luggage across the car, to her sights, directly in front of her. Now, I just sat and let my mind fantasize about what could possibly happen at this moment in time. I could get a wave of courage and say something profound or charming, I could make and hold eye contact, sending soft electricity into her spiky Central American head.

Instead, I sat facing her, but looking down or away, pretending to read the ads for laser eye surgery, reading and rereading the lame "poetry in motion" lines, trying to figure out how the authors got their stuff on these Barnes and Noble ads.

"Do you need a map?"

"Excuse me?" I replied.

"Do you need a subway map?" she asked again, holding up the map she was using as a fan.

Realizing that I looked like a tourist just off the boat with my luggage, I saw where she was coming from.

"No, I live here, I'm just getting back from work."

"What do you do?"

"I'm a flight attendant"—I cringed saying that; now I would have to make an effort to prove my heterosexuality—"I'm just getting back from San Francisco." Digging myself deeper.

She just looked at me for a second and then said in a straightforward manner, "Do you want to go to a party with me?"

I thought about how odd this was. The script of the conversation said this girl was a freak, but the look in her eyes and my sixth sense said I should go with it.

"Sure," I said with a nonchalant shrug, trying to sound as causal as possible, like that was something strangers asked me all the time, "but I need to go by my place to get changed and drop off my stuff."

That's how it started, randomly on the same train, randomly in the same car, and within fifty words we had plans for the night. I took a shower while I let her meet my flight attendant roommates, not knowing she was completely ignoring them and filling her notebook with line after line of brilliant prose and poems about the same things I was thinking about in the shower.

She said the party was way-the-hell-and-gone up in the seedier parts of Washington Heights, which was one of the reasons she talked to me in the first place. That isn't a neighborhood a young girl should be walking through alone unless she's familiar with it. At least not in the late 1990s. Even as the two of us passed the toothless drunks and hardened thugs, I didn't feel too comfortable. Every loud dominoes game was silenced as we passed. All eyes were scoping us out, sizing us up, and contemplating our agenda.

Audrey strode confidently down the avenue and side streets toward dark and lonely Riverside Drive. It was along one of the eerily quiet back streets that I realized I really didn't know this girl and she could be setting me up. We were walking through one of those nightmarish gray and black asphalt roads with lurking shadows stirring in the peripheral. I don't really remember, but I think she was smirking. I could be robbed and killed and no one would even know. I was sure a gunshot would be ignored around here. I was sure a scream would get no response at all. I told Audrey what I was thinking in a laughing/joking manner. She didn't reply. Gulp.

We did finally find the dilapidated building just across the Hudson from the Jersey shore. We buzzed the apartment, and the sound reverberated throughout the dusty building. Some guy who sounded wonderfully effeminate and not at all threatening let us in. The apartment was full of kids who had left home to make it in New York City. They were all aspiring musicians, playwrights, actors, and models, all celebrating gay pride in glittery pixie dust, short shorts, fabulous hair, gorgeous costumes, and numerous drugs. It was like the seventies had been wrapped up and shoved into this cramped apartment. Everyone was having a great time telling stories, prancing around, drinking cocktails, and enjoying the sweltering summer in the city (the hottest on record at the time).

There was one guy who stood out immediately. A very out of place, straight-laced, Jewish teenager in the middle of a living room full of queens and fag hags. He knew no one in the room when he arrived at the party. He was supposed to meet Audrey there, but I had delayed her a good hour. So this innocent, awkward, straight boy was at the mercy of the fucked-up queens and their desire for fresh seventeen-year-old tail. He was awfully glad to see us, though he did hand out water-colored flyers to the whole gang, inviting them to his next gig at the Sidewalk Cafe. (I still see that guy on MTV when I'm in Europe; Audrey too, for that matter.)

That was my first full summer in New York City and it changed my life forever. I'm sure it would've changed without meeting Audrey, but who knows where it would have gone? I know I'm at a better place because of it and I owe it all to changing my clothes as the passengers were deplaning.

Chapter 14

I hate coffee. I hate the taste. I hate the way people revolve their lives around it. People put a higher priority on coffee in the morning than a daily affirmation or quality time with the wife and kids. I hate the industrial giant it's become. I hate, most of all, what it does to the one saving grace of being awake in the early morning

Before the introduction of coffee to a room, office, or city, everyone is walking around in living dead solitude. Heads are heavy and still blurry from the half-wake dream state we walk in. People drag themselves around in sedation, in seclusion, in this waking-life surrealistic state. It's not an angry or an apathetic time, just not an outright friendly one. Still, there's an understanding in the silence and it's beautiful. We're all alone together and though we may appreciate the others around us, you'd never know it by the looks on our faces.

We're dreary. We're lost. We're contemplating this day and that day and all the days. Then some asshole is the first of many to order a large cup of joe. It hits the bloodstream and people snap out of it after the first piping hot sip. The room goes from various hues of gray to vibrant, radiant colors. The people open their eyes and lift up their heads. Things get back in focus. Now conversation begins, frivolous, inane chatter in very clear tones about ridiculous things as inspired by their caffeine high. Not only do people accept the transformation, they actually vocalize their thanks for the jumpstart.

Oh, now they feel alive! Just because of a little caffeinated energy, everything is how it should be. I say fuck that! What's so great about having bright eyes and a bushy tail? Tomorrow morning let's drink dreamy nighttime tea that comes in dark blue boxes with pictures of moons and stars. Why do we want to be alert and attentive so early? I hate the way coffee brings down its tyrannical hammer on such beautiful mornings of inward focus and catharsis. I love the smell, but I hate coffee. I even hate the word, those arrogant double

Fs and double Es. It's just so neat and proper and easy to handle, just like we all should be.

That's how I felt a week before I got hired with the airlines; not so much anymore. This job will turn even that guy into a coffee drinker. I hate that about myself, but I came to the dark side and so will you, if you aren't already a part of the evil empire. I think it took me just a few days of 3 a.m. wake-up calls during new-hire training for me to jump on the bandwagon. It's really the only legal way to put a spring in your step for those early morning flights or keep you awake on the all-nighters. Coffee will be your new best friend; that is, until you discover the farmacias.

Random interesting tidbits to share with people: The plane takes off at around 170 mph and lands at a slightly slower speed. Cruising altitude speed may be around 475-600 mph. The Mile High Club is really a misnomer; cruising altitude is around six or seven miles.

If someone asks you how many miles you fly in a year, the answer is roughly 420,000 if you fly just your schedule. If you fly more, let's say an extra 100 hours a month, which is pretty standard, then it will be somewhere near 650,000 for the year. If you just fly what they give you and don't pick up anything else, you should hit one million miles after two years and five months. That's your full-time job and it'll still take two and a half years. Think of road warriors who fly one million miles each and every year who also work off the plane! Understanding that might make you a little more kind to those frequent flyers whose dreadful lives make our job necessary.

Part 4: Welcome to New York City

Breathe through your mouth.

Don't make eye contact.

Chapter 15

If you work for any major airline and you're one of the younger people in your training class, that means you're going to New York City unless you speak a language and they need speakers in other bases. Our Spanish speakers all went to Dallas. The French speakers got sent to Chicago and the Japanese speakers to Boston. If you just speak English and Sarcasm, you'll be going to New York City, the Big Apple!

What you need to realize is something that I didn't think of when I was going through this process of moving to my base city and starting my new life as a flight attendant. As soon as you know what your base is going to be, which should be in the middle of training, find a good roommate. I didn't think of that at all. A third of our class got sent to New York and that included every person under twenty-five, except for the speakers.

I thought that we'd all be going together and we'd sort out who would live with whom once we got there. I was wrong. It turned out that people began making alliances even before the bases were announced. By the time I needed to find someone to live with, all the good people were taken. I wasn't an option for many of my classmates. The gay boys wanted to stay together, and most of the girls weren't allowed to live with a boy. Their daddies would kill them and since daddy was signing the lease, he was boss. The ones from New York already had somewhere to go. I was left out to dry, just like the girls I ended up living with. We called ourselves what we learned the cockpit windows are in the event of an emergency evacuation—the last resort! Luckily, I really liked the others that didn't have the foresight to secure roommates, at least for a while.

Being a young, single, straight male, you'll probably be inclined to live with a lot of girls. Sounds fantastic, doesn't it? I made that mistake. It was five girls and I in a tiny two-bedroom apartment in Kew Gardens, Queens. It sounded so good when I said it to my friends back home. They were so jealous that I was living with five young stewardesses. Even now it sounds good in theory.

I learned very quickly that living with all girls is just a horrible situation for someone like me. I needed a guy there. I just needed one person I could talk to about guy things. I needed someone to watch sports with. After a month we brought in a guy to live on our couch. I was so happy. I didn't even mind that he starting sleeping with one of the roommates that I'd had a thing with. Ah, to be young again!

The concept of bases is very important. You'll most likely start out in New York but you can transfer after a while, once the other bases need people. There's no timetable for transferring bases. Some need flight attendants several times a year, but others only have openings once every few years. Most airlines have several bases throughout the country and some even have bases in other countries. It seems like these would all be the same, but you couldn't be more wrong.

Usually, the base at the main hub of your airline is very by-the-book. Those people are just a little too close to corporate headquarters and have drunk a little too much of their Kool-Aid. Everything is done exactly as procedure dictates. There is no cutting corners during the service and the flight attendants actually wear the proper uniform pieces in their entirety. People do silly things in these bases, like tattle on their fellow crew members when they show up to the plane drunk or when they try to get a passenger into the lavatory for a quickie. Those people are the fun-burglars and really should give up the job and give it to someone who will really appreciate it. Yeah, the glory days are behind us but we're trying our hardest to keep the allure and lifestyle of the "flight attendant" alive and kicking. Keep the dream alive!

New York City is the junior base for most American-based carriers. The new hires get sent there, and then most try to get out immediately if not sooner. They simply hate New York and never give it a chance. Those are also the same people who move to Kew Gardens and think that Twin Peaks–esque neighborhood is what all of New York is like. It's not. Not by a long shot. Get into the city (Manhattan), or at least to a better Queens neighborhood like Astoria. Maybe give Brooklyn a try, even though getting to the airports is difficult from most Brooklyn neighborhoods without a car.

The ones that do give New York an honest effort and stay for a while inevitably grow tired of spending so much money on dirty, cramped apartments with several roommates, not including the mice, roaches, and slumlords. It takes some people a year to reach that breaking point. It took me ten. I had the time of my life in my twenties, but when I turned thirty I wanted more. Whatever the reason, generally New York bases have high turnover no matter which airline you fly for, even if New York has the best flying routes.

Chapter 16

I'm still based in New York, and us JFK people could not be more different than the master base near corporate headquarters. People just don't care as much in New York. I cannot remember the last time I've been on a crew where all flight attendants were wearing company-issued uniform pieces from head to toe. Someone (me) always wears their own pair of pants because the ones provided to us are hideous looking and scratchy. It's not like I'm wearing something that looks bad—I spent a lot of money on my pants—but technically I'm not supposed to wear them and could get in trouble for looking nicer than company-issue.

Someone else will be wearing a jacket they bought on a layover or a sweater from home they wear on the plane when it gets cold. Guys get sick of the three ties we have to choose from so we'll buy nice ones from Hermes. Girls will accessorize with scarves or shawls from Nordstrom's. None of this is allowed and we're constantly getting reminders from headquarters that this is wrong. No one cares about these messages. No one is there to enforce the dress code and so nothing changes.

When you see a JFK crew walking through the airport, it's impossible to tell that we all work for the same airline. Sometimes you can't even tell that we're employees. I'm one of the worst when it comes to this, but even I freely admit that it's embarrassing when you see us in other countries, walking beside the crew from one of the Asian carriers. They look sublime and flawless. We look like ragamuffins, but people based in New York just don't care and our supervisors care even less. No one is monitoring what goes on so it really is a free-for-all. In case you haven't noticed, that's one of the best things about being based at a base away from the main hubs; you don't have anyone looking over you. That's one reason so many flight attendants fall through the cracks when they get into trouble with drinking or drugs. There is simply no one there to notice. We'd never turn in another crew member to the company; it's us against them, not us against us. Even if you do turn in another flight attendant, they'll keep their job and you'll be the base pariah because you ratted them out. Never cross a picket line and never be a rat.

Our Miami and Los Angeles bases are known for the girls drastically altering their uniforms. Skirts are shorter and fewer buttons are buttoned on the tops. Some girls wear the uniform vest but with nothing else. No shirt or no jacket, just the vest and a whole lot of cleavage. You can get away with not wearing makeup when no one is looking at your face.

Miami is the party group. All of their layovers seem to be somewhere hot, as in the Caribbean and Latin America, so less clothing is worn on layovers and they're always getting into trouble. Miami is what makes New York seem well behaved. As long as Miami is up to their usual shenanigans, us JFKers can keep under the radar.

San Juan had a reputation for being a mafia. They had their own thing going and if you had to fly with a San Juan crew, you did things their way and didn't ask questions. They all spoke Spanish so if you couldn't speak it as well, you didn't have a chance with those guys. They could all speak English just fine, but they wouldn't; that's how tight they were. This was back when the DC-10 was flown. It had an elevator to go down to where all the ovens were. Passengers were never there, just the flight attendant who was in charge of cooking all the meals. Once the service was over, everyone else would go down there for lines of coke or shots of vodka, or so I hear. I only got to fly on that plane a few times before they retired it and I certainly didn't see anything like that.

Older flight attendants smile when they reminisce about working that "lower lobe" galley. They said it was so much fun; you could take off your uniform and wear whatever you wanted. You could also get to where they kept the animals in the cargo hold and take out all the dogs and play with them, though sometimes the proper dog wouldn't be returned to the matching carrier and their owners would get pissed, and a new pet. They'd just blame the baggage handlers. You could also bring cute and horny passengers down to the galley to party. This was common. These were the glory days of flying, back when I was still in grade school. Sigh.

So many drugs were going through San Juan and they were all in on it. Even the ones that didn't actively smuggle wouldn't dream of saying anything. Unfortunately, San Juan isn't a base anymore and the DC-10 is no longer flown by most airlines. Coincidence?

Right after that party ended, I got hired. If you're just coming on the line now, you really don't have a chance. You'll just hear stories about how great it used to be. You'll think that's just old-person talk, but they're right—we missed the glory days. You even missed the death rattle, my new-hire friend.

The senior bases are all about the rest breaks you get on longer international flights. After you do the food service for the passengers you get to take a little nap in the crew bunks on the plane. Most crews don't even think or worry about breaks until all the work is done and it's time to start the breaks. Then the lead flight attendant will go around and ask everyone if they want to take the first break or the second one that will start a couple of hours later. We're all easygoing so this process usually goes smoothly. If you don't get your first choice, it's no big deal; at least you get to get away from the passengers for a bit.

It's not as easy with the senior bases. They are ALL about the breaks. Those old ladies will figure out who's sleeping and when before the passengers even get on the plane. There's no waiting to see how you feel once the time comes. You pick a break and you're married to it. Never mind if you hit a wall and get really tired when you're on last break—you're stuck.

Even that got too complicated for our senior base people so they started a system where you sign up for a break when you bid for your trips. You get your trips one month at a time and it's all doled out by seniority. So in the middle of June you're thinking about when you want your breaks for all of July. Flight attendants are given position numbers on the plane and the odd position numbers get first break choice on odd-numbered flights and then the even number ones will get first choice on the even-numbered flights. All of our long-haul trips consist of an odd and an even flight number pairing so everyone gets a chance to choose their breaks first. It's complicated, ridiculous, and so unnecessary. People will actually take this into consideration when they're choosing their work schedule for the entire month—when they get to sleep on the plane the following month! Unbelievable.

    To make matters worse, some old flight attendants (and hungover ones) will buy your break off of you. They'll take first break and sleep for three hours, then they'll go to the people on second break and pay up to $100 for another three-hour nap. When I got hired for this job it never in a million years would have occurred to me that a commodity such as a crew rest break could supplement my income and fund my vacations. Like I said, though, at the senior bases, they are all about the breaks, and nothing else that happens on the plane inflight really matters.

Chapter 17

As a virginal new hire you may be living with a ton of people far from home in Kew Gardens, Queens, but that doesn't mean your life has to be all about that. Kew Gardens is located conveniently between the two major New York City airports, La Guardia and John F. Kennedy. Both of these airports are in the borough of Queens. As soon as you can afford it, get the hell out of the Kew and into a neighborhood that has a personality, something more you. Kew Gardens is all Jews and Stews, so don't be shocked when someone calls it Jew Gardens or Stew Gardens. I had no problem with the Hasidic Jewish community—that all fascinated me—but I hated being surrounded by airline people 24/7. You couldn't swing a dead cat without hitting a pilot, flight attendant, or local business that had special deals for airline personnel. Every waking moment you were reminded of the airlines and you couldn't get away. If for some reason the airlines all pulled out of New York City, Kew Gardens would shrivel up and die. It was such a relief to get out of Kew Gardens and into a properly functioning neighborhood with variety and personality.

To be fair to Kew Gardens, which does serve a purpose as a cheap place to live in the shadows of the airports, here are some people of note who have lived in the area: Jack Kerouac, Rodney Dangerfield, Charlie Chaplin, and Will Rogers. Another bit of trivia, one of the Son of Sam victims is buried in Kew Gardens' Maple Grove Cemetery. But honestly, when people talk and rave about New York City, no one is ever thinking of Kew Gardens. Most people don't even know it exists.

To get you excited about living in the greatest city on the planet, here are a few of my favorite quotes about New York City:

"New York City is a place where you can lock yourself up in

your little studio apartment, and not go outside at all, and not feel in the slightest guilty about it. And yet, you know that if you wanted to, there's every conceivable thing going on right outside the door, but you don't have to go. It's sort of like falling asleep when your parents are having a party." —Augusten Burroughs

"One belongs to New York instantly, one belongs to it as much in five minutes as in five years." —Thomas Wolfe

"There is no place like it, no place with an atom of its glory, pride, and exultancy. It lays its hand upon a man's bowels; he grows drunk with ecstasy; he grows young and full of glory, he feels that he can never die." —Walt Whitman

"A hundred times have I thought New York is a catastrophe, and fifty times: It is a beautiful catastrophe." —Le Corbusier

"There are roughly three New Yorks. There is, first, the New York of the man or woman who was born here, who takes the city for granted and accepts its size and its turbulence as natural and inevitable. Second, there is the New York of the commuter—the city that is devoured by locusts each day and spat out each night. Third, there is the New York of the person who was born somewhere else and came to New York in quest of something. Commuters give the city its tidal restlessness; natives give it solidity and continuity; but the settlers give it passion." —EB White

You will be in that third group so that's a tall order to fill! You better do it right and make the most of it! You will be giving New York City its passion—pretty cool, eh?

To further get yourself in the mood and to fully appreciate what it means to live and work in the greatest city ever imagined, watch these movies. In fact, don't even leave your apartment until the

checklist is complete; you're not ready and it'd all be wasted on you. Here is your assigned viewing list:
- Taxi Driver
- Goodfellas
- The Cruise
- Coming to America
- Donny Brasco
- Midnight Cowboy
- Breakfast at Tiffany's
- The Warriors
- Annie Hall
- Bronx Tale
- Eyes Wide Shut
- Cruel Intentions
- Carlito's Way
- Do the Right Thing
- Cloverfield
- The Day After Tomorrow
- Dog Day Afternoon
- Gangs of New York
- The Apartment
- French Connection
- The Basketball Diaries
- Kids
- King Kong
- Requiem for a Dream
- Miracle on 34th St
- Moonstruck
- Party Girl
- Serpico
- Basquiat
- Wall Street
- West Side Story
- And of course, The Muppets Take Manhattan

Chapter 18

One of the first things you need to do when you get to New York is to apply for all the free shows and tapings you can. Jon Stewart, The People's Court, David Letterman, game shows, sitcoms, whatever is being filmed in the city, put in your application immediately if not sooner. Saturday Night Live requests are only accepted in August. We applied for everything we could when we first moved to New York and within a month we'd seen both David Letterman and Conan O'Brien.

When it comes time to leave Kew Gardens you'll have a plethora of cool neighborhoods to choose from. Two things to keep in mind. First of all, it's hard to get to all three of the airports—LaGuardia, JFK, and Newark (New Jersey)—you have to cover when you're living in Queens or Brooklyn, and secondly, your friends who live in Manhattan will rarely come out to visit you if you live in an outer borough. Make no mistake, you will be the one always going to them if you choose to live in Queens or Brooklyn. It doesn't seem like that big of a deal, but it will when it's 4 a.m. and you're waiting for the damn train to show up to take you back home, drunk and needing to pee. I wish I had a dollar for every time I had to find a pillar to pee behind at the Lorimer stop when I was living in Greenpoint, Brooklyn, and trying to get home late at night.

Manhattan is definitely the way to go. I mean, you're probably going to live in New York City only once in your life so you may as well do it right. You'll regret having never lived in the city, even for just a year. You really have to do it when you're young and can handle the conditions a Manhattan apartment offers. I hear that all the time from my friends who lived in New York for years but never lived in Manhattan. They really wish they had done it. Just suck it up, tighten the money belt, and make it happen! The struggle is what makes you feel alive.

First thing you need to do is find a neighborhood that's right for you. If you're artsy and don't like to shower or groom, go to the Lower East Side. If you want to live near young professionals and have loads of delicious eating options, go to the Upper East Side. If you want to be near amazing art galleries and the gay scene, check out Chelsea or the West Village. If you want to live in a central location that offers no nightlife whatsoever, Midtown East is the place to be. If you want to be near all the theaters, Hell's Kitchen is a great and affordable spot. If you want to technically live in Manhattan but not pay Manhattan prices, try your luck in Washington Heights. If it all possible, try to avoid living across the street from a poultry slaughterhouse. Just trust me on that one.

Now that you have the neighborhood that's right for you, do some exploring. Go to your local hardware store and buy a loft kit. They're cheap, and by the end of the day you'll have doubled the size of your tiny room. Now two people can somewhat share the space, as long as they're both flight attendants and constantly going away. Technically, they're not bunk beds, but it's all semantics. It's pretty much a bunk bed, but that has such a nasty connotation. Having a loft in New York City is hip. Having a bunk bed is just sad. You want a loft. Starving artists have lofts. Five-year-old kids have bunk beds. Never mind the fact that either way you have someone sleeping right above or below you and a ladder is involved. It's a loft!

After that's set up, walk around your new neighborhood and collect every delivery menu you come across in a five-block radius. These will be more valuable than gold. Even if you don't like Bangladeshi food, get the menu anyway; you never know. You will soon have your favorite pizza, Thai, and sushi place. You may even find that one hole-in-the-wall spot that actually has halfway decent Mexican food, but probably not. There may be Mexicans there, but somehow the food doesn't come out the same. It must be the lackluster ingredients they get in New York.

Next order of business is to go around and have a drink at all the local bars. Find one that has a vibe that meshes well with you.

There may be some fancy hip places you'll want to take your friends to, but also find a comfortable spot that'll serve as your local. You should like the jukebox, the staff, the clientele, and the amenities, like darts or a pool table. This bar will be your new living room, and the other people sharing your living room will be your best friends. It's good to have a place where everybody knows your name and none of them are airline.

When I first moved to the corner of First Avenue and St. Marks Place in the East Village, that place was the St. Marks Bar. It was right next door. The Rolling Stones even shot a video there back in the day. Not only was it the local for the six people we had living in our three-bedroom/two-bath apartment, it was also the local for most of the other kids in my building. Any given night I could stick my head in there and see someone I loved dearly. Most of the time we wouldn't even change out of our uniform. We could get fired for drinking in uniform but that's the beauty of living away from the airline-heavy Kew Gardens; no one in a position to bust me would ever be in there to catch me. It's so important to have friends outside of the airline industry. Nothing is more pathetic than someone who can only talk about airline shit. Those people are called pilots and it works in their world but not so much in the stewardess world. Don't be that guy; at least the pilots get paid big bucks to be lame. Have outside interests and friends who don't care about your job at all. It will help you feel like a person, not just a flight attendant.

After you find where to eat and drink, you'll need to find all the other neighborhood things, like the Laundromat and grocery stores. You'll also need to find the nearest bus and subway stops and where those lines will take you. After you've discovered those, you're pretty much ready for anything.

The thing about neighborhoods in New York is that if you find the one that's perfect for you, you'll never leave except to go to work. Why would you? Everything you need is right there within walking distance. Uptown people act like they need a passport to go downtown. Us downtown people would get nosebleeds if we went above 14th Street. Forget about going to Brooklyn, that's like going to Sri Lanka. Try not to get too comfortable in your hood, though, it's so easy to do that. Go and see what else is out there. Baskin Robbins has got nothing on New York when it comes to different flavors. It's truly an effort to get motivated to leave your neighborhood, but you'll be glad you did.

The great thing about Manhattan apartments is that you will use every square inch of that place for something. You'll be like the Native Americans with a buffalo; even the tail will get used somehow. If you have a large living room in your new place, build a wall and create another room. Now you can squeeze another person in there and everyone's rent and bills go down!

It's amazing how quickly you stop caring how everyone knows everything about you. When you live on top of each other like that, there are no secrets. We could mimic one roommate's noises during sex exactly as they were happening. You quit being shy about going to the bathroom because everyone can hear and smell you from anywhere else in the apartment, though some people turn the radio on when they're going—I guess that creates a false sense of privacy and discretion. Most private moments in a Manhattan apartment are illusions, tricks you play on yourself.

You'll also quit caring about what your neighbors can see through your bedroom window. You'll walk around naked and not even give a second thought that half the city can see you from down on the ground. You might even start getting off on the fact that people can watch you have sex. You may even turn into an exhibitionist! The things you see in turn will cease to shock you. I knew I'd been properly desensitized when I didn't even blink when I saw in the window across the street two fat gay men having sex while smoking a crack pipe at the same time.

Chapter 19

Most people know that dating a roommate is a horrible idea, but hooking up is inevitable when you're a group of young, attractive kids really living away from home for the first time. Don't believe me? Just watch The Real World or Jersey Shore.

Try not to shit where you eat. It's not worth it and can only create drama. A good alternative is to date someone who lives in your building but not in your apartment. That's just as convenient but not nearly as messy. Just know yourself and know the other person. If you're looking for a fuck buddy in your building and you're worried that she might become clingy, only go for girls who live on the floors above you. You don't want to date the girl next door or on the floor below you; then she'll be watching for you every time you go up and down the stairs. If she's a couple of stories above you, then you have a decent chance of making it in and out unseen.

Once you find a neighbor you can trust, exchange keys with them, especially if they're going to be home every night. Getting locked out of your apartment really sucks and always happens at the most inopportune times. Getting a lock busted by a professional in Manhattan is outrageously expensive, and once you're in, you still have to pay to get a new lock put on. That costs a lot too. I once had a hidden key on the roof that not even my roommates knew about. It may still be up there. If anyone is around 126 First Avenue between Seventh Street and St. Marks Place, please go check for me.

There are many must-dos in New York City. Some you can do on your own, but most you'll do whenever you have out-of-town guests visiting and you're playing Tour Guide. Even after fourteen years I love showing people around New York City. I think I put together a fairly comprehensive tour. In general, though, you'll want to hit all the obvious places first: Central Park, the museums, the landmarks, and all that crap they put on postcards. After you do the

essentials, here are things I like taking newbies to do:
1. Have a meal at Tom's Diner, the diner up near Columbia on the Upper West Side that Seinfeld used as a facade for Monk's on the show. The interior is completely different but the outside is iconic. St. John the Divine's Cathedral is right around the corner.
2. Go to a minor league baseball game on Staten Island or at Coney Island.
3. Bowl and drink at the hipster mecca Bowlmor Lanes.
4. Have a drink at the oldest Irish bar in New York City, McSorley's. You can only order "light" or "dark" so don't complicate matters by asking questions. Honest Abe had a drink there and the New York Rangers brought the Stanley Cup there to drink beer out of.
5. On July 4th, be on a rooftop, any rooftop.
6. Check out 7B, aka, Horseshoe Bar. Everything from Sex and the City to Godfather 2 had scenes filmed there, plus it's just a bad-ass indie rock bar in Alphabet City.
7. Go check out the facade they used for the Friends house in the West Village. While you're over there go to the legendary White Horse Tavern, where Dylan Thomas drank himself to death and one of Jack Kerouac's friends wrote, "JACK GO HOME!" on the bathroom wall.
8. On a sunny afternoon hit the beer garden in Astoria or at least go to Zum Schneiden in Alphabet City.
9. You gotta do Coney Island in the summer and ice skating at Rockefeller Center in the winter.
10. Spend an afternoon going in and out of all the Chelsea art galleries and enjoy the elevated High Line that will take you down to the uber-hip meatpacking district. Make sure to stop by the infamous Chelsea Hotel and try to figure out exactly where Sid killed Nancy.
11. Eat and shop in Little Italy/Chinatown/Canal Street. Most people know about New York's Chinatown and they know

about Little Italy, but they don't realize that the two are right on top of each other. One street is one and the very next is the other.
12. It's obligatory and cliché, but the Empire State Building cannot be passed up. It should've been visited on your tour of "the essentials," but if you skipped over it, go do it now.
13. Very few people know that the giant cube on the corner of E. 8th Street and Lafayette has a name, but it does. It's called "the Alamo." Spin it around and then watch all the wannabe skaters who can never pull off any of the tricks they're attempting.
14. Take your 1970s rock fans to the corner of St. Marks and First Avenue to see the Physical Graffiti building, made famous by the Led Zeppelin album cover. Rumor has it that the song "Stairway to Heaven" was written about the apartment on the top floor where their heroin dealer lived.
15. Go to Korea town in the West 30s between Fifth and Sixth avenues and sing karaoke until the wee hours of the morning.

You've got to go for it though. Give New York a chance and get out of the Kew. You only live once and that life will not go on forever, at least not how you'd like it to. If there's anything I could push on the new hires of today, whether you're straight, gay, or undecided, if you're stuck in New York, even if you don't want to be, make the most of it. Do it the best you can. You have this insane opportunity that thousands of people would kill for. You get to live in the most exciting cities and on top of that you get paid to travel to dozens of other amazing places. Oh, and you get to fly on your own time to any corner of the globe for next to nothing. If this doesn't get you excited about living in New York City and being that group of transplants that gives the city its passion, or at least excited about your new career as a flight attendant, get the hell out now and let someone who'll take advantage have this ridiculous opportunity.

Chapter 20

One thing you need to know about the girls you meet in New York City is that they are a different breed entirely. It's not just the ones born and raised in the city either. Those are certainly unique, but the ones that come to New York are something else. It really says something about their personality if they've come to New York to make it, in any field. They are ambitious, strong, cut-throat, motivated, and all about networking. In order to make it in New York as a singer, banker, designer, artist, dancer, lawyer, accountant, or whatever, those are very good qualities to have. They're all imperative attributes; otherwise, you'll get chewed out and spit out, or you'll never make enough money to pay your rent so you'll have to slink back to Nebraska.

If you want to find a nice, sweet, simple girl like the ones from back home, you may be out of luck. Those girls don't last long in New York City and don't usually come to the city in the first place. The ones that are there are certainly there for a reason and their job might be the highest priority in their lives. They may not be looking for a boyfriend or, god forbid, children, at least not until their mid-thirties. Just know that going in; career comes first with a lot of the girls you meet in the city. They work hard, they play hard, and they don't have a lot of time to stop and smell the flowers. It takes a special gal to make it in New York and most are very intense. That's just a heads-up. The NYU or Columbia girls might be the way to go at first.

One thing I've noticed as I get older is that my range of what's acceptable as a companion gets wider and wider. More people are sexual targets or potential girlfriends than when I was in college and wanted a rail-thin brunette with blue eyes and a summery tan. You'll see that body type isn't really as important as you once thought. If you have rules about only dating someone three years older or younger, that might be thrown out the window eventually as well. What I'm saying is that if you're going to ultimately throw off these shackles, you might as well do it now and not ever have them. You'll be surprised what might float your boat.

One of the best things I ever did for myself was to sleep with a fat girl. She wasn't that obese, not embarrassingly fat, just bigger than anyone else I've ever been with or even kissed or even thought about kissing. Some guys would say she was a just a little thick, but I'm usually down with the thin girls, so to me, she looked big.

It wasn't a bad experience, even as my hands went over her body for a couple hours, but it changed me. That night I was a bit drunk, so I explored again the next morning when I had all of my senses up to normal levels. I didn't develop a fetish, I just learned to appreciate the classic Botticelli full figure that has been worshipped and celebrated in paintings and sculpture for centuries.

After that encounter, I left my apartment and I saw a whole new world. Now any girl with a pretty face was a potential hook up. Even if she was a little overweight, I could say to myself, "Well, you've had bigger and that was just fine."

The next time I was with a normal-sized girl I appreciated the hell out of it. I took in every gorgeous curve and the perfect amount of firmness in the legs and ass. It made me really get turned off by the anorexic ones. A handful of fat is so much better than a bag of bones. Pulp Fiction comes screaming back at me, something along the lines of how what brings pleasure to the eyes and what brings pleasure to the touch isn't always the same thing. These are more along the lines of "life lessons" than having anything to do with New York City or your imminent flight attendant career.

Here are some other pointers and random things you should know about living in New York City:
- Century 21 is your friend for cheap designer gear, but not on the weekends and certainly not around Christmas.
- The M60 bus will win a race over the Q33 to LaGuardia. So from the city go up to Harlem and catch the M60 over the Triboro Bridge.

- You will never know the price of a gallon of gas again, but when you go home you'll insist on driving because you miss it so much.
- When dealing with a cab, get inside and close door, THEN tell them your destination.
- I've never been in a wreck in a cab but if it happens I have a policy prepared. If I get close to my destination, I'll pay him most of the fare; that is, if it wasn't his fault. If it's my driver's fault, he gets nothing, especially if I get hurt. If we're just pulling away from where he or she picks me up and we get hit, then they get nothing for their troubles. Again, if it was totally not their fault, I may give them a sympathetic dollar or two. If the accident makes me late for something important or causes me to get out in the rain, then no money will be given under any circumstances.
- March is annoying because it should be getting warm but it'll probably still snow.
- November is when the mice seem to like to come out of hiding and run around inside apartments.
- By Halloween it's gotten cold outside, so keep that in mind when thinking about your costume.
- No matter how much you resist, you'll start supporting the New York sports teams.
- You'll fall in and out of love with the city every few months. The best remedy is to leave the city for a couple weeks or walk across the Brooklyn Bridge. Seeing an in-store performance by an author or band helps as well.
- The L train is the best subway line to meet interesting people, at least the ones that won't stab you.
- I'm usually the only white person on the E train going to Jamaica and I've learned to love that. I get mad at any other white person on that train. Don't get take this job if you're homophobic, and don't live in New York City if

you're racist.

That's about it for an introduction to New York City. Within two months you'll be an expert on your little slice of the city and before long phrases like "It's hotter than the bathroom at Yaffa" will make perfect sense to you!

Just remember the natural progression of a new-hire flight attendant: get based in New York, live in Kew Gardens, live in Manhattan, and finally, get sick of the city and commute from another state. You'll still be based in New York, but you'll just live somewhere else.

That means getting a place to stay for when you're in New York. You don't really live there, you just stay there a couple of nights out of the months before or after a work trip. You don't want to throw a lot of money to a place you're never at so you head back to the dreaded Kew and find a crash pad. Funny how things come full circle!

Chapter 21

Crash pads come in all shapes and sizes. Some have dedicated beds for everyone who lives there. No matter where you are in the world, you know that your bed is there with your sheets on it, waiting for you. It isn't being used by anyone else but you. No one is drooling, farting, or having sex in your bed. It's good peace of mind knowing your bed is YOUR bed. In my crash pad we have three bedrooms for fourteen of us. There are three bunk beds in one room and two in the other two bedrooms. I have the top bunk, but I'm patiently waiting for the guy below me to move out so I can upgrade. You always have your eye on the better spots. It's serious business. I've almost planted drugs in my roommate's luggage then called the cops just to get him fired and free up a bed that doesn't require a ladder. That's right, Larry, I'm coming for you!

Some crash pads have what are called "hot beds." That means you don't have your own bed. Theoretically there should be a bed somewhere in the apartment for you but you have to poke around the apartment with a flashlight, find a naked mattress, and throw your sheets on it. It's like musical chairs. Usually there are only a couple of people at the crash pad each night, which is good since hot-bed crash pads are overbooked and if every single person is there, someone might be on the sofa or futon, or worse.

Any time there are more than four people in on the same night, it gets incredibly claustrophobic and fights break out over what to watch on television. Nothing is more uncomfortable than a full crash pad, which often happens between Christmas and New Year's. Everyone just sits in one place and tries not to move around because there isn't any room to move.

Both pilots and flight attendants utilize crash pads. The turnover rate is high. The best part about the crash pad concept is that you may have five different airlines represented under one roof. You get to hear all about the drama your competitors face as well as all the ins and outs of how they do things. After getting all this intel, most crash pads could probably run an airline better than any CEO. We could take all the best aspects from each company and make a super airline. No one airline is perfect.

That's a crash pad in a nutshell. It has its drama, but it's better than sleeping in a chair at the airport or springing for an airport hotel every time you need to stay at base. The temptation is to join one of the party crash pads but that's just a horrible idea in the long run. The only time you're there is to sleep so you want to be able to sleep. It should be a sanctuary.

Part 5: Getting to the Airport

By far the worst part of your day.

Chapter 22

Welcome to the MTA and its myriad of delays, rerouted trains, and inconveniences! Sometimes the E train will run on the F line and the G train won't go all the way to its natural end. Sometimes local trains will suddenly run Express and skip your intended stop. Sometimes there are labor strikes. Sometimes rain and snow shut down the entire operation. You're going to have to deal with all of this. Know your route to the airports and come up with back-up plans. Sometimes it's faster to travel above ground and sometimes it's better to avoid roads and stick to the train. Learn what the best way is at various times, but having a contingency plan is imperative.

Always give yourself some extra time to get to the airport. It's very sad when you see a flight attendant in uniform freaking out on a city bus—one reason not to wear your uniform. The other is so that random people won't bother you with questions. Even if you have on your iPod and have your eyes closed, some stupid tourist will want to ask you something.

Taking the subway all the way out to JFK can take forever so make sure you have a book or game to play. You can tune everything out and for the only time during your day, have some alone time. Just a little bit of peace and quiet can go a long way. You're not going to get that at home with your roommates and you're sure as hell not going to get it on the plane. The heavenly break ends right when you pull into Jamaica station. It's really hard to tell who has Tourette's and who doesn't at Jamaica station.

> I got on the last car of the subway. I liked the idea that if I started there and walked forward from car to car, I would be traveling faster than everybody else on the train. As I stepped inside and looked around, I noticed a mood in the car. It was one of excitement coming from the people inside. Two Asian businessmen were smiling and speaking a mile a minute in Japanese, in unison.

It sounded like one long sentence, no periods, no commas, just an occasional break for laughter. I never knew when the break was supposed to occur, but the men did as they both quit talking simultaneously to let out loud maniacal staccato laughs. On the opposite side of the car there was a junior high choir group; they had big suitcases and larger smiles. The electric dozen had flown in from some small town in Oklahoma to compete in a singing competition. They were more excited just to be in the city, though. I moved past the group and opened the door to the next car.

This one was Desperation. A man was pleading with the passengers to give him their change. I've heard the speech so often I can recite it as easily as I can the PAs on the airplane: "Ladies and gentlemen, please excuse the interruption. I am not a drunk or on drugs, but I am homeless. I haven't eaten in three days and I'm asking you today for some help. I'm not too proud to take anything: a quarter, a dime, a nickel, even a penny, anything would be greatly appreciated. I'm sorry to disturb your ride. Thank you and God bless. We will be arriving at LaGuardia soon." He had lost his job and the police boarded up the building he was calling home, so he says. The man was insanely thin with blotchy skin and a terrible odor. A couple of people emptied their pockets. Most did not. I smiled and walked on under the row of Captain Morgan Spiced Rum ads.

The next car I entered was Hope. A Cuban man was sitting in the priority seats with his very pregnant wife. She seemed exhausted—her eyes were closed and her body was limp. He spoke gentle words to her and rubbed her stomach with a callused blue-collar hand. The baby would have an easier life than they had had. Two young black children with violins, a brother and a sister, were playing songs and taking requests. They had a sign saying they were trying to help their family buy food and clothing. They were also earning money to fix their out-of-tune instruments. While the boy would do a hoedown solo, his sister would walk around with a cup accepting contributions. I had seen these kids before; I gave them a quarter and kept on trucking.

This car was the Love car. There were couples and families, lovers and friends. One young Puerto Rican couple was sleeping hand in hand, her head on his shoulder. Another posh older white couple was standing close together. They hadn't been lucky enough to get two seats next to each other so they elected to stand; they didn't seem to mind. He would listen to her inane gossip while gently brushing her hair away from her eyes. I don't think he was really listening, just losing himself in her eyes. There was a family of four on vacation; they were all dressed up and on their way to see a Broadway show, the matinee. They were deep in conversation, discussing where they would go after the show and the following day and the day after that. They didn't notice they missed their transfer to the Times Square shuttle at Grand Central.

In the next car I found Giving. A middle-aged man was offering free food and drinks to anyone who needed it. Like me, he had also been traveling from car to car, going the other way. I guess he was the slowest person on the subway. He would lay sodas and sandwiches in the middle of the car and then walk to the next car and give his speech there. In a minute he returned and collected what was not taken. Nobody took anything; I should tell him about the homeless guy a few cars back. Club Med ads line the top of the car in the Giving car. I can't imagine any of these people at Club Med. I proceeded unnoticed into the car of Apathy.

A disfigured lady was making her way toward me; she couldn't use her legs. She didn't really have legs; they were mangled and shriveled. She scooted her body along with her arms, leaning forward, stretching out her powerful arms and pulling herself along. She moved like an inchworm. She couldn't speak clearly, but her grunts and open hat let everyone know she wanted money. The people who were wide-awake looking around only seconds before, closed their eyes and pretended to sleep or raised their newspapers to cover their faces. I stepped out of the way as she slinked by and waited for someone to open the rear door. I opened the door on the front side of the car and left. She was still waiting, helpless as a cat, for someone to let her out by the time I was gone.

The last car, or the lead car, I should say, was empty. No one was sitting, no one was standing, and no one was lying down passed out. I knew the conductor was in the little room at the front, but that was it as far as people. No talking, no soliciting, no emotion, just subway sounds and subway smells. I couldn't go any further. I walked up to the front window and watched the underground scene in front of me. I watched the stations come in and out of view until Sutphin/Archer/JFK. From here I get on the Air Train and enter John F. Kennedy International Airport.

Important tip: if a crowded train pulls into the station in the summertime and one of the cars is practically empty, don't go into it. At best, the air conditioner doesn't work and it'll feel like it's 130 degrees. At worst, a homeless man is sprawled out on the seats, covered in his own feces. Don't wait to see which it is, just cram yourself into the sardine tin next door.

Chapter 23

Once you're at the airport, you're going to head for your airline's Operations area and sign in for work. That's the equivalent of punching the time card, though you're not getting paid for anything yet. Most airlines have you sign in an hour before the flight is scheduled to depart and you need to be on the plane soon after to start setting up and checking all that emergency equipment. Of course, before you get to the plane you'll have to go through security. That's where we turn into little Fonzies and try to be as cool as possible, no matter what the TSA people say or ask of us. They have authority and even though they may be going off on a power trip, it's not your place to point that out. Just smile and nod and get through it. It's honestly the worst part about the flying.

Sometimes you have to go to the airport when you're not assigned a flight. Some airlines call this "Standby" or "Airport Appreciation Day." You're there "just in case," like if a flight attendant gets stuck in traffic, becomes ill at the last second, misses their commuting flight in, or is removed from the flight because they reek of whiskey. All four happen quite often.

Most "standby" flight attendants never get used. You'll just sit there for six to eight hours and watch everyone come and go, or maybe you'll just sleep through it. You have to put your entire life on hold and disappear into this black hole of nothingness. I like to pretend to be the official greeter to the Operations area, like the Walmart greeter. You're going to have to pack for anything, though, because you could be sent somewhere tropical or frigid. You could be gone for a night or maybe a week! Pack for the worst and hope for the best.

It's a great idea to always have a bathing suit packed even if you're flying to Oslo in January. You never know when you'll get reassigned to fly another flight. My first reassignment came in my first week of flying. I thought I was flying to Chicago and back in one evening, but the crew got reassigned. Next thing I knew I was sipping margis on the beach in Ft. Lauderdale. I didn't think to bring my bathing suit on a Chicago turnaround so I wasn't able to go swimming in the jellyfish-infested waters. I have had my trunks in my suitcase ever since. Also, some hotels have kick-ass indoor pools so just keep them in there; they barely take up space.

It's also a good idea to keep the correct uniform pieces in your bag as well. I have my fancy pants I purchased with my own hard-earned money to wear instead of the hideous ones we get free from the company, but I know I'll still get in trouble for having them so I keep a pair of the regulation ones in my bag, just in case. If I have a supervisor or Board member on my flight I can always duck into the bathroom and get into the proper uniform pieces. That's one bad part about not having an actual boss—any person could come up to you and tell you that they're a Flight Service Manager and you really have no choice but to believe them because you have no idea who the managers are.

Some airlines have fancy serving jackets that you're supposed to wear in the premium cabins during the food service. Some airlines look nice and ours used to be okay until they changed our uniform; now the serving jackets look ridiculous when worn at the same time as the new uniform. Still, though, the rules specifically say that the jacket MUST be worn during the service, so no matter how comical and unprofessional we look, we have to wear it. No one does, but I still bring it along with me just in case. It's yet another useless thing that weighs my bag down and takes up space.

Before you get to your gate make sure you stop by Duty Free to spray yourself with your favorite fragrance, for free, of course. Pretend you're interested in buying it and then just bolt of there. The minimum wage-earning kids will just apathetically watch you and roll their eyes as you scamper away, but it'll feel like you're getting away with something and that's a fantastic feeling. It's the simple things.

Slowly walk by your gate so that if a delay is posted you can just stroll right by and pretend like that wasn't your flight. If the passengers are upset and they know you're working the flight, you might get an earful of bad vibes. If you get the "On Time" display, continue on to the agent and have them check your ID and cross your name off of the crew list.

Once you get onto the plane you do the equipment checks in your designated area and then head up to first class for a briefing with the head stewardess and captain. These are usually ho-hum blasé nothingness, the same stuff you hear before every flight, but every now and then there's some very important information you need to hear. This is when the lead flight attendant will reveal whatever crazy neuroses and idiosyncrasies they have and the captain will hopefully give you a heads-up on possible turbulence en route. If you have an exceptional captain he'll tell you that he brought coffee and/or donuts for the crew. This doesn't happen very often but it's so wonderful when it does. Treat that man or woman like a saint because those people are few and far between.

There are a couple of lead flight attendants that will do asinine things like take roll, even though the agent just took care of that seven seconds prior. They expect a "Here" and if you say "Present," you get glared at. Yeah, it's even worse than in elementary school. A bitchy purser really sets the tone for the flight. You don't want to see that. And for God's sake, you know you're in trouble if they start their briefing with, "I'm really laid back and I hate drama." Those words are the kiss of death. If they have to tell you that they're easygoing, they're anything but!

Some pilots will take advantage of this fairly attentive audience in the briefing to preach about this or that and how he feels about certain groups of passengers. It sometimes gets racist, but not usually. Some have elaborate plans on how to deal with terrorists and they can get truly bizarre. One of our best pilots was also one of the worst for briefings. He always said the same thing before every flight, verbatim, for fifteen minutes. If you were hearing it for the first time, your jaw would drop. He took a possible terrorist scenario and ran with it to ridiculous and graphically violent conclusions. Let's just say the words "crash axe to the head" were used.

Most pilot briefings are the same. "Hey, guys, I'm so-n-so. There's nothing new security wise and nothing in the log book. Let's have a good flight." That's a damn fine briefing if you ask me. You can tell the pilots that can't get a word in edgewise at home—they really milk their audience in the briefings. They don't want them to end. Finally, someone is listening to them! Those briefings finally come to an end when the passengers start gathering on the jet bridge in front of the aircraft door.

Occasionally, the lead flight attendant will just do a quick briefing over the PA system. The lead flight attendant on a crew can be called many things depending on your airline. Sometimes they're referred to as "inflight supervisors," "cabin supervisors," "pursers," or "leads." Purser seems to be the job title of choice these days. They're not really the boss of the plane and hold no extra power, but they are the figure head, like the Queen of England. They are the official face of the crew and will deal with the most serious passenger problems and complaints. They also have to do all the paperwork when flying overseas. Pursers get paid a little extra and get slightly more respect from the world. Honestly, most of their duties involves settling disputes between two bitchy flight attendants who can't seem to get along.

The PA briefing a purser may do is something like, "Hey, guys, I'm blah blah blah, we all know what we're doing so I don't expect any drama. If you have a situation, deal with it yourself if at all possible. Try not to get me involved because I don't like paperwork. Later!" Sometimes you don't meet the cockpit until you arrive at the van to the hotel after you land. You might not even meet all of the other flight attendants until then if you're working the galley in the back of the plane. Galleys tend to stay in their galley and don't wander around in other cabins. They're like timid little mice. The chances of a main cabin galley meeting a first class galley before landing is pretty minuscule unless they met during the briefing. If there are any air marshals on board we'll get to meet them at this point, but I'll get into that group a bit later.

Some pursers or leads will treat the briefing like it's the most important thing in the world. They'll talk to the rest of the crew as if we're kindergarten students who can't possible think for themselves. It's ridiculous; it's not rocket science. We throw food and drinks at the people, make small talk, defuse bad situations with a smile, and then send them on their way. That's it. We can handle it.

Things can get a little hairy when you have several leads/pursers on the same flight. Every flight has just one designated lead, but eight of the twelve flight attendants may be qualified to be the head honcho. Sometimes there's a power struggle and everyone seems to think they know the best way to do the service. It can get very annoying when egos make a very simple operation absolute torture. You might want to be a lead flight attendant just so you can ensure a drama-free lead, but then you'd be opening yourself up to having to deal with all other drama that can happen on a flight. Sometimes it's an issue with an injured or dissatisfied passenger, but more likely it's having to mediate a fight between two bickering flight attendants. No, thank you! It's not worth the extra money to deal with all that noise!

During boarding the best positions to be are pulling the tickets in the terminal or directing the passengers at the aircraft door. You're removed from the overhead bin drama and you get first look at the cute passengers. You can see where they're sitting and make sure you work their side of the cabin.

If you're the directing flight attendant and greeting the passengers right in front of the cockpit door, you need to know if your pilots are proponents of the "stomping foot indicator." I once got in trouble during deplaning for not adhering to the stomping rules. I had no idea what he was talking about until he explained that as greeter, it was my job during boarding to stomp my foot two times if a hot girl was coming on. That would give them the heads-up to slip off their wedding rings and come out for a look-see. Even after I started doing the stomping bit I was still getting scolded for not stomping enough.

There were some uglies that the pilot said should have been stomp-worthy. If he had his way I would've exhausted myself by stomping nonstop during boarding. I would've looked like a mental patient with a horrible tick.

The galleys are usually the most senior positions and you'll figure out why very early on. They work really hard during boarding, but then the rest of the flight is cake. They rarely have to deal with passengers and don't have to walk around at all. They stay in their kitchens and watch the cabin with a fantastic sense of detachment. The aisle flight attendants are the ones that have to deal with 99 percent of the terrible things that could happen on a flight.

The galleys also get first crack at the food. If you're working in a premium cabin you can just snack from takeoff to landing on the stuff you're supposed to be serving to the passengers. It's fantastic and a very coveted position. Asking a first class galley to swap positions with you as an aisle flight attendant is like asking a contestant on Survivor to give up their immunity necklace; it just ain't gonna happen.

Setting up a main cabin galley on a smaller plane where no meal will be served may go a little something like this. First, I get on my McDonnell Douglas MD-80 single aisle airplane and make my way back to the main cabin galley. After I check all of my required safety equipment I have to get everything set up. I have my routine and it never varies. There may be better ways of doing things but flight attendants are creatures of habit and we'll stand by our method through hell or high water. To start the galley set up I throw all the racks of food into the ovens and count the entrees, making sure we have more meals than the projected passenger load. Next I set up the inserts that will go on top of the beverage cart.

One insert contains two pitchers of coffee (one with milk), two cartons of low-pulp Minute Maid orange juice, and two large bottles of Evian. The other: three stacks of plastic cups (approximately 30 thirty in each stack), two stacks of Styrofoam cups (15 in each), 120 or so napkins, a half-pint carton of two percent milk, cups full of sugar and Equal packets, lemon and lime garnishes, the non-dairy creamers which nobody ever requests, stir sticks, and Lipton tea bags. I put those away and get out the two inserts of ice that reside inside the beverage cart on the top shelf. I throw away the two chunks of dry ice they put on top of the ice to keep it cold. Later in the flight when I dump out the coffee into that same trash can, the combination of the dry ice and unused coffee creates some great fog. You can really scare the shit out of the passengers by telling them there's a fire in the trashcan. Good clean fun.

I use the metal mallet to break up the ice, then put two milks under the ice, and throw in the ice scoop. I put the ice inserts back inside the cart. After that I put bags of coffee into the coffee makers. If it's a tea-heavy market I'll brew a pitcher of black tea in one.

I'm supposed to do this before we start boarding, but I wait until I see the passengers get on the plane. This way I can hide out during boarding and not be amongst the people trying to fit their oversized carry-on items into the overhead bins. When it won't fit, they look around for a flight attendant to help them, but I'm hidden in the galley, looking busy. I don't have to hear about how "it fit on my last flight. That's the basic run down on how to set up a meal/beverage service on the smaller, narrowbody aircrafts. If you're organized it's incredibly easy, much easier than dealing with whatever is going on in the aisle during boarding.

You'll find that the ice you get from catering in Tokyo is the best ice you've ever seen in your life. It looks like the fake stuff they use in soda commercials. Each cube is a perfect square and they are all identical to each other. It's beautiful. I dream about that ice sometimes.

If catering neglects to give you an ice-breaking mallet, your backups will be the large wine bottles; they can certainly break apart the ice. If you don't have wine bottles then use the metal coffee pots or the can of cranberry juice (never a carbonated canned beverage!). Some people just take out the large bags of ice and slam them onto the ground. That's the quick, but annoying way to break the ice.

Point of fact: some older flight attendants who live alone or with cats will take the mallets home with them. They say the mallets work better than Mace if you think you're being attacked in a dark Walmart parking lot.

Chapter 24

The most annoying position to be during boarding is the premium cabin aisle. The passengers like to stand around in a very entitled way and chat with their friends, completely blocking the aisle so the lowly coach people can't get to their torturous seats with no leg room. They want to make sure everyone notices them in the premium cabin. They'll sit there and wave their jackets at you with the urgency of a four-year-old about to pee in his pants.

Some of the ballsier flight attendants will run up to them with a fire extinguisher, pretending that they thought the jacket was on fire by the way the owner was trying to get rid of it. Others will ask the owner why they purchased it in the first place if they're trying so hard to get rid of it. I can't get away with stuff like that. I can't pull it off like some of the pretty girls can. They can say the rudest things and then flash a smile and be celebrated. Not me. I have to work hard to be tolerated.

On the smaller planes you don't get the luxury of a purser. Any old flight attendant can be the lead on those because technically, there is no lead. The only thing that makes that flight attendant look more important is that they're the one making all the PAs and working in first class.

If you're on a plane without a video system then you have to do a manual safety demonstration. That's the song and dance everyone and their mother knows how to do. It's far better to be the one reading the spiel than the ones in the aisle making fools of themselves and donning a bright yellow life vest.

Our company-issued safety manual gives many hints on how to effectively make your public announcements. It says you must always be welcoming. You do this by facing the passengers and trying to make eye contact when making all announcements. Don't hide behind the wall or curtain. Speak clearly and with a personality, not like you're reading from a card, which you are. Deliver PAs in a helpful "did you know" tone rather than a preachy one. Tell the passengers what they CAN do rather than telling them what they CAN'T do. Be honest during delays.

No one is honest about delays and I hate that. No one seems to get that passengers will like it more if you say it's going to be a three-hour delay and it ends up being two rather than saying it's going to be twenty minutes and it ends up being forty-five. Any delay is a pain in the ass but if you throw out a number, no matter how ugly, and you get out before that target time comes, you look like you did something right.

It's all perspective but for some reason it seems to be policy to promise half an hour and then when that time is up, you promise it'll just be another half hour. This goes on until people are ready to revolt and I don't blame them at all. You can't keep poking an alligator in the eye with a stick and expect him to take it every time. Eventually he'll snap at you.

Being cheerful is very difficult right after you touch down after a thirteen-hour flight. It's hard enough to read your watch and figure out the time difference, much less deliver a flawless PA, full of personality. If I were a purser and needed to make those long announcements, I think I'd take advantage of today's technology and prerecord all the basic ones and have them on my iPod. That way they would always be perfect and I wouldn't have to think about it. If you fly lead enough you don't have to think about it anyway, though. You memorize all the PAs and can rattle them off while setting up the galley at the same time. Without even trying you'll memorize everything you say over the PA system.

Lucky for the aisle flight attendants doing the safety demonstration, the passengers don't pay attention at all. We could be naked or on fire and no one would notice. Thankfully, no one is watching when we do that effeminate thing where we blow into the red manual inflation tube on the life vest. It's hard for anyone to take us seriously when they see us do that. Be suspicious of anyone paying attention while you're doing the safety demonstration; they could be giving you a dreaded "check ride"! Nothing good comes out of check rides, only trouble.

After the demo is over you have to make a safety compliance check to make sure they heard you when you told them to turn off their electronic devices, fasten their seat belts, and return their seats to the upright and most uncomfortable position. The ladies and gay men love doing this. It's also known as "package check." You'd think the straight guys could make a cleavage check but it's not the same thing. You can easily get busted for looking at tits when you're supposed to be looking at where the seat beat buckles. There's no way you can get caught looking at bulges when doing the same thing. Lucky bastards. At least you get a look at the passengers and if you notice the cute ones are all on the other side of the plane from where you're supposed to be working, you can kindly ask one of the other stews to swap with you. They'll be happy to do it. They understand. We've all done it before. We work together very well in those sorts of situations.

When you're doing the check never assume that an obese passenger needs a seat belt extension, just as you'd never assume a girl is pregnant and congratulate her. Even if they're oozing over onto the seats next to them, don't offer that extension until they ask for it. It's easier for everyone that way.

After the compliance check is completed you're ready to go up into the great blue yonder. You're going to take your jump seat and prepare for takeoff. On some planes your jump seat will be directly in front of the passengers. You'll be knocking knees. Sometimes you have to sit for a while before it's your turn to take off so those are good people to schmooze with. They may be on their way to their dream vacation so make sure you get it started on the right foot. You can set the tone right then and there for their entire holiday.

It might also be their first flight ever. I know it seems unlikely that someone out of college hasn't been on a plane before, but you'd be surprised. Hook that person up and make them a loyal customer for years to come. Make them feel special. A free drink costs nothing to you but goes a long way with them.

If you're lucky enough to have a cute girl in front of your jump seat, you need to be prepared. Remember your ratio. As the amount of time you spend sitting there before speaking increases, so does the quality of what you have to say. If you're going to nervously squirm in your seat for five minutes, what you come up with better be pure gold. It better be something that belongs in the Poetry Hall of Fame. If you plop down and ask, "How are you," from the get go, whatever you say next won't have to be that clever. You just seem like a friendly guy who will chat with anyone. Conversation will be easy breezy. That's a good life lesson, not just for use on the passenger-facing jump seats.

Part 6: Pilots and Air Marshals

A love/hate story.

Chapter 25

The relationship you'll have with the pilots will be very complicated. You can't live with them, you can't work without them. They're your old ball-n-chain, except there will always be at least two of them, sometimes four!

Even non–airline people know all the stereotypes from how they're portrayed in movies, television, and romance novels. They're cheap, they cheat, they're bad dressers, they have multiple ex-wives, no personality, have short names like Bob, Dan, Bill, Tom, or Ted, and always talk about aviation. If that's your thing, then they'll seem as interesting as anyone else out there. This is the stereotype anyway. There are many wonderful exceptions, but you don't need a briefing on the normal ones.

Commercial airline pilots certainly have a reputation. We're all somewhat jealous of them, though. They honestly have the best job in the world. They get paid so much for doing what they love, which happens to be very little if you really watch them. Potentially, they have to use their skills and save our asses, but luckily that doesn't happen too often. Pilots don't have to deal with the passengers and all those hassles. That's a huge plus. They don't have to get dirty or exert any effort during the flight. They still have fingerprints and forearms without scars. They get all the respect, admiration, and most of the girls. Kudos to the pilots, though, really. They figured it all out and we didn't. The best part is they truly love their job and make a fantastic living doing it. I wish every person on the planet could be so lucky. We all want our sons to be pilots. We all want our daughters to stay away from pilots.

You're going to have a love/hate relationship with your pilots. Think of them as your bratty big brother or that senior in high school that gave you swirlies when you were a freshman. Sometimes there's weirdness between them and the male flight attendants, both gay and straight. Oftentimes the pilots are conservative, especially the military ones, and they're not really down with the gay boys as much as polite society should be. They tolerate them at best. So you'd think they'd really appreciate working with the straight ones, wouldn't you? Well, not so much. Any flight attendant with a penis is a bad flight attendant in their eyes.

You see, you're seen as competition when it comes to hooking up with the stewardesses. There are some cool pilots out there, but you will see this phenomenon over and over again. Be ready for it. Let me add that most pilots are very normal, some are super cool, and some are the biggest pricks ever created out of God's own image. I'm not talking about all pilots when I talk shit, I'm just warning you about the worst ones. Please be nice to the pilots and assume they're normal until they demonstrate otherwise. Coming onto the plane and hating on the guys just because they're pilots is not the way to do this job or live your life in general. Be respectful, and most of the time you'll be respected, even if you have absolutely nothing in common with them.

At times you'll be treated like a matchmaker for the pilots, or better yet, a pimp. It's not unusual to hear the pilots say, "Hey, we're lonely up here in the cockpit, why don't you send Brenda up here to hang out." They won't call Brenda directly, that's not their style. Side note: if you see a stewardess go into the cockpit with the leftover hot fudge, butterscotch, and whipped cream from the sundaes, don't ask questions and don't stick your head up there. You don't want to see what's going on.

You will also hear, "Hey, man, come down to the bar tonight and I'll buy the first round." Then, as an afterthought, "Don't forget to bring the girls!" It can be annoying because you know they're just using you, but getting a free drink out of a pilot is something you should take advantage of anytime you can. It's as frequent as Halley's Comet. It's as special as catching a leprechaun. Never turn it down because it may be years before they offer to buy you something ever again. They use you, you use them, it's the American Way.

If you're lucky enough to be flying with several cute girls and they actually want to hang out with the pilots, stick with them as long as you can stand it. Ride that train as long as humanly possible! Like a Playboy bunny with an elderly billionaire, close your eyes and just do it. The worst-case pilots are most certainly cheap, but there are only a few of them stupid enough to buy the drinks for just the girls and exclude you, though that does happen. Most pilots quickly learn that girls don't respond well to excluding the male flight attendants from drinks when they're buying a round. The girls will still take all the free drinks but at the end of the night they'll slam their hotel room door in their faces. Lesson learned—next time don't be a cheap bastard, and go all or nothing. Cabin crews stick together like Thelma and Louise.

Chapter 26

One thing I was shocked to see was that quite a lot of pilots have no interest in sports whatsoever. I've stuck my head up in the cockpit on Super Bowl Sunday and asked what the score was in the "big game" and they had to ask me what big game I was talking about. Unbelievable. I thought these men of men would for sure share in the universal love of sports, but somehow that gene is missing from their genetic makeup. I thought that might be one of the few topics of mutual interest between them and me, but I was sorely mistaken. I thought that travel would be something else we could talk about since we're both in the airline business and get insane discounts on almost every airline in the world. Yeah, not so much. The pilots as a species don't do a lot of traveling unless they're getting paid for it. Again, there are some exceptions, but the majority just like flying planes and talking about flying planes and dreaming of the time they can fly a plane again or reminiscing about a plane they flew years ago.

If they're not talking about planes then they're talking about the company. It blows my mind how pilots can talk about airplanes, layovers, work sequences, and what the company should be doing for hours in the cockpit during the flight and for hours at the bar during the layover. Every day. For years upon years. Kew Gardens was made for people like that.

It's often said during the pre-flight briefing by the captain that he has our back 100 percent, and if we don't like the looks of someone and want them off the plane, then he'll make it happen. They'll say, "If you don't like him, I don't like him. Let's remove him before we get airborne." That's what we want to hear. It makes us feel good that they trust our judgment. It really makes us feel like we're on the same team. So it's shocking how many times a drunk person will come onboard and you'll want them removed and the captain will pull a 180 and tell us to just let them on, that they'll probably just pass out once we take off. The ones that really do follow up on their promises and deliver by kicking Drunky-poo off the plane are my favorite pilots. I respect the hell out of those captains and treat them so well. It's a little thing for them, but it goes a long way for us and it's pathetic that others can't do the same. That's the fastest way for a pilot to lose the respect of an entire base, not to back us up. Word travels fast and reputations are formed quickly.

One of the worst experiences I ever had with a pilot was when he didn't even do anything to me directly; in fact, he was really nice to me. I liked him quite well until "the incident." I was working first class from LAX to JFK and we had Chris Rock on board. The first officer noticed this during boarding and asked me how he was. I said he was really quiet, but seemed nice. The pilot muttered something under his breath and then made his way over to him while we were still trying to board. I knew nothing good was going to come of this. I followed after him, pushing past some passengers trying to get to their seats. When I caught up to him he was asking Mr. Rock why he doesn't like white people. Oh god, why?

Chris took it very well and laughed it off. With a huge grin he said he does like white people, but yeah, his act does play around with racial stereotypes and he'll poke fun at white people just as he pokes fun at black people. I thought that was a very good way to respond and I hoped the situation would be over. Nope. The pilot apparently didn't hear a word or just chose to ignore the words. He went on to warn Mr. Rock that he better like white people tonight. The smile from his face faded and he asked the pilot why he should like white people tonight. The pilot looked stern, pointed a finger in his face, and replied, "Because white people are flying this plane."

I'm not sure what exactly he meant by that, but his intentions were obvious. The pilot, satisfied with his exchange, turned and went back into the cockpit. My mouth was gaping. I turned to look at Mr. Rock and he had the same look on his face, only slightly less bewildered and more indignant. Great, so the pilot pissed off my cabin and then got to walk away and I had to deal with it for the next six hours. That was super. I was a robot the rest of the flight. I did my job but didn't even try to make amends; it wasn't going to happen. I just closed my eyes and waited for it to all be over. It was so uncomfortable, and the worst part was that I knew the pilot was up there in the cockpit, so proud of himself, most likely bragging to the captain and trying to get a high five. I hope the captain left him awkwardly hanging.

Whenever your pilots need to take a bathroom break they're going to need one of the flight attendants to come up and take their seat. Only one can leave at a time, obviously, but two people have to be in the cockpit at all times. Always try to be the one to go up there, especially if it's in the middle of the food service. You'll act like you don't want to be stuck up there with the other pilot, but secretly you're happy to get out of doing work.

The conversations you have during the bathroom breaks are hilarious, and they are always the same. The non-peeing pilot will ask you how it's going back there. You'll answer and return the question. He'll ask if you live in whatever city you're based at or if you commute. If a commuter, he'll ask if its an easy commute and if you'll be able to get home after the trip. If you live local he'll ask which neighborhood. You'll return those questions as well. Next he'll want to know if you're flying that trip all month. You'll respond in turn and at that point the phone rings and the peeing pilot is ready to come back in. That's how it's scripted.

The pilots are good about taking their potty breaks in pairs so when one comes in from the lavatory, the other one will go out. Then you'll have the same exact conversation with the other pilot. Verbatim. If you've covered your schedule and the phone hasn't rung yet, it can get pretty uncomfortable. After you talk about how the flight's going, where you live, and what you fly, there really isn't too much to talk about. You'll just stare in awkward silence. I usually look around at all the instruments and gauges. If it gets too painful I'll ask if we're still getting in on time. That's a total desperation move.

Eventually, both of you will be staring at the phone, subliminally pleading with it to ring. If still no ring and it's obvious the pilot is taking a dump, one of us will ask the other about the layover we're about to have or just had, whatever the case may be. Then back to staring at the phone, maybe picking it up and making sure there's a dial tone.

    I know some nasty flight attendants that volunteer to babysit in the cockpit just so they can fart in there. That's just mean. I bet it is pretty funny for the cockpit, though, when one of them lets one rip. It's not like you can blame anyone else; it's obvious who the culprit was. I wonder if they acknowledge the fart or if it's an unspoken thing and they just pretend it didn't happen. I'm going to have to find that out. Maybe the victim goes on oxygen until the air clears.

Chapter 27

My favorite quote from the pilots is when you ask them inflight if they want the cereal or the omelet for breakfast. They'll think about the question, make a pondering face, take a deep breath, let it out slowly, and finally say, "I think I'll try the omelet." They say it like the idea of an omelet is something so obscure and foreign to them, like maybe we just started offering omelets and they're not sure what they're in for. I've been flying for over fourteen years and we've ALWAYS served cereal or omelets for breakfast, since day one! Never anything besides! Every single time they're on the plane they're offered an omelet, every day for years and years. I love that every time I offer one they act as if it's brand new. Love it.

One of my flight attendant friends is married to a pilot and for their anniversary she initiated him into the Mile High Club. It was his leg to land the plane and apparently he had the smoothest landing of his career. Maybe that's what it takes to calm the nerves. So if you ever have a super smooth landing, assume the pilot just had sex in the last hour or so, somehow. Don't ask questions, but you know what went down.

Worse tha≠n the passengers on one particular flight was the cockpit. I'd already been yelled at by the captain for keeping my first class galley too messy. The nerve!

"I'm sorry. Screw off, sir. Why don't you concentrate on driving and leave the kitchen to me? It isn't much, but it's all I have!" Later he yelled at me for making him spill his coffee all over the plane's consoles and the first officer's arm.

"Jessie, get in here!" he said from the cockpit as the first officer cleaned up his shirt. He thought my name was Jessie.

"Yes, captain, my captain."

"Look at this mess. Do you know how this happened?"

"Looks like you spilled your drink all over the controls of

this multimillion dollar aircraft, sir. Got the first officer, too."

"Yes, there was an accident and it happened because my cup was filled to the rim with piping hot coffee."

"Yeah, coffee shouldn't be filled that full, especially inflight. Even if you're on the ground and parked at the gate you can still spill so easily. That's why I don't fill it past two-thirds capacity when people ask me for a piping hot drink."

"Then why is Glen treating his arm for burns and why is this brand new plane covered in sticky coffee?"

"I have no idea, sir, I didn't pour that cup of coffee. Someone else poured that for you, didn't they? Was I the one that handed you that cup?"

"Well, go find out who poured this cup, I want to have a word with them."

I went back to my crossword puzzle at that point. During one of the inflight PAs to the passengers, the captain mentioned that this was a brand new plane, second trip ever. During deplaning one of the passengers asked the captain if he was serious about that. The good and proud captain radiantly beamed and said, "Absolutely!" He said it even has that new car smell in the cockpit still. Chuckle chuckle nyuk nyuk. Everyone laughed as I rolled my eyes and said that actually it smells a bit like stale coffee. The captain glared at me as I laughed at myself.

Chapter 28

Your love/hate relationship with air marshals is going to be a little more complicated because they don't work for your airline and you don't see them all the time.

Air marshals serve a very important function in the airlines for both passengers and crew members. They are deployed to "detect, deter, and defeat hostile acts targeting the United States, promoting confidence in civil aviation." Sounds like a fantastic idea, doesn't it? I'm all for it, but for all practical purposes and your normal day-to-day operation, they will just annoy the hell out of you—at least, the new ones who think they're saving the world will. The older ones are cool as can be and are a welcome break to some of the other regular passengers. Again, let's dwell on the worst-case scenarios because you're gonna need to know this.

The federal air marshals can be the worst passengers and it's not really their fault. They have to stay awake the entire time they're onboard. While the rest of the cabin is asleep, as the good passengers should be, they're sitting there wide awake and bored out of their minds. They try to talk to us way too much. They constantly need coffee or this or that and so you never really get to take a break as you would when your cabin is full of normal passengers.

It's not really a problem in main cabin because there are always other people awake, but in first class it's a different story. In first class, the paying passengers are very low maintenance. Your biggest headache is dealing with the pilots and air marshals. Since the air marshals don't always work in the same cabin they get really excited when they're in first class; at least, the new ones do. I get that, I really do. I would be too if I were them, but they turn into the most high-maintenance passengers ever thrown onto any mode of transportation. I don't think Miss Daisy was that bad compared to some of these guys. They don't turn down anything and often make requests that just aren't what you'd expect from your first class passengers. We have this thing called "sequence of service," where we give the passengers everything they get coming to them in a predetermined order based on time, need, and natural flow of the dining experience. We have many experts spending years studying this and they've come up with a decent system that works brilliantly, if you let it.

The newbie air marshals don't care about that. They could not care less. They like to have the dessert when it's time for warm mixed nuts. It never occurs to them that maybe at the beginning of the flight the ice cream is still on dry ice and isn't ready for human consumption. Adversely, they may pass on the main course entrée but then request the meal that got away at the very end of the flight. I'm sorry, but I'm not serving a dried-up piece of beef that was cooked seven hours ago, especially one that has been sitting inside a cold, dirty cart for the last four hours. Why would you even ask for that nasty thing? The new ones are horrible about that. After they've been around the block a time or two they settle in pretty nicely and are much better. The old pro air marshals are actually wonderful passengers.

Like the pilots, there are a good chunk that are all about the female stewardesses. As with the pilots, there are some girls that are really into that authority type and throw themselves at them. Like the pilots, the girls seem to love them or hate them but all end up getting screwed over by them sooner or later. After you get used and abused by a federal air marshal (FAM for short), it's said that you've been "famboozled." That term was coined by one of my colleagues who was famboozled once upon a time. It fits.

One of the most annoying things about the new hire FAMs, other than that they think they're single-handedly saving the world, is that they don't even pretend NOT to be air marshals. They dress like military guys. You can tell they bought their $15 button-up shirt the day before the flight. They have military haircuts. They don't really sit comfortably in those nice seats. While everyone else is reading Money, The Wall St. Journal, or at least OK magazine, they're reading Soldier of Fortune and Guns n'Ammo. They play war games on their

PSPs. They ask for things that other passengers don't usually ask for and it puts us in a weird position when we have to tell the normal passengers that they can't have a second meal while the undercover dude with a gun next to him has three.

The worst is when they fall asleep in first class. We're supposed to wake them up like a schoolteacher would with a sleeping student, but then the rest of the cabin notices us waking up a passenger for no good reason and gets curious. They think that we're just being mean not letting a passenger sleep if they want. It puts us in an incredibly awkward position. You really have to be an idiot not to notice air marshals on your flight. They might as well just put them in uniform so that everyone knows who they are. I don't see what would be so wrong with that. I love why they started the air marshal program and I think it'd make everyone feel better if they wore bright orange hunting vests (I know they have them at home) and let their presence be known.

Just got back from London tonight. We had FAMs on board. This isn't unusual, I'm even starting to recognize a few of them. These three I've never seen before. I don't pay them much attention, I just go to the back of the plane and start getting things set up in my galley. Then over the next fifteen minutes the girls I was flying with come back holding their hands in pain. Apparently one of the air marshals has a very hard handshake. When the first lady came back I thought she was just being dramatic. When the second lady came back and also put her hand on ice, I took them seriously. A few minutes later the purser came back and said that she thinks her hand is fractured. She went off on the guy about how you can't shake a female's hand like that and he just laughed. Almost immediately, the hands started to swell up. I could see it from across the galley.

In the midst of the bitching session about the FAM another lady came to the back with a hurt hand. The captain was notified immediately so he went to see for himself. I wasn't about to go shake his hand. They told me all about how he would squeeze down on all four fingers until it would snap. I know what that feels like, and if he's doing that to the older ladies, no telling what he'd do to me. A minute later we get a call from the captain saying that his hand is also hurt now. Wow! Really? After we reported all these hurt stewardesses he's going to try his luck? Genius!

The captain told the asshole FAM that he's going to get reported for his handshake and maybe even arrested for assault. It was an inconvenience to have the flight attendants hurt, but it was scary to think that the pilot couldn't use his right hand either. I'm sure he needs to push some very important buttons with that hand!

By the end of the flight all the hands were at comical size. One lady went straight to the hospital after landing and another was going to one as soon as she got home to Los Angeles in the morning. The air marshal was sitting in first class and probably got the worst service you could ever get from a flight crew. He retaliated by going to the bathroom a lot and not flushing the toilet and not draining the sink after he washed his hands. The ladies think that he has a really small dick. I think a flight attendant just dumped him, viciously and abruptly.

Whatever. He spent the entire flight reading his magazine about new martial art fighting techniques and playing combat games on his laptop. Nooooo, nobody could tell that he's a fucking air marshal; tons of businessmen read Soldier of Fortune and play assassination games for seven hours. I thought I'd seen everything there is to see on a plane until tonight. A damn FAM single-handedly (chuckle) takes out four flight attendants and a pilot in record time. He didn't even care either; he just laughed and said that he usually shakes hands harder. He totally got off by inflicting this pain. It's scary to think that guy carries around a gun. I was actually worried when the captain said he was going to confront him. He doesn't have a gun; he just has the ax from the cockpit. He didn't stand a chance if the nut-job went berserk and pulled out his gun. I could totally see it; the kid is obviously insane.

All that being said, there are some very nice air marshals that I've gotten to know very well, and they can freely admit that there are some people exactly as I've described, especially when they first start. They don't get paid enough for having such a boring job that keeps them away from their families so much. The recruiting brochure made the job sound a lot more exciting and important than it is in reality, I'm sure. I love the idea of having them patrolling the skies, waiting for bad guys to attack so they can protect us all. I just wish they were allowed to sleep while doing it, and weren't allowed to shake our hands so that people have to go to the emergency room. A good high five or chest bump might have to be the standard greeting from now on.

Part 7: The Flight Attendants

Us vs. the world, and each other.

Chapter 29

When I got hired, one of my main concerns was whether or not I'd have anything in common with the people I'd be sharing a beverage cart with. I had in my mind that the girls would all be brainless cheerleader types I really wouldn't have anything in common with. I'd lived with a gay roommate before and he was/still is very close to me, so I knew I'd get along fine with most of the gay boys, as long as they weren't overly bitchy and dramatic. I don't like bitchy and dramatic no matter whom it's coming from.

Before I got hired, I guess I never paid attention to the crew when I flew on planes. The only thing I had to go on was stereotypes and how flight attendants were portrayed in television/film. I figured it'd be a nonstop sorority/fraternity mixer with the pilots being the Alpha-Betas and the stewardesses being the wasted blonde Tri-Delts. I wasn't sure where I'd fit into that scene. That was not my thing in college and I avoided it as much as possible.

When I turned up at training that first day I was thrilled to see that these days flight attendants come in all shapes, sizes, religions, colors, and socio-economic backgrounds. You're going to see everything from bright-eyed college dropouts who can't even legally drink yet to retired policemen and everything in between.

Whatever it is that you're into, you're going to find some flight attendants that share your views. I was shocked by the amount of artists that become flight attendants. I was also shocked by the amount of Bible-beaters that would pull out their fancy leather-bound, personalized King James version any chance they could and silently judge the crew while reading Leviticus. I didn't think the traditional stewardess lifestyle would appeal to those people, but they found their niche just like everyone else does.

If you have a family at home and want to use your layovers for rest, there are plenty of others that do the same. If you don't really go out at home and work is where you go crazy and have YouTube-worthy nights out, that crowd is easy to find too. If you're adventurous and like to explore a city and check out the cultural sights and museums, you'll have no problem finding someone to join you. If you're sexually repressed or stuck in a miserable, loveless marriage, there's always a coworker who can tell you the best places to find hookers. Whatever it is that you're into, you can always find a partner in crime.

Flight attendants are somewhat superstitious, or at least sentimental, and most of us fly with something that we cannot fly without. They are no-go items. Some ladies have something their kids made for them. The religious ones wear St. Christopher around their neck, the patron saint of traveling. Some have a stuffed animal or a lucky bag tag. It's not so much a superstition for most of us, it's just a little piece of home. It's something to remind us of the near and dear we have waiting for us for when we get done working. Even that little connection can get you through some hard times if you happen to be stuck in Amman, Jordan, for a week.

I have a red bouncy ball that an ex-girlfriend gave me as I was leaving to take my first road trip when I was a teenager. I keep it in my toiletry kit. Whenever I go to a new city I'll take it out in the bathroom of my hotel room and bounce it. I've had that thing for nearly twenty years and it's been bounced in Australia, New Zealand, Turkey, Jordan, Italy, Costa Rica, Argentina, Tunisia, Brazil, Japan, Germany, and thirty other countries. It's now old and cracking and not really red anymore, but I still have it. I also have a St. Christopher medallion and a Turkish evil-eye I keep in my toiletry kit as well. I'm not sure if my items are really keeping me safe, but I'm still here, so there ya go. I won't leave without them.

When you first come on to the plane and meet your crew you'll either recognize the people or you'll pretend that you do. Even if it's a complete stranger you'll probably say, "Oh, we've flown together before!" You really don't know, though, because all the trips will run together. You may honestly remember someone and think that you just flew a trip together last month but when you figure it out, it turns out that the trip was over a year ago. You will have no concept of time at all. I swear I just flew a trip with this girl to Brussels a couple of months ago. She didn't remember. I refreshed her memory, reminding her that we snuck up on the roof of the hotel and watched the planes take off and land since we were right at the end of the runway. She pointed out that we haven't stayed at that hotel in over four years. Oops.

What shocked me after my very first trip was that nobody said goodbye. We flew to Los Angeles, had a great layover, and worked well together coming back to New York. I thought I did a great job and bonded with those people. I knew their story and they discovered mine. I wasn't expecting us to all add each other on Facebook or anything, but I thought we'd at least say bye. No, not so much.

As soon as the last passenger was off, people were rushing to catch their commuting flight home or the next bus to the employee parking lot. A purser may make a quick PA saying thanks for a good trip as she sprints toward the jet bridge, but that's about it. It wasn't the way I wanted my first trip to end but I've gotten used to it. At least you'll know going in that's how it goes and won't get your feelings hurt like I did.

Right after you pretend to know each other when you get on the plane, you have the mad dash to the newspapers. Most of our customers don't even know we offer USA Today because the pilots and flight attendants have taken them all. The crossword is what we're really after, and the rest will get thrown aside. If the flight is boring enough, however, we'll read every word of that thing, even the Money section.

Lately, it seems like half of the crew will be girls and half will be gay men. It's a good balance. I don't really like working with just ladies, especially if it's a crew of ten-plus. I'd much rather work with all gay men than women. I didn't expect I'd ever be saying that when I started, but you'll see that it's true. There is far less drama with all-male crews, unless they're all lead/purser qualified. Then you get too many cooks in the kitchen. Some of the worst, nastiest, most difficilt flight attendants we have are older ladies set in their ways. They're much worse to other girls than to guys, but it's still not fun when you have crew drama, even if it's not directed to you. If you stand up to those bullies, then the drama usually stops, so don't take no guff off of those swine!

The best scenario is that you get to work on a smaller plane with two pretty, single girls and the pilots don't lay over with you. Small crews tend to hang out together more, especially in lame cities. That's one secret that our senior people don't know. If you're going to a fun city like Los Angeles or Miami, you'll have a ton of options and people will usually do their own thing, or maybe they have friends there. If you're laying over near the Tucson airport and the only thing to do is go to the hotel bar, everyone will go there and make the most of it. Some of my craziest layovers have been in the least likely spots. A good crew can make anywhere fun. I'll always have a special place in my heart for Raleigh/Durham.

Chapter 30

The dynamics of your relationships with other straight male flight attendants are very complicated, more so than in normal society because we are so isolated. It's a fascinating case study. We are a small fraternity of brothers and it seems every year we're losing members to the other side, sometimes members you'd never think would fall to the dark side. Sometimes our most successful members put in a trade request. Ultimately, everyone gets their trade request, no matter how much their parents, best friends, or ex-lovers object. For the most part all the straight guys get along really well. It's welcoming to have another dude around you can talk to about straight guy stuff for a couple of days.

If you're at a base long enough you're going to hear about every other straight guy at the base and people will be shocked that you don't all know each other. "What?! Of course you know Kenny! He's straight too, slept with half the base. Really funny guy. Yeah, you have to know him." Of course, that's as silly as asking a black guy if he knows this other guy Ty that also lives in Atlanta. "Oh, I'm sure you know him, he's black too."

Some flight attendant bases are massive and you can go years without meeting everyone. After fourteen years, I still meet people for the first time when I get on a plane to work a trip. You sure hear about the other straight guys, though, especially if they're single and active. It's always funny at that moment when you finally meet another Straight for the first time. You know so much about him. You've been hearing about him for years and you know about all the other flight attendants he's slept with and you probably have a couple of girls in common. That's usually a good bonding point and will be discussed later in the bar over some whiskey drinks, SportsCenter, and ball scratching. Of course, whoever got there first will have bragging rights for all time. A word of advice, though: when you start laughing about a girl you had a fun layover with and you know that he has also been with her, make sure she was just a fling and not a serious girlfriend. Nothing is more uncomfortable than making comments about a girl and then finding out that your new straight friend used to be engaged to her, but she broke it off at the last minute and he's still heartbroken. Trust me. AWK-WARD!

I love meeting the other straight ones. It's like coming face-to-face with a long-lost brother, or a unicorn. There may be a little competition on the plane or at the bar to win a girl's favor, but after you've been flying for a few years you really don't care if you win or not. It's just fun being a guy with other guys and talking about guy stuff.

There is another faction out there, but thank god they're becoming extinct. I haven't seen them in years, but they're out there for sure. They are the straight homophobes that wear the Superman pin on their uniform. I noticed this once when I was brand new and asked the guy if he was a Superman fan. He looked at me with an intense seriousness and dragged me into the galley so he could tell me about his secret organization, much like the Masons or Stone Cutters. He said that the S Superman pin meant something much more important than liking some silly comic book character. The S meant that he was a Straight and that was how he let the world know that he wasn't just another "faggot flight attendant."

I was shocked. I figured most people could tell by talking to a person for a few minutes if they were a Straight or a Gay, but I guess he needed to accessorize in order to spell it out for them. He said us Straights need to stick together and that he'd put a Superman pin in my mailbox at the airport so I could join the club (cult). I think he was planning a revolution or something because this was all done very hush-hush with constant checks around us to make sure no one was listening in. I guess we can't let the Gays catch wind of the coup d'état!

I'm not sure how he thought the passengers would instinctively know that the S pin meant that he was straight. I never did get that part. I was apparently being groomed for fast entry into the club and

I didn't even know what it meant. What chance would anyone else have? Lots of flight attendants wear pins on their jackets or aprons during the service and no one bats an eye. So watch out for those guys. They are the Scientology extremists of the airline industry and completely whacked out. I think most of them quit the job once they realized they just weren't going to eliminate the Gays from the flight attendant profession. There are still a few stragglers, though, I hear stories from the underground. They usually hang out with the pilots on layovers.

The Straights will either support you in your endeavors or cock block at every chance. Mostly we help each other out but you'll definitely come across one greedy bastard that has to have the monopoly on talking to the female passengers or flight attendants. It's fun to help your fellow Straight out though; that's what life is all about, isn't it? Plus it's just great entertainment. Here's an example of both types of Straight. See if you can tell which is which.

The crew is heading to the layover hotel in Los Angeles. It's five guys, two girls, and me. I'm not the only straight one; one of the older guys is straight as well. We were on the plane for six hours together and on this van for half an hour and he still hasn't introduced himself to me. He's one of those macho guys who's been the King Cock for many years. He's used to being the only straight male and prefers it that way.
I could tell that he was sizing me up when a few of us were talking in a group earlier.
First, he was scanning for gayness, giving him the opportunity to accuse me of being a closet case. It wasn't there so he held his tongue. When we were checking in I stood right by him and kept looking at him until he acknowledged my presence. He's much bigger than I am. He's older, but works out and it shows, just as it shows that I don't work out but do have a trim semi-fit body. He has that cheesy-ass buzz cut that looked tough years ago, when he was in his prime. He found a look that worked for him and

by God, he's going to stick with it until the day he dies!

Finally, he looks at me and says something. He asks how I'm doing and calls me Sport, just a little bit nicer than Boss. His condescending tone is not wasted on me. The only attractive female on the crew asks me to re-pin her wings to her jacket because they had fallen off. I do and she makes a joke about me feeling her up in the process. Everyone laughs and I say something clever in response. Everyone laughs again. Everyone but the straight man, who I decided looks like the asshole jock in Encino Man. He says something about how that's cool that I touched her tit, but he's touched her taco. He actually used the word "taco." No one said a word and it got awkwardly silent for a second, except for the crickets, of course. I realized then that this guy was even more of a joke than I had originally anticipated.

Usually there is some sort of camaraderie among the straight flight attendants, even if they're competing for the girls. There are enough potential mates to go around and you win some, you lose some, so why fight with each other? Most guys think that way, not just straight stews.
Not this time. I've never in all my years of flying been seen like this.

The old rooster is seeing me as someone who might replace him, though I don't even want to be thought of like that. I could not care less. There are plenty of girls in this world to go around and most certainly enough in the confines of our job, where boys are already in the minority and most of the boys like burritos and not tacos.

Also, although he hates the attention he gets from the gay flight attendants and bitches about it to his buddies, he's a little jealous that now I'm the one they're saying inappropriate things to. I handle the comments with just the right amount of humor and masculinity. I know how to take the comments, decline any notion of whatever, and still have the gay boys respect me and enjoy having me around. After a trip of them flirting with me and me not freaking out about it, they're chill and appreciate me being around. I know this other guy complains about getting hit on by the boys, but it's just as obvious he misses the attention tonight.

On the van ride over to the hotel I got a couple of calls and the boys made comments about me being Mr. Popularity, Mr. Ladies Man, and all that. Everyone laughed and made their little comments. He just glared out the window in silence. Since only one girl came to the hotel tonight and since she's cute, I just know she's the current target. She's the prize we're fighting for, though only one of us is in this competition. I know her, I've flown with her before, and I wouldn't even think about hooking up with her. I'm not sure why, because she's hot and has a great personality. She's also hilarious. I'm single and in the mood to go out and have fun, so I'm not sure why I'm not interested.

Doesn't matter; if I'm not feeling it then I'm not feeling it. I'm not usually looking to hook up anyway. I just want to hang out and have some drinks with my friends. He's going to make her the challenge, though. I wonder if she senses this.

We're all supposed to meet up in her room in ten minutes. I bet he's dressed to the nines. I guarantee he'll be wearing Cool Water. I could not care any less. I'm going to go in and have my drink and be social. I'll have another one and hang out. Another girl I'm interested in is coming in to the hotel tomorrow at around noon. I'm looking forward to that the way the stud is looking forward to tonight's competition. He's going to be well-groomed and his hair will be flawless. He's going to be wearing something that shows off his muscles. He could kick my ass in two seconds and he's the sort of guy that gets off on that fact. He can always fall back on that and feel good about it.

Everyone is meeting up just about now. I'm going to take my time, make a phone call or two, and come in fashionably late. Just when he thinks that I chickened out of the "debrief" in the girl's room, I'll come in and everyone will be glad to see me. They'll have a couple of drinks in them so their reaction will be slightly more excited and welcoming. I'm not going to be dressed up. I'll be very casual. I don't even carry around nice clothes with me in my suitcase, just jeans and a couple T-shirts. It kills guys like that when a girl chooses a scrawny, slacker, artsy kid who looks like he just rolled out of bed rather than a well-groomed, fit, older, stylish person who takes great pride in his appearance.

I'll give myself another ten minutes before I go over and see how this plays out.

So was that Goofus or Gallant? Here's another straight guy being a straight guy:

> It was January 3, 1999, on a Boeing 757 from Newark to Los Angeles. I was working on the beverage cart behind the two flight attendants who were passing out the meals. I was going faster than they were, so I had to keep waiting for them to move their cart back before I could serve more people. I felt like an idiot while I was waiting. I was just standing there in front of one hundred sixty-six people, blocking the monitors showing the movie. Finally, I bent over to the person on the right and said, "So, you going home or away from home?"
>
> My subconscious was looking out for me. I didn't realize that this passenger was one of the most beautiful creatures I had ever seen. If I had noticed that, I don't think I could have spoken to her so casually, even though it is my job. Maybe it wasn't luck; maybe I had a sense she was there. I honestly was surprised when I saw to whom I was speaking. I had noticed her earlier writing in a notebook; my curiosity was piqued. Girls who write in notebooks are out of this world, even if they're just making a list of all my flaws. Nobody owns notebooks anymore.
>
> All the way from Newark to Los Angeles I sat in the aisle and talked to this girl. Anytime there was any sort of a lull in the conversation, I'd run back to the galley and get her another rum and coke. It was the perfect setup. I asked her what she was writing in her notebook and she said it was mainly poetry, song lyrics, and

whatever else popped into her head. She kinda closed the book when I tried to look at it. She was blushing. She said she even wrote something about how I walked down the aisle with this slow, sexy attitude, like a runway model. This came out before the cocktails were provided. Damn, the girl was fearless. I was impressed with all of it, though I did think her imagination was working overtime. I hate myself in the uniform. I feel like all my personality is drained from my being as soon as I button up the shirt and tighten the tie. I feel like a tool. Now I was the one blushing.

I was impressed she wrote so well, I was impressed she was so comfortable about sharing it with me, and I was impressed she could find inspiration out of something so blasé as a flight attendant walking down the aisle making sure everyone's seat belt was fastened. I also knew I was in trouble—she had it all planned out and there wasn't anything I could have done about it. She had me in her tractor beam. Though she was sitting I could tell she was probably taller than me, but barely. She had red wavy hair that was naturally brown but her current employer needed it red. Her eyes were blue/green and sparkling behind long flowery lashes. Her lips were light pink and I could tell by the way they moved while she talked that they were soft and sweet. She had the perpetual LA tan, even in January, that suited her well. After kneeling for so long, my knees were killing me; I had a new respect for baseball catchers.

I was in everybody's way; there was only one aisle on this particular plane so anybody going anywhere had to climb over me. But still, the other flight attendants would not let me do any work. The other male flight attendant was insistent. "For the sake of all us straight men in this profession, you are not to leave this plane without her number. I am senior to you, and that is an order. You don't have to lift a finger on this plane if you keep talking to that girl." I was entertaining them as well as everyone seated around her. Some say entertaining, others would say annoying.

By the time we landed, we knew each other pretty well. The

alcohol helped. We knew all about the other's past, dreams, family, interests, favorite bands and movies, and obsessive-compulsive behaviors. I got her number and told her I'd give her a call as soon as I changed clothes. Somehow in the van from the airport to the hotel I lost the number, but after digging through the seats for ten minutes, the driver found it for me. He received an extra dollar tip for that one.

I had twenty-three hours in Los Angeles before I returned home; she was with me every minute, always within three feet. Before we even spoke, she knew we were going to be together that night. She always gets what she wants. She came up to my room and I was all ready to go. She seemed impressed that I dressed like a slacker and not like some snotty prep or Abercrombie model.

The room I had was pretty amazing. The fourth wall was all windows and overlooked downtown Los Angeles from twenty-something stories up. Though there's nothing to do in the area, I've always liked staying there. In any case, we didn't have to stay there; she had her little beat-up blue car with hundreds of random CDs and mix tapes in the backseat. She took me to one of her local bars near Venice. It was dark and empty so we sat up at the bar, ordered some screwdrivers, and started to really get to know one another. She was already tipsy from all the drinks I made her on the plane so she made me do a couple shots to catch up.

I had my camera with me but I thought it was too early for that. I doubted she'd mind, as she was used to being in front of a camera for work, but still, I needed to play it cool. She told me stories about how her dad used to hang with Jerry Garcia and that she dated one of the Faith No More guys. I didn't know how much to believe but when we stopped by her place so she could grab a jacket, I saw photos of her with everyone she mentioned. There was one with her at four years old, holding hands with Jerry Garcia. I thought that was pretty badass. I noticed her modeling card for the Ford Modeling Agency. She showed me some of her portfolio and I was shocked and ashamed to discover that I had had one of the photos up on my wall in high school. I kept that information to myself because it was quite possible I had used that photo during a certain private activity in the shower.

I met her roommate, a wannabe actor from New York, but he didn't seem impressed by me. He just asked if I planned on staying over tonight. For two seconds he was happy to hear that I wasn't, but then she mentioned the beautiful hotel room I had downtown. He was afraid to ask if she was going to be coming home tonight. I didn't want that to be settled at that point either. I was hoping she'd stay over but it was way too early to be thinking about that.

We quickly left the poor guy, who was obviously in love with his bad-ass roommate, and headed to another bar she liked to go to. As the night went on we just keep praising each other more and more. Our hands were all over each other, though we haven't had the first kiss yet. I liked her because she was spontaneous and fun. She's liked me because I was laid back and creative.

After the bars closed we went to a coffee shop with thousands of books in cases on the walls. We spent an hour in a drunken haze reading to each other. I finally remembered my camera so we had a little photo shoot in the back corner of the coffee shop. When she took me back to hotel I didn't even have to ask if she was going to come in. I invited her up anyway and she just laughed and took my arm. It didn't strike me until I took off her last piece of clothing that this was a fucking gorgeous model that lots of guys would recognize and pay money to be with. I didn't see her that way at all; she was just a cool chick that I got along with famously. Honestly, if I had been blind I would have slept with her just on the basis of the conversation, but then I'd be pleasantly surprised when I ran my hands over her body.

I had always wanted to take this photograph; it was a lot like the scene in Lost Highway when Balthazar Getty and Patricia Arquette are lying on the dirt road, making love in front of the car headlights. There was something about that scene that got to me. Maybe it was the camera work and the editing, or maybe it was the isolation and immaculate freedom of the moment, that magic moment. It reminded me of where I grew up in West Texas, out in the desert, in the middle of nowhere. That silhouette was exactly what I wanted to capture and I knew she would be perfect for it; she had the ideal body and would be totally into it. I didn't feel like I knew her well enough at the time to ask her, and I regret that now. If she was fearless enough to tell me what she thought of me before we even met, I should have been able to pitch the photo idea. I dropped the ball big time.

    We stayed in the hotel room until the last second, when I absolutely, positively had to get ready for work. Even then she joined me in the shower and accompanied me downstairs to the lobby. We thought we were stealthy coming down the back elevator, but the entire crew still saw us going out the side door out to where I needed to catch the van back to the airport. The straight guy who helped make it all happen was beaming like a proud father. He had a slew of questions but I was way too tired even to respond. I think he was happier than me, though.

So you see the difference, right? Don't be an asshole, do the right thing. Treat others how you'd like to be treated.

Chapter 31

The people you work with will confide in you and tell you the most outlandish stuff you've ever heard, before they even learn your name. Something just comes over flight attendants when we're sitting on our jump seats together. It even has a name: "Jump Seat Therapy." It won't shock you after a while; at least, it shouldn't. I thought I'd heard it all until one girl was telling us how she's obsessed with putting her tongue in her husband's ass. We tried not to judge so I offered up some encouraging words. "Well, that's cool, do you make him wash up prior?"

She responded, and I quote, "No way, I like some flavor."

If I was talking with my good friends I'd be a little surprised that they told me that, but it might seem like a normal thing to say after a few drinks. No, this was a flight attendant I'd just met ten minutes ago and she was completely sober, I think. Just when you think you've heard it all, along comes a female with a fecal fetish.

You'll hear about affairs, diseases, threesomes, unruly children, fist fights with in-laws, stealing money from spouses, swinger parties in Buffalo, and that's just to get things started. I'm not sure why flight attendants think it's okay to share this stuff with their coworkers but it happens on every single flight. EVERY. SINGLE. FLIGHT. After a while you won't remember people by their name, just by their story. I have no idea who that lady is that likes a little anal flavor but the next time I see her that's all I'll be thinking about.

The thing is, you can get fired for talking about half that stuff. Most airlines have a list of things that you can't talk about because it offends people or makes them generally uncomfortable. You can't joke about sex, religion, race, or gender. You can't be a normal human being for the most part. Making sex jokes is half of what being a flight attendant is all about, but technically you can't do it and if you have an uptight coworker, they can turn you in and say that you offended them and you're done. You're fired, just like that. Union or no union, you're out of a job. You'll feel a lot like Austin Powers when Miss Kensington won't let him joke around and flirt with her. That's what being an International Man of Mystery is all about!

It got so bad at my airline that they made a section in our company's rules about it specifically. It's called "Article 32." Of course, being flight attendants, it didn't take long for us to rename it "Article 69" and later on "Article Doggie Style" and finally the title settled on, "Article Reverse Cowgirl." I think the people who can't handle jokes about religion, an occasional smack on the ass for a job well done, or the random racial generalization should probably not be in this field. We're a jokey group and talk a lot of shit, though nothing is malicious. The flight attendants who worked during the heyday of sex and drugs must be rolling over in their graves right now about how the industry they made famous has turned so prudish.

> It's been a really strange day, but only because of the last fifteen minutes. I got up early, flew to the Dominican Republic, flew back to New York, and got on the subway to come home. Nothing unusual there. In fact, very blasé nothingness. Well, the two landings we had today ranked as number 1 and number 2 in the all time hardest landings I've ever had. I guess it's just the M.O. of this particular pilot. I liked the guy, though; he was young and actually treated me as an equal and not a servant.
> I forgave him for those two terrible landings and subsequent headaches. The other flight attendants weren't so forgiving. The old Latino steward said that's what happens when egg rolls fly the plane. It took me a second to realize he was using "Egg Roll" as a racial slur against the young Asian pilot. I guess the flight attendant was hoping that if I had any racist tendencies, he could direct them against the slants and away from the spics. If anything, it backfired.

If you're not hearing outrageous stories while you're strapped into your jump seat waiting to take off, you're probably having to hear about someone's kids, or worse, their pets. Flight attendants are very crafty when it comes to showing off their little pride and joys, whether they be of the two- or four-legged variety. If they come at you inflight, it's easy to get away from these people. You just do a walkthrough and check crotches, making sure everyone still has one. If you're strapped in and ready to take off, however, you're stuck, and there is no way to get out of it. You're a fly trapped in a spider's web. You'll be at their mercy for at least fifteen minutes. Well played, crazy cat lady, well played.

Now that everyone has a smart phone with picture-taking capability, it's just gotten that much worse. There were only a few offenders when I first started, but now it's just out of control. I have no problem looking at travel photos, because I honestly enjoy seeing those pictures, but I really don't give a shit about how your bathroom remodeling job is going or about your new grandson. All babies look exactly the same to me. If I've seen one baby photo then I've seen every baby ever born, so unless they're dressed up as something hilarious, don't bother showing me.

I certainly don't care about seeing your two cats sleeping together in a ray of sunshine, I really don't. I love cats more than most people but enough is enough. Showing horribly boring photos to crew members really should be included in the Article 32 umbrella of things that can get you fired. The worst part is that those ladies (and they're ALWAYS ladies) are the sweetest ones so you can't tell them to piss off. You're going to just smile, nod, and innerly cringe while they beam. It's torture.

If a crew member is sobbing alone in a corner and talking about the loss of her "child," don't assume she's talking about a human being. We had a lady who had an entire crew mourning the loss of her "special little guy" for three days before it finally came out that it was a cat that had died, not a child. The crew was pissed; some of them had been in tears before they realized the lady was useless on the plane because of one of her damn cats and that there were still fourteen left at home. They had given her a free pass and let her take a passenger seat while everyone else worked a little harder. They applauded her for being brave and trying to get back to work after such a devastating loss. It's rumored that the same lady kept a different dead cat in the front window for a few days after it died, because it made her feel good. It wasn't until the smell became unbearable that she threw it out. When you think of the stereotypical stewardess you don't really think of a lady like that now, do you?

Chapter 32

It's a smart idea to have a code word for hot passengers and for assholes so you can talk about them on the cart right in front of them. Some flight attendants will even have a special ring for when they're dealing with a super annoying customer. While they're getting yelled at, they'll hit that Flight Attendant Call button a certain amount of times, just to give a heads-up to the rest of the crew. It doesn't resolve anything, but it's a secret way of letting off steam and letting your coworkers know which one is the problem child so they won't reward them with any free things later on. Everyone comes up with their own way of dealing with nasty passengers in nonchalant ways so that it doesn't end in a fist fight. It's what you gotta do.

When I'm on the cart with my friend Frank and there's a hot girl we want to point out to the other, we say, "Did you get that message from the extra flight attendant?" It's an inside joke that no one would understand, but that's the point. It's certainly more subtle than tapping your foot during boarding for the pilots.

Flight attendants might not be the smartest people on the planet, or even on the plane, but there are some things we can do very well. We're all math geniuses when it comes to certain calculations that are important to us. We all turn into Rain Man when it comes to figuring out our rest breaks, currency conversions, Fahrenheit to Celsius, or when we go illegal because of the length of our duty day during ongoing delays. We may not be able to count the passengers correctly, but we sure as hell can tell you exactly when our sign-in needs to be pushed back to the next day in order for the crew to get their legal amount of layover rest.

Your coworkers are also very creative when it comes to making kick-ass meals out of random ingredients. There's usually food left over for the crew to eat, especially in the premium cabins.

You'll probably eat your way from cabin to cabin and from takeoff to landing. You'll have a little salad from first, the cheese and crackers from business, and then finish up with the beef from coach. If you're still hungry you'll go back to first for an ice cream sundae.

Your coworkers can do amazing things with those random scraps of this and that. My specialty is cheesy roasted potatoes with a dab of blue cheese dressing on the side. Flight attendants will look at what's left over and treat it like a challenge on Top Chef, making amazingly complex and delicious dishes out of nothing. At first you'll love the food on the plane; it's really not that bad. I praise the tortellini in the creamy pesto sauce and would order it at a restaurant if offered, but after having it literally a hundred times, even that starts to get disgusting. Eventually, it will all be unappetizing and you'll resort to bringing food from home or paying exorbitant amounts for food in the terminal.

Flight attendants are also very good about killing time on the plane. If the flight is light the last row might be blocked for the crew. That gives us a comfortable place to sit and monitor the cabin. You can also watch a movie. If you've got a full boat you can read books or magazines; those are all obvious. The more creative people find other ways of passing the time on the longer flights. One guy (not a Straight) can make a very elegant-looking skirt out of the paper doilies in first class that we put the ice cream on. He also makes a kick-ass vagina by shoving the salmon appetizer into a breakfast bagel. I've never met a gay man so obsessed with female genitalia. Needless to say, I love working with him.

One purser brings a Scrabble board on every flight and takes on any challengers. Sometimes a flight attendant will have a deck of cards and we'll get a game of poker going in the back galley, using sugar packets and non-dairy creamers as betting chips. One time coming back from Puerto Rico we got a game of Horse going with the trash can in the back galley. The toughest shot was standing on one foot, banking it off the oven door and into the tiny garbage opening, all the while sticking a finger in the stewardess's ear. On our larger planes the back galley is big enough to play hacky sack or throw dice, both of which have happened and are well documented on my home videos. One flight attendant swears you can use the dry ice to burn off corns, moles, and warts. She'll be more than happy to take care of your foot/skin problems in the downtime during the flight.

If you get really bored you can always take the Soda Insert challenge. This is reserved for when you have exhausted all other forms of entertainment and it's done purely in desperation. You have one person close their eyes while you take out one soda can from the insert and replace it with another one. We all know those beverage inserts by heart so it doesn't take long to figure out that a tomato juice is missing and has been replaced by an extra Diet Coke. Occasionally, you get all three clear sodas: Sprite, Sierra Mist, and Seven Up. We had blind taste tests and I was shocked that I hate 7UP. All this time I thought that was the one I preferred, but after doing the taste test, I'm now a fan of the other two. So kudos to the 7UP advertising team for making me think that their product was the best. Shame to Sierra Mist for having a great product but horrible marketing.

That kills a little bit of time. If you're still bored you can always make grills for your teeth using the aluminum foil. As dire as the boredom situation gets, just remember you're in a better place than sweating over INS reports or climbing down a mine shaft and inhaling harmful air.

Chapter 33

Because of the flexibility of this job, some flight attendants have second jobs to supplement their income. It's not unusual for someone to fly and also bartend or work in a store. I know others that work in hospitals, own restaurants, own bars, own strip clubs, do real estate, teach yoga, sell cars, read cards, do interior design, act, build houses, or work as photographers. That isn't unusual at all. It is unusual for flight attendants to have part-time jobs WHILE they're on layovers. Usually those jobs aren't exactly legal, but some are. My old roommate used to bartend on her layovers back in her hometown. One girl teaches yoga classes in her layover cities.

I've known several other stews who have turned tricks on their layovers or smuggled drugs in from other countries or electronics out to other countries. The guy that did "massages" was very smart about it. When he got his schedule for the month he'd post which cities he'd be in on what nights on his special website and then just take reservations. It was a good system.

He'd carry his oils and whatnot with him so he was always ready to make some money. Even if he didn't have a client lined up he'd come prepared and hope that someone would beep him for an instant meeting. I don't think he's working for us anymore.

Chapter 34

That brings us smoothly to our next topic: how flight attendants are like flying pharmacies. Very quickly you'll learn which layovers are known for which pills. Even if you don't care to know because it doesn't matter at all in your existence, you'll hear all about it anyway. Some flight attendants will fly to Argentina just to get their Xanax, Paris to get their sleeping pills, and Caracas for their birth control pills. We have only nine hours to sleep after we land in Sao Paulo, but that doesn't stop some flight attendants from running down to the nearest farmacia to replenish their supply. Some pharmacies like the one in Buenos Aires will deliver right to the hotel. Recently, I heard the going rate for Xanax on the streets of America is around $4 a pill, and that's if you buy in bulk. You can get them for about $.30 a pill in Argentina. Do the math.

Since you probably won't be working international flights right away, you can always get layovers in McAllen, El Paso, or San Diego and then make a run over the border. Or else you can just ask your senior colleagues for whatever you need. Pilots and gay boys usually have Viagra. The waif-thin boys will also have speed. Waif girls are a good source for diet pills. Older ladies are good for Xanax and Valium. The gym rats often have supplements on them. Actually, the older ladies are good for anything else you might need. They cherish their pills the same way they do those photo albums they have devoted to cats that have died twenty years ago. You will always be missed and remembered, Sprinkles. Tear.

If you do get in trouble for drugs or alcohol, you're going to have to go to rehab to save your job. Your insurance covers it the first time and it'll only cost you around $800. It's usually at a nice place filled with celebrities. I use the term "nice" loosely. You might not call it nice until you see the place you have to go to if you get busted a second time. That place is a shit hole and your insurance won't cover it. It will cost you A LOT of money and self-respect. You should be scared straight by the end of that ordeal. The key to passing a drug test even if you're dead in the water is to dilute. Dilute like there's no tomorrow. If you get the call to head to Medical for a post-flight test, start chugging as much water as you can. A properly diluted sample can't get you in trouble. True, you'll be spending the rest of the day in the bathroom but it'll be worth it.

You're probably wondering about dating the girls you work alongside. Yeah, it happens and it happens quite a bit. I can't think of many straight male flight attendants who have been single while doing this job and not dated a coworker at some point. Who wouldn't want to date a cute stewardess every now and then? There are pros and cons in doing this and some might not seem so obvious.

First and foremost, don't go crazy when you first start. A base with over two thousand people might seem massive, but after a few months you'll realize you're seeing the same people over and over again. Don't think you can just sleep with someone and never see them again. You will see that girl again, so be respectful. Also, word gets around fast so you don't want to get a reputation for being a whore.

Your entire base will know your business and discuss it. It's annoying, but it's what flight attendants do. Rumors are started every single day and spread like wildfire throughout the base, morphing into fantastic stories of fiction. If you hook up with a girl on a layover in Las Vegas, I guarantee by the time you land back at base everyone knows about it. What happens on layovers ends up on Facebook, or Twitter, or whichever social media is popular that day. I'm not saying don't have fun, just don't be a prick and screw girls over.

One positive about settling down and seriously dating another flight attendant is that you'll be with someone who understands your schedule and the flight attendant lifestyle very well. Some "normal" people never really get used to the randomness and the fact that their loved one is gone so much doing god knows what.

Another great thing about dating a flight attendant is that you can sometimes fly together. Even if you have a horrible crew, just one person can make it tolerable, and if you're flying with your girlfriend, you know you're going to have that one person. It won't even seem like work. It'll seem like you're going on vacation. The best part of having the same schedule as your girlfriend is that you're not only in these fun cities with them, you also have the same days off back at base. You can have a normal life at home and a lot of fun on your layovers. It really makes going to work a pleasure.

The downside to that, of course, is when you can't work it to where you fly with your honey bunny. If you're holding opposite schedules and she's coming when you're going and vice versa, you may NEVER see her. That can be very difficult to deal with. In times like that, having a girlfriend who lives and works in your base city seems like the way to go; at least you know she'll always be around when you're in town.

A great perk of dating a flight attendant is that you both have very flexible schedules and excellent flight benefits. Taking dream vacations is so easy. It's not like you're dealing with someone who will only get time off around the holidays, when the flights are the fullest and most difficult to fly standby on. Take advantage of that for sure.

There really aren't too many drawbacks to dating a flight attendant except that neither of you will make any money, and raising kids is very difficult. It's a struggle on our paycheck, but even harder when you think about who will actually watch the kid if you're both having to fly. You can work it out where one of you is always with Junior while the other one flies, but then when are you all going to get to see each other? It's a problem.

Another potential calamity is that the girl will know how to look up your schedule. If you need a day or two to get away and have some precious alone time, you can tell a "normal" that the company gave you a trip and you have to go to Paris for a couple of days. You're not happy about it, but hey, your hands are tied.

The non-airline person will accept this at face value and let you go. If you're dating a stewardess, she'll know that trip wasn't on your schedule and you purposely picked it up when you previously had the day off.

After you're done dating and you find out she's a Stage Four clinger, you have to worry about her just showing up on your flights and assuming she can spend the layover with you. I once dated a girl based in Dallas, and every time I had to pass through there I had to worry that during boarding to wherever we were going, she'd turn up with her overnight bag. It happened only once but that was enough for me to be scared of DFW for years. It's one of those things that if you're excited about the girl it's the coolest thing ever, but if you're not into her, it's downright scary.

The worst part about dating a flight attendant is what happens after you break up and you have to work together. It's hard to get over a breakup the normal way when every day you're flying with mutual friends who always ask about it or try to help. Again, everyone knows your business and nobody can mind theirs. Even when most of the base knows about the heartbreaking split, for months and even years later someone you haven't seen in a while will show up on your trip and ask how your gorgeous sweetheart of a girlfriend is. You'll have to relive the breakup all over again while you tell the out-of-the-loop person that you got dumped a year and a half ago. Thanks for bringing that up.

If you are going to break up with your stewardess girlfriend and you're flying together for the month, never, and I repeat, NEVER break up at the beginning of the month. Suck it up for four weeks and do it after the last trip is completed. It seems like common sense, but I wish someone would've told me that ten years ago.

The best situation is probably to go interline. Date a flight attendant, but not with your airline. Pick another one. It's far less dramatic that way. You will still have that understanding of the lifestyle and the amazing travel benefits, but the stalking and coworker gossip will be in check somewhat. Not wanting children is also a huge advantage in making a flight attendant couple work.

The various crew match-ups range from common-as-a-cold to extremely rare. To put it in terms of animals, it works out like this:
- A Female flight attendant hooking up with a Male pilot would be a "pigeon." You see those everywhere, every day.
- Female flight attendant + Male stew is a little less likely so we'll classify that as a "Weinie Dog."
- Female pilot + Male flight attendant = Snuffleupagus
- Female pilot + Male pilot = Loch Ness Monster
- Male stew + Male stew = House Fly
- Female stew + Female stew = Bald Eagle
- Male Stew + Male Stew + Female Stew = Koala
- Female Stew + Female Stew + Male Pilot = Siamese Cat
- Female Stew + Male Pilot + Female Pilot + Female Stew
- Male Stew + the chambermaid = A Caracas Layover.

Part 8: Passengers

Without you, I am nothing!

Chapter 35

Ahhhh, the passengers! Our sole reason for being! It's so easy to get down on the passengers because directly or indirectly they have their hand in almost every little drama that can befall a flight attendant. They are, however, the reason we're needed on the plane so try your best not to take it personally when they come to you with problems. Most of the time they don't even want you to fix the problem, they just want you to listen and sympathize a little bit. Tell them you understand and that everything is going to be all right. Nothing takes the steam out of a good tantrum faster than saying they're 100 percent justified in it.

Others that come up to you red in the face are angry and dag-nabbit, they intend to stay that way no matter what you say or do for them! There's just no pleasing them and they don't want to be satisfied. It's easy to spot those people so don't let them suck the life out of you. Don't let them hijack your emotions.

Your attitude is going to be the bigger determinant in how the flight will go, not theirs. Even though we like to think we're there for passenger safety, we're not really. We are for the FAA, but for your airline, you're there to defuse bad situations and turn those frowns upside down.

When the passengers need to complain, they don't get to talk to the CEO. They can't look the reservation agent in the eye. They'll never see the baggage handler that mishandled their suitcase. You're the one they come into contact with so you're responsible for everyone else's actions as far as they're concerned. I know it's ridiculous, but that's the reality of it. Get over it. No matter how ugly one of these passengers is to you, you'll deal with them for a few hours and then they'll get off the plane and you'll never see them again. Just remember that. At the same time be very conscious that you're also the only one within punching, spitting, and kicking distance of the angry passenger.

Try looking at each passenger as a problem that needs to be solved if they seem angry or stressed. If they seem normal, then be thankful and keep them that way. First of all, kudos for that passenger for getting off their ass and seeing a different part of our world. Not many Americans really explore the planet so give props to the ones that want to know what's beyond their backyard!

If you're meeting people from other countries and they seem cool, stay in touch with them. Since almost everyone is on some sort of social media or has email, get their information. Having friends all around the world is a fantastic thing. My best holidays have been visiting people in other countries. You have a free place to stay and a local to show you how to live like a local. The flight to get over to them won't cost you much at all. Cheap flight, free place to stay, free tour guide who has friends, of whom I'm sure at least a few are cute—you can't do much better than that. It takes so little effort to make friends but the benefits could be through the roof!

On most of the larger planes you have three classes. You have noble first class, envious business class, and shameful steerage. Sitting in first class does not make you a first-class individual just as sitting in coach doesn't make you common. This isn't the caste system in India with Untouchables and Brahmins. Andrew McCarthy, Patrick Dempsey, Chloe Sevigny, Emile Hirsch, and Crispin Glover are not common people. They all proudly sat in coach on one of my flights over the years and didn't mind at all.

Typically, the first class people are very low maintenance. They fly all the time and they just want to be left alone. They know what to expect from the service and they know what we will and will not do for them. They don't usually get wasted or complain or ask for things that make our job more difficult. If anything, they'll request things that make our job easier, like forgoing the long, drawn-out process of giving them their tray with bread, then appetizer, then salad, then entree, then dessert. No, they'll say skip this and that and just have certain elements all at once, so they can get to work or take a nap. I love those people. You might feel like you're not giving them your best, but you will be giving them exactly what they want. That's the point.

The business class crowd can be a little tricky. When people from coach use their miles for upgrades, they don't get to go all the way to first class, they have to stop at business. You can only upgrade one cabin with my airline. They can be a little fussy, demanding, rude, and high maintenance. The business class people behave as if they're in first class, but they're not. I don't think they realize that the people really sitting in first class aren't snapping their fingers or ringing a little bell to summon us. I honestly think they believe that's going on in first class, so they try to act that way as well. Those are the people that can get a bit of a superior attitude. They act like they're happy in business, like they're doing the smart thing by saving the money and not moving up to first, but given the chance, they'd knock down their own grandmother for an upgrade to first. They're just playing hard-to-want.

On our largest plane we have nearly forty seats in business class and only two flight attendants working the aisle. Can you imagine if all forty were prima donnas? It happens sometimes. On any flight where all cabins are full, the business class flight attendants will work the hardest out of anyone on the plane. Some people don't mind that, it keeps them busy. I avoid that cabin like the plague. I have nothing in common with those people and they have nothing to offer me. Some of the single stewardesses like to flirt with the male business classers, but that doesn't really help me. The worst thing I've seen in business class was when a businessman was flying home from Dallas after a big meeting. He took off his shoes and propped up his feet on the seat in front of him, gross but not uncommon. What repulsed me and sent shivers down my spine, making me question how far evolved we really are, was what he did next. I guess he felt like his socks were a little sweaty so he took them off and proceeded to dry them out by putting the dirty sock over the air vent on full blast. The sock blew up like a windsock and instantly filled the cabin with dirty foot smell.

We had people all the way back in main cabin complaining about the smell. That was the only time I gagged on a flight without having alcohol involved. I really thought I was going to throw up.

The "Shaking My Head" moment certainly goes to business class, though. We were on a smaller plane so we only had fourteen passengers in business, but four of them were small children. Halfway through the flight they got bored as hell, as they do when their parents don't think to provide them with activities or an iPad. The lead flight attendant went through the galley, trying to find something entertaining and/or distracting. Unfortunately, the most fun things to play with were the most dangerous, but the girl did find a lot of aluminum foil that previously lined the bottom of all the racks that went into the oven. She used her Origami 101 skills and fashioned little pirate hats for the kids. They loved them.

The stuffy old business men just glared and returned to their newspapers, not even cracking a smile over the overjoyed children. The children got their parents in on the pirate game and soon the flight attendant was making hats for them as well. She went ahead and used up all the foil, making as many silver pirate hats as she could. She offered the extra hats to some of the other people sitting in business class. They kind of looked around and eventually took one, not putting it on at first, not until the kids forced them too.

Once the hats were distributed, they all had a pirate party, until two business men who weren't offered a hat started to get pissy. They were the ones rolling their eyes and not at all hiding their disapproval of what was happening in their classy cabin. They asked why they didn't get a hat when everyone else had one. The flight attendant had to explain that they didn't have enough foil to make pirate hats for fourteen people. Can you believe that one of the guys wouldn't let it go? He didn't see why he wasn't able to have a hat whenever everyone else got one. I never thought I'd see the day when a grown man would pout about not having a silly hat made out of aluminum foil, but that's the mentality of those passengers. If everyone else has something, by God, they want it too! If that flight attendant would've given herpes to everyone in the cabin, I bet he'd want that too. Unbelievable! I never would've believed it if I hadn't seen it. No way! At least you know what to expect from business class. You know it's going to be hard, and it is, but you're ready for it.

Chapter 36

You can never be ready for what happens in coach, though. You just never know. You can have the nicest people in the world on one leg, but the very next group might be straight out of hell, or the trailer park, or a from a trailer park in hell.

If you get tired of the mundane and predictable, work in main cabin. Every calamity known to befall man will happen in the back of an airplane. You will see things that make your head spin. There will be biting fights, amorous couples, loud music, screaming kids, drunk rugby teams, and many arguments over reclined seat backs. Most of your medical situations will occur in coach as well. You're dealing with many more people in coach, but I like it back there. Those are my people and they'll keep you on your toes.

You'll notice that if your airline collects money for any sort of charity, the people in coach always give the most money, by far. Not just as a cabin—I mean of course two hundred people in coach are going to give more than the sixteen in first class. I'm talking about individual donations; the average middle-class passenger will give more than the rich business owner nine times out of ten. You'll see the same thing on the subway when homeless people beg for money. It's the ones that don't look like they have any spare scratch to give who give the most. You can see parallels to our society all over the place.

When you're working in main cabin you're going to see passengers take on certain roles. The aisle seat will be the spokesman for the row and the row leader. They'll be in charge of when people can and cannot get up and go to the bathroom. They'll also collect the row's trash when the market bag comes around to pick up rubbish. The window seat is in charge of the window shade. It doesn't matter if you want it down to make it darker in the cabin; if the window person wants it open to stare at clouds, then it's going to stay open.

If you're in the middle seat then you have no power at all. You are the bitch of the row and have to go along with what everyone else is doing. You have no voice. You are a woman in Brunei, you have no vote. For this reason I think the middle seat should get the lion's share of the armrests.

The debate on who gets the armrest has been going on as long as they've had armrests on planes. Many articles have been written about it in every conceivable form of publication, from a flight attendant's blog all the way up to The Wall Street Journal. Many experts have weighed in on the subject: frequent flyers, etiquette experts, CEOs of airlines, flight attendants, and fat men.

There are many theories and most have holes in their logic. Taking turns doesn't work. One person using the front part of the armrest while the other person uses the back part doesn't work either. First come, first serve doesn't work.

The fact that there isn't a clear-cut system is what drives people mad. Even if you had a system in place that said the middle person doesn't get either armrest and the other two people get to have two, that would work out better in the long run, once everyone got used to the rule. Having a right and wrong way to sit is much easier for our minds to comprehend than this vague and confusing battle of comfort versus manners. Someone will complain to you about the armrest and you're going to have to have a solution—don't think it won't happen. Maybe by the time it happens the airlines will have a solution. I bet it involves paying more in order to have full access to the communal armrest. Situations like the armrest debate is another great study on human behavior and why we crave boundaries and rules.

Even more often than the great armrest debate, you'll have problems in coach with passengers reclining their seats and encroaching on the person behind them. It happens more often than the armrest brawls, but it's also an easier fix. If it's during the meal service and someone can't get to their food because of a seat back, I think it's all right for you to ask the person to temporarily put their seat up a couple inches. They can always put it back down after they're done eating. Only a few people grumble about that.

If there is no meal service and someone is demanding the person in front of them to put their seat up then the answer is obvious: No! That person has every right to be comfortable and put their seat back as far as the seat allows. If a passenger feels like they're being crowded, then tough shit. They can always recline their own seat and gain back the precious space they just lost during the encroachment.

You'll also find that people like to tattle on other passengers, usually about stupid things. They won't tell on someone from their own row, though; that would just make things awkward afterwards. It's sweet how the row will come together as a team and not bring each other down. Usually the tattletale will snitch on someone in the row ahead of them, behind the offender's back, so that the guilty person isn't aware that they've been ratted out. Mouthing words, gesturing, and finally pointing gets the message across. I like to make an example of that person who tattles. I'll pretend like I don't understand what the tattletale is getting at.

"What? Oh, the person in front of you doesn't have their seat belt fastened? Oh okay, thanks for bringing that to my attention!" If you do that you don't even have to say anything to the sinner. They got the message loud and clear. They'll buckle up and then shoot a look back at the little Cindy Brady. The passenger who takes it upon themselves to enforce the Fasten Seat Belt sign is usually the same kid who took names for the teacher when she stepped out of the classroom back in elementary school.

One exception of a row turning on themselves occurred one afternoon when we were flying back from London to New York. I was on break, so I was busy tasting what food the other cabins had to offer; thus, I missed it actually happening and I'm so sad that I did. As soon as I came back to my coach galley the flight attendants involved told me all about it.

It seems a little old Indian lady came to the back of the plane and meekly complained about something going on in her row that she didn't want her little son to see. The responding flight attendant rolled his eyes and asked her to be more specific. She mumbled something and motioned for him to follow her. The steward, still clueless about what was going on, followed her up to the first rows in main cabin, thinking, "What could really be that bad?"

It was a day flight where everyone was awake and the cabin was filled with sunlight. So he got up there and saw what the problem was and took care of it. That was all he said at first. He teased us with the details, but we could tell it was something brilliant. Finally after he was sure we were all hanging on his every word and about to burst, he continued with what happened.

It seemed that a young American law student guy and a comely lass from Scotland had hit it off during the flight. They started talking, then they ordered some drinks. From there they started cuddling and then things got out of hand.

We asked how far they got before the lady came back to complain and he said, "Well, I can't say that I saw nipple, but that's only because his mouth was covering it." We lost it at that point. So this girl let this random guy take her tit out and start sucking on it in front of the entire cabin on a full flight in broad daylight, with a little Indian family seated directly next to them? WOW!

I asked him what he did about it and he said there wasn't much to do. The cabin was full so they couldn't separate them. The guy got really mad and started talking about how once he got his law degree he was going to sue the airline, denying him his God-given right to get to second base in front of a crowd. The girl was mortified. She could not have been more embarrassed. Once the guy started giving us attitude the flight attendants knew what they should do—they upgraded the girl to first class. That's what happens when you show remorse and apologize rather than talking about lawsuits! Case closed.

I've heard stories of couples partaking in simultaneous oral sex in the seats in coach, but I've yet to encounter that in my travels. I don't doubt that it's true though. I'm still trying to figure out how I'd handle that situation. I'd have fun with it and embarrass the hell out of them for sure. That's a given.

Chapter 37

The most difficult passenger you'll ever come across is the first-time upgrade to first class. You can spot them immediately. They're dressed nicer than everyone else, can't operate the fancy chairs, and tell you that they want items that everyone gets automatically, like mixed nuts. My mom does the same thing at Olive Garden about the breadsticks.

The first-time upgrades will sample every wine we offer, including the port, ice wine, tokaji, and sherry, and that's before the meals have even been passed out! They insist on being woken up for breakfast, but then snap at you when you wake them up. They don't seem to realize that when you fly from New York to Paris the time between the end of the dinner service and the start of breakfast is only three hours. They think just because one is "dinner" and the other is "breakfast," there must be plenty of time to get a nice long sleep in.

We used to have a big problem with them not knowing how to use the hot towels before the drink service, but now everyone has seen The Wedding Singer so that potential obstacle is met with quiet confidence. It's hard to get mad at the upgrade because they really are excited to be up there. It's not their fault that they don't know how to act. I probably did exactly the same things they did during my first time up there. I'm sure I wanted to try every wine; I wanted everything I had coming to me. Who knows when you'll be up there again, so hell yeah you're gonna take advantage!

Every now and then you'll get passengers from coach who decide mid-flight that they are too good for coach. They'll take it upon themselves to right things with the universe and place their sacred ass into a business or first class seat. Usually we discover this right away and explain that only the cosmos has the power to reassign passengers into better cabins, not the passengers themselves. They scowl and embarrassingly slink back to their seat where their former seat mate is laughing his or her ass off. Instant karma.

On one all-night flight to London we had a lady get up from her main cabin seat, bypass business, and find an open seat in first class. When the flight attendant confronted her on this, the indignant lady called the flight attendant "a dried-up cunt" and stomped back to coach, but not before barreling over an elderly man who was stretching his legs near the business class bathroom. When she got back to main cabin she went to the very back of the plane, called us all "miserable bitches," picked up the stack of UK Landing cards, and threw them all over the cabin. She made it rain.

She was arrested when we landed and if the case would've gone to trial, the crew would've been flown in to testify. We were all hoping for that. Turns out in that sort of situation the crew gets to deadhead to the city in first or business class and gets removed from any trips already on our schedule during the days of the trial, with full pay! I love that the airlines already have a plan for how to handle situations where crews need to show up and testify against passengers. It must happen quite a bit.

We asked the arresting officers about the chances of this going to trial and he said very good, unless she pleaded guilty. I guess that's what happened because we never heard another word about it.

After you've been flying for a while you'll start to notice certain traits from different markets or groups of people. It's really fascinating. You'll feel like Jane Goodall and want to document everything you observe.

The Italians like to stand the entire flight and chat with each other. The Dominicans like to party. It's not unusual to have to tell them that if they're going to listen to their boom box, they're going to have to put in the head phones. The response I received the last time I had to do that was, "But this music is meant to be heard LOUD!" Fair enough.

When you work a flight to the Dominican Republic you'll find that a lot of the women suffer from DDS. When they come to the back of the plane and tell you that they don't feel good, your first question should be if they drank last night or earlier today. The problem is usually pinpointed there and you send them back to their seats with a Pessi (Pepsi) or Esprite (Sprite). If they say no, then check the tightness of their clothes. They like very tight clothes, and not much of them. Sometimes what they're wearing is three sizes too small during boarding. We all expand in the air, so it's very possible that their circulation is getting cut off. Solution: tell them to find something looser to wear or at least unbutton their jeans, if they're wearing underwear.

If that isn't the problem then it's obviously DDS. Tell them that it looks like a bad case of DDS and that they need a Sprite to make it go away. They'll believe you and everything will be fine. Don't tell them that DDS stands for Dramatic Dominican Syndrome. Another great cure is to get them the supplemental oxygen we have for emergencies, but not turn it on. That seems to work wonders and they'll thank you appreciatively. Oh, and if someone asks for Wikkey, that means Scotch whiskey. Penis = peanuts.

The Japanese passengers are quiet as church mice and leave their area tidier than it was when they boarded. LOVE me some Japanese passengers! The Indian crowds are nonstop tea drinkers so you have to block off the galley with a heavy cart to avoid them coming back to the galley for tea. All the other flight attendants will just make tea after tea after tea and keep them out on top of the cart for all the people coming back. You're pouring tea nonstop, they're drinking faster than you can set a new batch down.

The Finns like to drink and the French do as well, until you run out of the French wine; then they get indignant and teach you a lesson by not drinking your Californian swill. They don't understand that it doesn't really hurt the flight attendants' feelings when we don't have to do anything for them.

Every now and then you'll get a group of refugees from Nepal or Somalia. They are so nice, but completely out of their element. They'll want to try Coke because they know about it, but don't give it to them! Their bodies can't handle it so they end up spending hours in the bathroom, yet they don't know how to use the toilets. It's flights like those that make you thankful that you don't have to clean the lavatories.

The Haitian passengers don't always know how to use the toilet either. They'll get their business in the hole, but neglect to put the used paper in there as well. Those will be left on the floor. Sometimes you'll see footprints on the toilet seats from where they stood on the bowl and squatted down. Flight attendants block off a bathroom for crew use on the Haitian flights. You'll love the Haitians, though, they are so sweet. They don't have a lot of nice clothes, but they'll wear the nicest thing in their closet for the flight. They try, at least, which is more than I can say about most American passengers who show up in their pajamas.

Someone once said that the Haitians will put their dying on a plane because they want them to die in America. I think they get a free burial or something. I'm not sure if that's true. It's just the opposite for the Puerto Ricans, though. Their dying try to get back to the mother island from the States before they pass. Another rumor is that the Haitians will put their pregnant women that are about to burst on a flight to America so that they'll be citizens. That doesn't sound right either. I'm not going to question it, though; many voodoo priests fly on those flights and I'm not messing with that.

Chapter 38

On the domestic side of things you'll quickly discover which flights or markets to avoid. Miami-New York is notorious for high-maintenance ladies who order four drinks at a time and refuse to say thank you. Even when you give them exactly what they want, they complain. The coffee will be too hot, the ice will be too cold, or the salted pretzels will be too salty. It's just in their nature. Having a trip that goes to Miami and back in one day is a lot like moving day or a breakup—no matter how smoothly it goes, it's still excruciatingly painful

Los Angeles-New York has a lot of attitude but if you pretend like they're hot shit, they'll be fine. San Francisco flights can be trying because of all the damn vegetarians and their special meals. I get so fed up with them whining about the food choices—and I'm one of them! I'm also a vegetarian! I'm a self-loathing vegetarian, I guess. It's a mode of transportation, not a restaurant! If you have special dietary needs, you might want to address them before you get on the plane. Just sayin'.

Anything flying into Las Vegas is going to be tough; that crowd is ready to get the party started. You can make good money on tips with them at least. We're really not supposed to take tips but we're also not supposed to start a fight by declining them. The rule they'll tell you in training is to refuse three times. If they still insist, graciously take the tip. Of course, in real life that means grabbing the money as you say "No, no, no! You don't have to do that. Thank you."

Flying to Chicago in the winter sucks, but that's mainly because of all the damn coats. The flights to Vail are the absolute worst because it's all rich New Yorkers who are too good for East Coast skiing but not good enough for European skiing. Every single person in coach has a fur and they're outraged when you tell them that there isn't room in the closet for nearly two hundred coats and that they're going to have to put them in the (gasp) overhead bin.

Telling them that is like telling them that their children are going to be tortured with sewing needles.

Any flight in or out of Orlando is going to be a ball buster because of all of the kids. The silver lining on those is when you get a Make-a-Wish foundation child going to Disney World. If you can get through one of those flights without crying then you're a stronger man than I am.

I'm not a very religious guy, but I want to read the Torah from start to finish just so I can see where exactly it says that all people of the Jewish faith must wait until the last passenger deplanes before they can start getting their stuff together. It's got to be in there somewhere, because they all seem to know about it. Luckily, you're a straight MALE flight attendant so I don't need to explain being "clean" when you serve the kosher meals, but it has to do with monthly vaginal bleeding.

Chapter 39

As big as I am about being honest about delays on the ground, I'm equally against being honest in the air. You're going to want to tell those people whatever they want to hear so that they stay calm, even if you know it's an outright lie. Will they make their 4 p.m. connection when we land at 3:50 p.m.? Sure, that's plenty of time! Since we're landing right as the last flight to Rome is taking off will they hold the plane for me? Sure, they'll hold that plane for you! Will their bag make the connection as well? Sure, those bags get moved faster than you can get from one gate to the next! Will a wheelchair be waiting for them when they get to the gate? Sure, the airport special services is very good about being there on time!

It's just so much easier to tell them what they want to hear if it involves something that can't be changed anyway. Why panic them? By the time they realize you're full of crap, you're on another plane going somewhere else. At the very least you gave the chump a few hours of peace of mind when you could've been honest and freaked them out. It's just a little white lie. Fair play.

Always promise fearful flyers that it'll be a good ride, even if the captain tells you specifically that it's going to be rough. There's a chance that it might miraculously be smooth. The mental anguish waiting for the scheduled bumps to come will probably be worse than the turbulence itself for that passenger. This way they have a sporting chance. If the turbulence does come, act like it's not a big deal. They'll be looking at you for reassurance so pretend like it's nothing, even if it gets bad. A passenger could probably handle a wing falling off at 35,000 feet if the flight attendants acted as if it was supposed to do that.

On domestic flights, passengers have this overwhelming need to know where exactly you are after you've been in the air for a couple of hours. They start to get bored or antsy so they'll look out the window and wonder what they're looking at. Rather than trying to figure it out or bothering the cockpit, just tell them you're over Kansas. No one seems to know exactly where Kansas is, but it always sounds like it could be the right answer. They're always satisfied with Kansas. If you're near Chicago and they ask which ocean you're flying over, it's not an ocean, it's Lake Michigan. Don't blame them, blame the school system.

On every flight there will be a couple of people who will try to come up with any reason to why they should be getting free drinks. Some examples are as follows:

- "We pushed back forty-eight seconds late, I want a free drink!"
- "My seat reclines too far, I want a free drink!"
- "I don't like the food, I want a free drink!"
- "I don't like the inflight movie, I want a free drink!"
- "Braniff used to give us free drinks! Why don't you?"

The truth is that we don't really mind giving out free drinks. They aren't ours, why should we care? A happy passenger is a loyal passenger. If someone is pleasant and doesn't expect the drinks to be free, I might just forget to charge that person. Or better yet, if someone whines about having to pay for drinks, I might give the person next to them a free drink, just to teach everyone a lesson.

Quick tip: if someone is drunk yet keeps trying to order cocktails, instead of making them a seventh jack and Coke or cutting them off and risking a bad scene, give them a glass of Coke, but put a little whiskey along the rim of the glass so it'll smell like a stiff drink while they're drinking it. They'll also get a little taste of whiskey as well. I've never had anyone bust me on that one.

Some people deal with air travel better than others. I actually got airsick on my flight back from my interview. I wondered if this was really the right job for me. During choppy flights several people might get airsick. Even on smooth flights some people might get nauseous. It's normal, it happens, that's why each and every seat has a barf bag at it. What to do with the used sick bag is up for debate. Most flight attendants look at a passenger coming to the back of the plane with a full bag as if they were holding a dead sewer rat by the tail. They'll dry heave and then refuse to take it, making the person wait for the lavatory to be vacant so they can throw it away themselves. I do that. Messy problems occur when I catch a whiff of someone else's vomit.

Some flight attendants like to pretend they never knew that the person got sick and will just let them leave the used bag at their seat for the cleaners to find. That's just disgusting, but you'd be surprised how many passengers will do just that. They'll just leave it there for someone to find. They won't hide it; they want it to be discovered. They're like a cat that's leaving its family a gift of a dead bird. Never trust a vomit bag. At the very least it'll have used gum but it could have some things in it that are much worse.

If you see a passenger running to the back of the plane and it looks like they're going to throw up, run away, especially if you glance at the lavatory and notice it's occupied. Grab a trash bag, throw it toward them, and run for cover. That's the only way you can be helpful, honestly. It's better to be safe than sorry. A third of the flight attendants I know have been puked on by a passenger at some point, sometimes when they were a good five feet away from the sickie. Maybe it's the pressurized cabin, but projectile vomit at altitude can get an extra three feet in distance than in the frat house on the ground. Nothing can ruin your day faster than getting thrown up on and still having eight hours left to go in the flight with no back-up uniform in your bag.

Another interesting phenomenon is that grown men turn into twelve-year-old boys when they take massive dumps on the plane. They feel the need to show them off for all to see, so they won't even flush them. It's not like they tried and it didn't go down. I've seen guys come out of the lav without hearing a flush, so I'll go in to wash my hands and then see the sickest remains imaginable. I don't know why you'd be proud of that, but you'll see it.

It's always disgusting when you see passengers go into the bathrooms without shoes or socks. I don't see how you can do that. I know I've missed the toilet when I've been trying to pee and we hit some bumps. There's no telling what wickedness lives on the bathroom floor. Some of your coworkers will yell at adults that go in there barefoot; I don't say a word. It's none of my business. When parents let their babies crawl around right in front of the bathroom door, however, that's another story. Babies don't know any better. Broken glass is the best-case scenario for what you may encounter in front of the bathroom door. That really ought to be a form of child abuse. Babies repeatedly exposed to the floor by the lavatories will either die at a young age or achieve superpowers like some hero in the comics.

Another peculiar thing passengers like to do is when they ask for a cup of water to take medication, they'll show you the pills, to prove to you that there really are pills that need to be taken. It's not just a bullshit story they've concocted to swindle you out of a cup of water, as if you weren't going to give them water if they didn't produce the pills to corroborate their story.

"No, I don't believe you have aspirin back at your seat, sir, I'm afraid I can't give you any water. If only there were some way you could prove to me that these pills exist, then maybe I could help you!" There are great opportunities to mess with the passengers when they do this. Personally, I like to ask them if they're sure they wouldn't rather have vodka to chase their Ambien down with. One guy said, "Yeah, that's a good idea, thanks, Brian." Of course, that guy is the one that remembers my name, never the ones I give good advice to.

Chapter 40

One of the great things about this job is that you never know what to expect. Every single flight is different. You might have to fly between Chicago and Detroit five times in a day on the same aircraft, but I guarantee that those flights won't be remotely the same. That's one of the good and bad things about the profession, depending on what type of person you are. If you like consistency and knowing what you're in for every day, this might not be the right job for you. If you think that variety is the spice of life and think it's exciting not knowing what to expect when you step into your office, then hells yeah! You're in for a treat! There's a comfort in having a dependable routine, but air hosts and hostesses are a rare breed. We thrive on the unexpected and the chaos.

The stories you'll hear and the questions you'll be asked will make your head spin. I really wish I would've started writing them down from the day I started, so that's my advice to you: document all the insanity. You only get the ridiculousness every now and then, but if you document all of it, by the end of your career you'll have the most interesting book ever imagined. And it's all true.

The most unbelievable thing I've experienced on one of my flights so far was when an older Jamaican lady was taking her super elderly mother from Kingston to New York. After we shut the door the daughter came up to the first class galley where we were discussing how the entire country smells like weed. She very politely asked if we could refrain from mentioning over the PA that we were flying to New York. She didn't want her mom to know. So of course we wondered why. Why did she not want her mother to know that we were going to New York, and where exactly did she think we were flying? She went on to explain that it wasn't the destination that we were supposed to avoid mentioning, it was the fact that we were on an airplane. Right.

Her mother was terrified of flying and would never have made the trip if she knew that you had to fly to get to America. So again, it begs the question, how did she think she was getting from the island nation of Jamaica to New York City? Well, the mother threw up a Hail Mary and told her elderly mom that they were taking the train from the Caribbean to New York. A bold move indeed.

At this point we all leaned out into the aisle to get a good look at the lady. Was she really that dumb or senile? She was just sitting there, happy as a clam with her little purse in her lap. The daughter had secretly closed all the window shades in the cabin so you couldn't see all the other planes parked at the gates. I'm not sure how she didn't notice them before, like when they were in the terminal area. I really should've asked how she pulled that part off.

We didn't think this plan had a chance in hell of working, but we said we'd do our best. We were taking bets to when mom figured it out. I thought we'd be fine until descent for landing.

We even had the captain play along and not say anything airline specific in his announcements. Of course, we didn't let him call himself captain; he was Conductor Bob. He was happy to do it and actually did a fantastic job getting all the pertinent information to the passengers without blowing the cover that we were on a plane. He played it just right, to where the elderly lady didn't know she was on a plane and the rest of the passengers didn't know that they weren't supposed to be on a plane.

I have no idea what happened when they got off the plane/train in one of the biggest and busiest airports in the world, but I guess it didn't really matter then. She pulled it off. I never would've thought to even attempt something like that, but I can now picture her at the time she came up with the idea. I see her hands clasped in front of her face while she looks shiftily about, whispering to herself, "It just may be crazy enough to work!" It just goes to show that you can't accomplish what you don't try.

That sweet old lady was duped, but she was indeed very old. Sometimes you hear of even more stupid things coming out of very alert and seemingly intelligent people. My favorite questions are: "Which way is the plane flying?" I thought it was a straightforward question so I answered, "Mostly south, maybe a little west." No, she meant were we traveling the way that we were all facing or were we going backwards. I pretended to think about it for a second. I stood up straight and looked forward and backwards. After biting my lip in deep thought I gave a confirming nod and answered that we were heading in the direction that we were all facing. On this particular flight the cockpit was in the front part of the plane.

 A health-conscious passenger once asked, "Is the ice onboard the plane made from the water onboard the plane?" I guess some newspaper did a report on the purity of our tap water and she was worried that our ice was made from that same water. To save you from the embarrassment of asking your coworkers, no, our ice comes from the caterers. It's not made onboard the plane. That's just stupid, just like when people think we have microwaves in the galleys.

 "Won't that mess up my hair?" was a question asked when we requested that a passenger lower her window shade so that the cabin would get darker. No, it's not like rolling down the window in your car, the window will stay shut. You just have to bite your lip and pretend like it's not the dumbest thing you've ever heard, because actually it's not. No matter how stupid a question, it'll be topped on another flight. There is no rock bottom, it keeps going and going.

 On one flight from London to New York on November 9, I had a European lady ask me about the light load we had in main cabin. It was the last flight of the evening back to New York and it's not typically a popular flight for us, so I told her that. She thought about it and said that she didn't believe me; she thought it was because people were scared to fly on 9-11.

 I realized right away what was happening. She was from France and they write the dates backwards from how we do it stateside, so if she were going to write September 11, she would write it as 11-9-2001, whereas November 9 would be 9-11. She'd heard 9-11 so much on television that I guess she thought the attacks on the World Trade Center and Pentagon happened on November 9.

I politely told her that she was mistaken and that they happened on September 11. I thought that would clear up the confusion and we'd get a chuckle out of it, but I couldn't have been more wrong. She snapped at me. Through clinched teeth she informed me that she was not an idiot and that she was well aware that the attacks happened in September.

So now I was the one that was confused. If she knew that 9-11 was September 11, and not in November, then why in the world would she ask if that's why we had such a light load? So I asked her, at risk of getting snapped at again. She put on an air of superiority as she adjusted herself in her seat. Then she told me that she reckoned that everyone else in Europe didn't realize that 9-11 was in September and they all thought it was in November and that was the real reason nobody was in main cabin that day. Reiterating that the late flight to New York is always empty didn't dissuade her at all. She had figured it out and she wasn't going to be convinced otherwise. She was the only smart person from Europe apparently.

She was so adamant about the entire continent being backwards that I took a poll of all my European friends that night to see if they knew the month of the attacks in New York. Every single one of them got it right so that pretty much blew her theory out of the water. I only wish I'd bump into her again to tell her that, just to rub it into her smug little face. That would've given me as much satisfaction as I get when a passenger goes off on me and tells me that they'll never fly my airline again, only for me to see them on another flight a few weeks later. I love that. They always recognize me and at that first moment of recognition they seem happy to see me; then they remember what all had happened in that first encounter. The smile drops from their face and they get a bit sheepish.

Chapter 41

All airlines offer comparable amenities on the plane. What United does from one market to another market is probably very similar to what American and Delta do between the same cities. So why would passengers choose one over another if the flights are all priced relatively the same as well? It's because they like the experience one airline gives over the others, or maybe that they're members of that airline's loyalty program and it's too late to switch now, but let's go with the crew creating an enjoyable atmosphere and a painless flight.

In most cases it doesn't matter if you don't have the nicest entertainment system or best on-time arrival numbers. If the customer feels like they were treated well and the headache of air travel was somehow a pleasant experience, that more than anything will keep them coming back. So while being professional and providing a nice service is important, so is just being cool and fun.

Our airline has phases of service, and I'm sure that all airlines have something similar. Our third phase is when we go around after the meal service and chitchat with whomever wants to talk, schmooze a little bit. It's this little bit of personality that goes a long way. In training they teach you that Phase Three is the "phase that pays." It's true, so go socialize a little bit and make some friends; don't just run to the back of the plane and hide out until it's time to land.

I like to have fun with the passengers. One month we were showing The Ring on the plane, even in main cabin. How that movie fell through the cracks when they were supposed to be picking general-audience approved movies is beyond me, but it was a fun month.

When it got to the point at the end of the movie where Samara walks toward the television and ultimately walks through it to kill the male lead, that's when we had our fun. I was flying with a girl with very long dark hair, so if we were lucky enough to notice that part of the movie coming up, she'd run to the front of the cabin. While the passengers were glued to their monitors, she would be brushing her hair down over her face, looking exactly like Samara. She'd wait until that shocking moment when Samara came through the television set and all the passengers came out of their skin. After they jumped and squealed, the passengers would invariably look around in embarrassment because of the way they reacted. That's when my colleague would walk slowly up the aisle with her arms out in that freaky zombie way with her face totally covered by the long hair. When they saw that they'd scream even louder. They were truly terrified. It was fantastic. That's the sort of experience that keeps them coming back. Maybe.

We've already discussed how to chat up passengers inflight and we just learned about Phase Three, the Phase that Pays. For all practical purposes, it's also the Phase that Lays. But much like a good check in hockey, make sure you do it the legal way. There's no shame in the game if you follow the rules for your purposes.

As much as you want to look at the Passenger Information List and get the cute girl's name so that you can look her up later on Facebook and send her a message, don't do it. I'm not sure if it's illegal, but it's certainly unethical. It's way creepy at the very least. I don't know too many girls that would be flattered by that. You may call it "resourceful," but they'll call it stalking and so will the courts. It's funny how guys would be okay with a girl doing all that legwork but the same isn't true the other way around. Don't try to figure it out. Women are from Venus, men are from Mars.

If you're like me, you probably like a good accent. Some guys dig the Swedish accent, while others get off on Italian, Australian, Russian, or Caribbean. For me, it was always the British accent that would cause me to melt. I thought it was the sexiest thing ever. After working almost one thousand flights to and from England, I lost that loving feeling for the Brits. At one point I could get turned on listening to a British girl read the Bible to me, but now all I hear is one of my passengers complaining that we don't have the special meal they ordered two weeks ago or that they don't like our wur-tah. It's pronounced wah-ter. W-A-T-E-R. If you see a T in a word, make that sound, don't add an R to it. You see that R at the end of the word? Make that sound, you lazy wanker! It's a sad thing when you love something and then this job takes it away.

On a more serious note, flight attendants these days are taught to be suspicious of young girls not ordering anything to eat or drink on long flights or of the ones that avoid eye contact, especially from Central and South America. So many girls are being used as drug mules. Every other person they come into contact with sees them for about three seconds, but you get them for hours, and you're really the most likely person to catch this. Yeah, this job isn't quite what it used to be. Now we have to look out for drug runners and terrorists, along with the fact that traveling 600 mph in a tin can through highly elevated levels of radiation is just wrong on so many levels.

You probably won't get much "joy" doing this job. You won't get that internal satisfaction from doing a great job on the plane the way you might if you were a nurse and helped a sick person get better or if you were a teacher and taught a child to read. You deal with the "work" aspect of it in order to get to the kick-ass layover and the chance to enjoy your flight benefits on your own time. That's where the internal satisfaction comes. The job is good for your soul, just in a different, more roundabout way.

That doesn't mean that it's not enjoyable, it's just not that fulfilling. We're all capable of so much more. You serve drinks, you pass out food, and that's about it. No one ever accused flight attendants of being overachievers. If anything, the general public will see the job more like a phase, something you ought to grow out of. It's fine and dandy when you're in your twenties; people can accept that. They don't feel the same way about you if you're still doing it at fifty, though. They wonder why you wasted your life. Things like that will either bother you or they won't, but you shouldn't let it. Never apologize for your life if you're truly happy, no matter what you do. So many people will talk shit about your life because they're envious that you're doing exactly what you want to be doing. People are generally scared of people who do exactly what they want.

Chapter 42

You probably got hired because you're at least a little bit of a people-person. You seemed like you'd be the type to enjoy interacting with people, and they seemed to react favorably to you. I don't do as much chitchatting with the passengers as I did when I was a new hire, but I still enjoy hearing what they have to say. Everyone has a story and I love to hear the bizarre ones, especially if they're traveling stories.

> Fantastic flight today. I met this one guy from Florida and I could just tell that he wasn't having a very good day. I figured it was just a long, exhausting trip with his wife and it was taking its toll. We see it all the time leaving Orlando. He ended up hanging out in the back galley for a long time while she read a book at her seat, so I started chatting him up. I didn't want to pry, but I asked some questions that got him talking about things. I was so glad that I did!
>
> Turns out the couple had won $30,000 in some lottery and they picked up their prize earlier today. They had hit five out of six numbers. They played every week and always used the same numbers: 3, 14, 6, 22, 12, and 31. They used those numbers because he was born on December 31st, she on June 22nd, and they got married on March 14th. If they had married on the 15th, they would have won eight million dollars. The winning numbers were 3, 15, 6, 22, 12, and 31—they missed only one number and they missed that number by one!
>
> He had wanted to marry on the 15th, but she was afraid to get married on the Ides of March. There was a fight before the wedding about the date, but he eventually caved in. She thought that was settled and would never be brought up again, but ten minutes after the numbers came in, it was again an issue. For ten minutes they were the happiest couple. They were screaming, hugging, laughing, planning purchases, and generally loving life and

their good fortune. The man remarked how they were so close to the big jackpot.

"Oh, honey, just one number away, isn't that something! We need to thank our mothers for bearing us on those God-blessed days. Just think, baby, if only we had married on..."

It was just about then when it clicked. He realized that it was her fault. As far as he was concerned, she cost him nearly eight million dollars. So there they were, avoiding each other on a full plane, $30,000 richer, but eight million dollars poorer.

A friend of a friend of mine told me a great story about a trip he took overseas for an acting job. It was his first big break and might have even been his first trip abroad, I don't remember. He was cast in a new show and they were going to shoot the pilot as soon as the cast showed up. The guy couldn't have been more excited about the whole experience. When he was going through customs they asked him why he was traveling that day. He replied enthusiastically, "To shoot a pilot!" A few hours and many interviews later, they decided he wasn't a terrorist.

Okay, I take it back. Business class passengers won't be the worst you see. It won't be the first-time upgraders either. The worst group of passengers I've ever had were the whores the Germans flew in from the Dominican Republic to work during the World Cup in 2006. Yeah, they literally paid for prostitutes to fly to the various cities for the soccer tournament. Those Germans thought of everything! I have never met a more self-centered, egomaniacal diva with delusions of grandeur who was a bigger problem than those "ladies." They thought they were rock stars. They thought they were just the shit. I can't believe I didn't take a photo of these outfits. I must have been in shock. It looked like they were going to walk off the plane and go straight to their street corner, but they thought they looked sublime. By the way they were acting, you'd think that the only reason they were even having a World Cup was to showcase the girls' talents. The soccer thing was secondary. So watch out for roaming packs of

Dominican hookers; they are not an easy bunch to please.

You might always want to be wary of the passengers that actually subscribe to your airline's inflight magazine. I bet you didn't even know that you could subscribe to that, did you? Surprise! Yes, you can, but why in the world would you want to? It takes a special kind of person to care that much about what your airline has to say about where to get a drink in Miami. I don't trust those people!

It's absolutely fantastic when you unexpectedly get your friends on one of your flights. Those will be the best flights ever. I've had it happen quite a few times and I love being able to give them the VIP treatment. If at all possible I'll get them in first class and pamper them with good food and chilled champagne. You're really not supposed to upgrade your friends if they're flying on your buddy passes. You can get in trouble for that for some reason. But if you know someone who's a full-fare passenger, then there are always legal ways to get them moved up. You'll be allowed to upgrade passengers if they go above and beyond during the flight, or help out during boarding in some substantial way. At the very least it's cool to have your friends watch you in action. They've all heard your stories a million times but very few get to see what you really look like doing your thing.

Any time you know a full-fare passenger personally, have them write a good letter about you to the company that might offset the bad ones you'll be getting. You can't have your Buddy Pass people do it, but an independently traveling friend cannot be traced back to you. It'll seem like you earned the praise from a perfect stranger. That's huge.

Part 9: Inflight

It's business time!

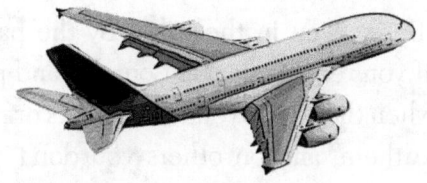

Chapter 43

Once you get up to cruising altitude things are usually smooth sailing. People are settled in. Whatever drama they had getting to the airport or with boarding is over and they're on their way. You're also in between the two most dangerous parts of air travel—takeoff and landing. I think I'd rather crash during landing than takeoff; there's less fuel in the wings during landing.

The Food Service manual you will be given demands that the drink service commence eight to ten minutes after takeoff, but that's just silly. You'll still be hearing about your coworkers' love life or looking at photos of cats wearing hats well past the half hour mark.

You can always look busy by doing a walk-through and seat belt check. Being seen in the cabin by the passengers is very important, even if you're just checking out tits and packages. This is usually the time when they'll ask you for blankets or pillows. On some flights you'll have them, and on others you don't. The best flights are the ones where every seat has both a pillow and a blanket. That should satisfy everyone, but of course there will always be a couple of people who will insist on multiple blankets. They'll either wrap themselves up like a mummy or hoard the pillows in case a cabin-wide pillow fight breaks out. If that happens, they'll instantly have the upper hand. Honestly, the airline pillows are not that great. It takes at least three of them to provide the amount of cushion that one normal pillow does. Those neck pillows are a wonderful suggestion.

Do not give the blankets to anyone you like. They are incredibly dirty. Even if they come sealed in plastic wrap don't think that the blankets are brand new. I know for a fact that sometimes the used ones are wrapped up again and passed off as clean. I've seen those blankets get doused with everything from urine, feces, wine, ejaculate, and vomit. I always throw those blankets that get spilled on straight into the garbage, but I know some get left on the plane and who knows what happens to them after cabin service gets ahold of them. Most likely they get a spin through the washing machine, but is that really enough after a hormonal teenage boy on the all-nighter to Las Vegas uses the blanket as a cum rag? I gag whenever I see passengers cover their faces with those vile things. I dare you to take a black light to an airline blanket. I dare you!

Just as passengers will always try to find a reason why they deserve free drinks, flight attendants will always look for justification in only doing one service for the passengers in main cabin. You'll hear lame excuses like, "It's going to get bumpy," "We'll give out cans and that's the same as two services of just cups," or "These people seem hungry, let's skip that first drink service and go right into the meal service."

Sometimes it really does make sense to feed the people right away if you've had a long delay, or to rush the service if turbulence is a probability, but it's amazing how quickly these one-off situations turn into normal flight procedure. Once you cut the corner one time, you really don't have much of an argument against doing it a second and third time. Before you know it, you've completely rewritten the Food Service procedures and the passengers don't get what's coming to them. Flight attendants are excellent at rationalizing anything, though. They'll say that if a passenger really needs that second drink they're getting screwed out of, they'll ring their call button and ask for it.

The operation of receiving catering items and distributing those items to the people is very much the same as when rich countries send humanitarian aid to corrupt African nations. The best stuff gets taken by the Haves and very little makes it way down to the Have Nots. Oftentimes, the best items that make it onto the plane never make it to the intended passengers.

For a while we were supposed to serve lemonade to the premium cabins on the afternoon flights, but those usually ended up in someone's apartment. If the lemonade did get made, it certainly didn't get offered to the passengers; it was for flight attendant use only. They don't give us the lemonade anymore for some reason. The same holds true of the fancy box of chocolates they used to give us to offer the passengers after the meal service. They were delicious. Those would get served to the passengers, but only after the crew would pick out the ones they wanted first.

If you're going to offer six beef, six chicken, and four pasta entrees to first class, the galley might take one of the beefs off the menu and have it for themselves. They usually give you a couple extra meals in case you run out of one choice or if a meal comes out bad, but some flight attendants will claim one before it even gets offered to the paying passengers. Occasionally the catering will be exactly the same as the passenger count and so there will be no room for error. If you accidentally drop a steak on the floor while you're plating it, someone is going to have to eat it. You can wash it off the best you can, but it's going to be served. Hopefully on legs like that your cockpit gets to eat. That way you can serve the important full-fare passenger a good piece of meat and the pilot can have the one that's been scrubbed with hot tap water.

One of my favorite sides we get in first class is this gnocchi that comes with the beef entrée. We invariably run out of the beef so I never ever get a chance to eat that gnocchi. If I'm the galley flight attendant in charge of plating all the dishes I can remove two little pieces of gnocchi off of each plate I send out into the cabin. The passengers don't notice, and after doing that several times, I have a nice sized gnocchi dish for myself and no one is the wiser. Win-win.

In main cabin you're supposed to count the meals and then make sure you have enough when boarding is complete. The problem with that is that you never know the exact number of passengers until the door is about to close. If you are short then there's no way in hell you'll be able to get the extra meals on. If that happens, then you can try a couple of different things. If it's an all-night flight you probably won't have to worry about it because you'll have people who go right to sleep and won't eat. If it's a day flight you can make an announcement. You can either ask parents who know their kids won't eat the food to kindly pass so that everyone else can get a meal. In turn, you can ask other adults to give up their meal so that every child can be assured of something to eat. Both of those tactics will usually free up a couple of meals.

If you're still short after playing to the passengers' sympathies, then you can go for the old standby, free drinks. Let the people know that if they give up their meal they'll receive a couple of beers or whatever. There's always some young guys who will jump at the chance for that. If all of that is done and you're still short, then that really sucks. It's embarrassing and painful and you're going to hear about it. Don't get defensive; they have every right to be irate, especially if it's a long flight.

Try your best to be on their side. Pretend like you're just as pissed off as they are. Blame catering. Your airline doesn't provide the meals; they have catering services do that, so you can totally throw them under the bus. You know the South Park song "Blame Canada," right? Well, same concept here: "Blame Catering."

Flight attendants really do feel bad when that happens. Not having anything to eat is just unacceptable if we've promised the passenger a meal. We're far less sympathetic if we run out of choices when we get to the last rows though. Yeah, it sucks for those people but hey, at least they're getting something. It's impossible to cater all the choices to 100 percent of what the cabin holds, so the airlines do the best they can. There's simply not enough room on the plane to do that. There are people who study who eats what to where and when. They come up with the numbers and go by that. It's not an exact science but they certainly do a lot of research on it. Still, though, some egocentric prick might through a tantrum so just let him do his thing and you can sing the Blame Catering song.

Passengers, especially American passengers, think that having a choice is our god-given right. I mean, that's what it means to be an American, right? Oftentimes, it'd be better if we just gave everyone the same thing and there wasn't a discussion about it. Having a choice and then having one of the options taken away is what really gets people mad. That's just way too Nazi-istic. Remember, though, there is always a choice—to eat or not!

Chapter 44

When you're doing the drink service inflight, the bane of your existence will be the coffee drinkers. They'll never tell you how they take it and even if they do, they'll change their mind as you're trying to ask the next person. It's a cliché and it happens on every single flight ever flown since the Wright brothers took flight, so just get used to it. Don't let that get you upset. You'll see 80 percent of your coworkers snap at someone during breakfast flights and yeah it's annoying, but there isn't anything you can do about it. I've tried everything in the book. When someone tells me they want coffee I ask, "How do you take it?" in every way imaginable. I tried putting the emphasis on every word and none of them work.

"HOW do you take it?"
"How DO you take it?"
"How do YOU take it?"
"How do you TAKE it?"
"How do you take IT?"

It doesn't matter, half the passengers will answer incorrectly. I've even tried making a helpful, but polite announcement to the entire main cabin that goes something like this: "Ladies and gentlemen, in just a few minutes we'll be starting our breakfast service. Since we don't know you personally just yet, please let us know if you take milk or sugar/sweetener in your coffee or tea when ordering. Also, remember that 'coffee regular' means something different in every part of the world so please be specific. Thank you."

It doesn't matter. They won't listen. Just get used to it. When you think that the coffee song and dance is usually the worst thing we have to deal with at our job, you should be very appreciative that you're just dealing with that and not having to do something disgusting or dangerous.

Usually after that little scenario plays out the very next person will ask you what you have. Try not to roll your eyes. Go through the basic list: soft drinks, juices, coffee, tea, water. Alcoholic drinks are also available for a charge. Some flight attendants won't go through the list. They'll just say, "What do you like and I bet I have it." When asked, "What do you have," some of the wise asses will respond with "Everything but time, honey." Even pretty girls don't really get away with that particular smart-ass retort.

I used to answer with, "Whatever you want, I bet we have it," but lately I've been getting way too many orders for Fanta, pear juice, grapefruit juice, root beer, and Snapple. So now I give the subset groups and then we take it from there. If they're interested in the colas then I can expand on that selection: Coke, Diet Coke, Pepsi, Diet Pepsi, Sprite, Diet Sprite, and ginger ale. Usually the ones that want to hear every liquid we have on the plane are the ones that end up asking for the most common choice: water or Coke. You think they'd just take a stab at "water" or "Coke" before asking what all we have.

On select flights you'll serve these disgusting-looking barbecue sandwiches in coach. You heat them up a hundred at a time and by the time they get moved from the oven to the cart and onto the tray, they're all mangled and smushed in their foil wrappers. The foil will say "Caliente" to warn you and the passenger that it's very hot temperature wise. When you go through the aisle to offer them to the passengers you should say something like, "Barbecue beef sandwich, careful, it's hot!" Don't be the idiot that doesn't understand that "caliente" is Spanish for "hot" and go throughout the cabin offering the passengers hot caliente for dinner, thinking that "caliente" is the name of the dish. I've seen it.

During the meal service there's usually one passenger who decides they need to get to the bathroom immediately. You'll roll your eyes and start to pull the heavy cart back so they can make it to the lavatory, but they'll insist you don't need to move. Those carts are about seven millimeters skinnier than the width of the aisle but for some reason everyone thinks they can squeeze past in that amount of space. They can't make it. Don't let them even try. Consider it your daily exercise by moving that cart an extra few yards for that special little passenger, but don't you dare let them return right to their seat after they're done. They can wait patiently, and hopefully they learned a lesson by the time they get back to their cold meal.

One trick I've learned for getting a good letter is to secretly, yet openly, praise your aisle flight attendants when you're the galley stew in the premium cabins. One time as a joke I told everyone that they did a great job and gave everyone high fives behind the curtain in the galley. No passengers saw this happen. I didn't think anything of it until a month later when I got a glowing letter sent to my supervisor about what a great crew we were and how it was the best service he'd ever had. What impressed him the most was that after we delivered this service (which was very ordinary), he heard me recognize and congratulate my colleagues. He was impressed that we realized that we "nailed it" and that props were given to all involved.

I cracked up when I read that letter, but now I make sure I loudly congratulate my crew after every service so that the people in the first row can hear. I'm still waiting for that second letter of praise.

Even though ideally you'd like to sleep across the world or watch as many movies as possible, don't rush the service too much in order to go on break. At least pretend that serving the passengers is what you care most about when you're on the plane. It looks tacky when you're in a hurry to get the food out and cleared as quickly as possible.

Once the service is over on those longer flights and it's time to go on break, you'll find that flight attendants are geniuses at finding places to sleep or at least making themselves more comfortable. I've seen crew crawl into cart compartments on the Boeing 767 and into closets on the McDonnell Douglas 80. I've seen them remove the jump seat headrest from the 757 and use it as a pillow on the emergency door in the very back, out of view of the passengers. Flight attendants are a very resourceful bunch.

Some flight attendants will treat themselves to a drink after the service. Red wine in a coffee mug looks very much like coffee to the naked eye. If a flight attendant asks you if you want French coffee, she's asking you if you want some Cabernet.

Chapter 45

A quick word about the lavatories. Guys will have to learn to use their bodies as a tripod to pee during turbulence. Spread your legs and then lean forward to rest your head against the wall so that your body is touching the plane in three different places. You should be able to not piss all over yourself if you're positioned that way. The obvious solution to peeing in turbulence is to sit down to pee, but no self-respecting man would ever do that!

The lighting in the bathroom is harsh but also great for seeing zits that will be seen in natural light in a couple of days' time. You can get a head start on fixing your skin. It's like a magic mirror that can see into the future! Girls and metrosexual boys alike love using the lavatory light to pluck their eyebrows. The light is perfect for it.

If you're a smoker and can't survive a long flight without a cigarette, there are always ways to smoke in the lav and get away with it. Some do the college trick of exhaling into a toilet roll crammed with Bounce. Others will exhale into the drain while it's open and the air will get sucked out. On the Boeing 777 there's some crazy thing the smokers will do in the business class bathroom but I don't know exactly what that is. It can only be done in one bathroom out of the eight we have and I have no idea what goes on when they go in there. You'll have to ask a smoker about that one.

If you have Wi-Fi on board and you brought your computer along, get online and befriend your heavy-drinking passengers. That way, instead of ringing that pesky call button every time they need a refill, they can just poke you on Facebook or send you an instant message and you can hang out in the galley behind the curtain. It's a great system and hopefully the wave of the future. The flight attendant that first implemented that program got a $50 tip from the couple that utilized it. Win-win again.

Though medical situations are few and far between, they will happen to you and you need to be prepared. Learn the phrase "I was not involved. I maintained service." That's what you're going to say on your report when you talk about the incident if you weren't directly involved. Even if the event occurred while you were in the bunks sleeping, you'll still have to write everything you know. Just remember those two lines.

If you are the flight attendant who discovers the medical situation, it's yours and don't try to pawn it off on the more senior flight attendant or to the purser. It's first come first serve so you need to know what to do. If you're qualified on several different aircrafts, then you'll have to remember where about a hundred different pieces of emergency equipment are located.

This is just impossible. It's way more than most people's brains can deal with, especially us mindless trolly dollies. If we had minds that could retain all that information then we probably wouldn't be stewardesses, we'd be scientists or professors. For sure know where the AED lives. That's a bare minimum. If you can handle more information than that, memorize where all the fire extinguishers are. Those are the most important things, and not knowing where they're at is a big deal. Take it seriously.

One of the most frightening things about flying is the missed approach. It'll happen when you're not even thinking about it. You'll probably be thinking about what you're going to do on your layover or where you'd like to get a bite to eat in the terminal if you have some sit time between flights. Hell, you may even have your phone out and are checking your messages if you're out of sight from the passengers.

You'll be just a few feet from the ground when all of a sudden the engines rev up to full force and you shoot back up into the air. It's loud and scary. This usually happens because the plane that landed in front of you didn't clear the runway fast enough and you're going to slam into it, but sometimes it's for really bizarre reasons, like a goat wandered onto the runway. Whatever the case, it'll terrify you at first, but once you realize that you're going to be okay, you'll be pretty stoked. It takes a while to get back to a normal altitude and rejoin the planes that already have their landing sequence. It may add half an hour to your flight time, and that's cold hard cash in your pocket, my friend!

Part 10: Celebrities

A short chapter.

(I don't want to get sued.)

Chapter 46

After someone asks about your near-death encounters and whether or not you're really straight, they're going to want to know about the celebrities you've had on your flight. Even if you're working in a different cabin and never say a word to the celebrity, the civilian you're talking to will want to hear all about it.

You can tell a lot about a person by how they behave on a plane, especially on the longer flights, when they really drop the persona and behave the way they really are. Obviously, the flights from New York to Los Angeles and vice versa are where the celebs usually congregate. You can have several on one flight, and in really bizarre combinations. Once we had Snoop Dogg in the same cabin as Barry Williams (Greg Brady) and Joan Rivers. The seating chart looked like Mad Libs.

First of all, you need to know your celebrities. Don't assume every young, gorgeous person sitting in first class wearing Wayfarers throughout the entire flight is someone famous. They might not be flying out to audition for the remake of Less Than Zero, they may just be a douchebag no-name hipster trying to look cool. If you suspect you may have someone important on your flight you really need to do your legwork on the ground unless you get Wi-Fi inflight.

First of all, ask the agent when he/she comes down with the final paperwork and Passenger Information List (PIL). They should know. If they don't, check the name on the PIL and do a quick Google search on your smart phone. If they are a television or movie star then you can make a quick trip to IMDB.com and pull up everything they've ever done.

One of my pursers really impressed a certain Gossip Girl by knowing about all the random side projects she'd done. Of course, he gave her kudos and raved about them to no end. At that point she was so flattered that she would've followed him to the end of the earth. It was all bullshit, though, he'd just looked up her résumé and pretended to be a fan to mess with her.

When I had Chloe Sevigny on a flight from New York to Los Angeles I didn't do the appropriate research and I regret it to this day. To be fair, this was way back in 1999 when no one had a smart phone and IMDB didn't exist, but still, I could've looked at the paperwork and found out who she was. I just thought I was smiling and flirting with a random cute blonde sitting in coach. It wasn't until we were taxiing into the gate that I realized to whom I was speaking. For some reason that realization of who she was prevented me from saying another word to her or even looking at her. I got so embarrassingly shy. I think I ducked into the bathroom during deplaning and I regret it to this day. I swear to God she was flirting with me and I totally blew it.

Because mega-celebrities are getting harassed by people every second they're out in public, you really should just leave them alone when they're on the plane. The duration of the flight might be the only bit of peace and quiet they get all day. I don't recommend disturbing them either, but if you're going to play the part of being a wannabe star-fucker, at least wait until they go into the bathroom before you try to talk to them. When they come out you can calmly and discreetly give them a short synopsis of your obsession and politely ask them for a photo or for them to sign something. Some say yes and love the attention. Some think it's mildly annoying, but will oblige. Some will rip you a new asshole. If they get angry, apologize. Then call TMZ and sell them your story.

If you're going to attack them with these requests, have your supplies on hand right then and there. If you want a photo of you and them, have the camera out and a partner-in-crime ready to shoot the photo. If you want something signed, have a Sharpie and whatever object you want out and ready. In a pinch I've seen people use the ceramic coffee mugs. I may or may not have one in my kitchen right this second signed by Samuel L. Jackson.

The very first time I had to bug a celebrity was when we were taking Judge Judy from her home in New York back to Los Angeles so she could film her show. She was on that flight all the time and most of the flight attendants at my airline have had her at one time or another. I certainly knew who she was, but didn't really care that much, at least not enough to disturb her. One of the other flight attendants I was working with was freaking out. She was a huge fan and was so starstruck that she couldn't even be in the same cabin as the judge. Somehow I got roped into going up to Judy and asking for an autographed photo because my coworker was too shy. I reluctantly obliged, but was incredibly nervous doing it.

When I got to her seat I crouched down and in a soft voice explained the situation. Judge Judy laughed her ass off and quickly produced a promo picture from her briefcase and signed it with a sweet message. I thanked her heartedly for it but before I could get up, she asked if I wanted one as well. I really didn't, but are you ever going to say that to someone? She was sweet as can be, but what was I going to do with a signed headshot of Judge Judy? I nodded in fake excitement as she wrote a long, personal message to me. She beamed as she gave it to me and at that moment I really wished I were a bigger fan of her show because she was one of the nicest people ever. I took that photo and kept it on my wall in my tiny East Village bedroom for years, until it was finally time to move.

If you do have Wi-Fi on your flight, then you can do some serious homework inflight. When you pounce on them as they're leaving the lavatory you'll be ready with all the useless trivia you've found out about them online. One time we asked Joel Schumacher to name every movie he'd ever directed, in order, while we checked his answers as he was saying them on IMDB. Amazingly, he got them all right except for one omission, and this was after many cocktails.

There are certain people who are known for being the nicest people ever and others for the opposite reason. Some you are not allowed to speak to directly or even look at because you're "stealing their energy." Some washed-up, born-again pop stars will leave behind their napkin in their seat as they deplane in Minneapolis. Their assistant will explain that he left it there as a gift for the crew.

Some are exactly how you'd think they'd be and some are exactly the opposite. Some want to be left alone and others you'll want to strap down to their seats because they want to talk in the galley the entire flight.

Like I said before, the best judge of character is when you see an A-list celebrity when they're forced, for whatever reason, to sit in coach with the riffraff. There are some actors I absolutely hated until I had them on a flight and they were nauseatingly nice, even in a middle seat in coach. Then I respected the hell out of them. I thought others would be cool and they ended up being worthless, self-righteous pricks.

If you're inflight without the benefit of Wi-Fi, and you have a group of leather-clad misfits who reek and are obviously a band, get the oldest flight attendant to ask them who they are. That way you don't seem unhip if it turns out they're someone massive.

Here's an example of a celebrity encounter that went horribly wrong. It could've been avoided if I had done some proper research before we pushed back. Maybe.

> When we boarded the passengers in Los Angeles, a young couple asked us if their dog could ride up in the cabin. I was told this gray poodle was on its way to New York to be in a movie with Billy Crystal. The dog hadn't been in anything yet; this was its first big break. I don't like dogs, especially poodles, especially gray ones. At the same time, though, it was kind of fun having this dog on the plane; it could be the next Rin Tin Tin or Spuds Mackenzie. We allowed it to ride in the seats. After all, we only had about twenty of the one hundred sixty-six seats occupied on the all-night flight.
>
> When the passengers were deplaning and the couple passed by me, holding that beast like an infant, I decided I would make nice and show the mutt a little affection. I reached out and went for the top of his curly head to give him a quick pat, just to tell others a year from then that I knew the dog before the academy award and the seven-film movie deal. Right before I made contact

with the shaved forehead, the dog turned and snapped at me with primal savageness. Stunned, I drew my hand away and stared at the owners. They hadn't seen, but they did hear the snarl and the chomp.

"Did he get you?" she asked.

Embarrassed, I replied, "No, he tried, but missed me. I guess he has that Hollywood attitude already."

I grabbed my bleeding finger and headed for the lavatory. Two entry wounds in the middle finger of the left hand. It would be quite a lawsuit if the dog was already a celebrity. He wasn't, so I let it go.

A few months later I had Billy Crystal on a flight. I usually don't bother the celebrities, but I felt like he would be interested in this story. I sure would be if I were him! I wanted to know if he had problems with this dog as well.

I finally got the nerve to go up to him. I knelt by his seat and softly asked, "Did you recently film a movie with a large gray poodle?" Expecting him to say yes, I was ready to go right into my story about my encounter with the dog in the most abbreviated version I could come up with. It took me three hours to come up with that version.

"No," he replied, somewhat annoyed. This was bad; now I looked like an idiot. How do I explain a stupid question like that, it sounds like a lame opening line to start a conversation. I might as well have said, "Is it fun to be famous?" or "You look marvelous!"

Feeling like I had nothing to lose, I explained why I asked him that and showed him the scars on my finger to back up my story. He wasn't amused in the slightest. I decided to cut my losses and forget about the whole encounter. I retreated back to main cabin with my tail between my legs.

Chapter 47

I have an idea to start a paparazzi ring. I want it to be comprised entirely of airline people in Los Angeles and New York. Agents on both ends can tell the other station if there's someone newsworthy headed their way. They can also tell the flight attendants working the flight.

You always see the TMZ people hanging outside the terminal at LAX, but we have access to inside the terminal and the plane itself. We get first crack at them and maybe could even get some au naturale photos of gorgeous leading ladies before they duck into the bathroom to put their face on. You'll be shocked when you see how some of these ladies look when they first wake up. After fifteen minutes in the bathroom, however, you see the person you see in the rag magazines. They know the photographers will be down by baggage claim and they're ready for their close-up. My ring will get them before they're ready.

Just be nice to the celebrities and treat them like anyone else. Assume they don't want to be bothered until they show you otherwise. Sometimes they like to forget that they're something special and just want to be anonymous. Give them that.

Yeah, you may get a little nervous serving Tom Colicchio or Anthony Bourdain his meal when you're working in first class, but that's okay, just do your job. They won't hold you responsible if it tastes like shit. You may feel embarrassed wearing that horrible uniform when you're serving Diane Von Furstenberg, but again, suck it up. Above all else, don't verbally attack an actor because you don't like what their character did in the last movie you saw them in. Robert Carlyle is a very nice man; he's not Begbie. Billy Zane didn't really indirectly kill Leonardo DiCaprio in Titanic. Just because no one understood you the way Morrissey did when you were sixteen, clumsy, and shy, that's no reason to tell him your life story and expect him to care.

At this time I'd like to thank Diana Ross, Steve Guttenberg, Patrick Dempsey, Eva Mendes, Jackie Chan, Chris Rock, Joan Rivers, Sean Lennon, Sherman Helmsley, and Elizabeth Berkley for being above and beyond nice people. I'd also like to thank Abigail Breslin for saying that she would thank our flight crew in her acceptance speech at the BAFTAs had she won Best Supporting Actress for her role in Little Miss Sunshine. She said she would and I'd like to think that she would've remembered and acknowledged the crew that flew her out to London for the award show.

Nicolette Sheridan, I admire your Scrabble skills.

Samuel L. Jackson, thanks for making a Snakes on a Plane joke before we got a chance to.

Sandra Bullock, thanks for pretending to be interested when I was telling you about my favorite places to hang out in Austin.

A very special thank you goes out to the band members of Jimmy Eat World. I was never much a fan of their music, but they were hands down the nicest first class passengers I've ever had on a flight from London to New York. I enjoyed them so much that I went straight home and gave their music a second listen, with a much more open mind. Alas, I still couldn't get onboard with their artistic endeavors, but they were cool as shit and I wish them all the success in the world.

Not all the celebrities you have will be Hollywood stars or rock icons. You'd be surprised how often royalty and political leaders from other nations fly on commercial airlines. True, they'll usually buy up all of first class and only their entourage will occupy those seats, but they're still out there in the boarding area with the masses and subject to the same hassles. Reflections on a few...

The President of Sri Lanka is on board in first, but I'm in coach so I don't have to deal with him. I hear he's high maintenance and ordering ridiculous things like cappuccinos. All his bodyguards are back here with me, but they're all 5'7" and 135 pounds. I don't see them stopping anyone if the President is getting fucked with, but then again, who'd want to fuck with the President of Sri Lanka? Half our crew doesn't even know where Sri Lanka is.

The President of Uganda and his wife are onboard. There are some pretty fucked-up things going on in their legislature right now and we're all dying to ask them about it.

If you're gay and have AIDS, you get the death penalty, which is a redundant thing to say down there. If you are gay and don't have AIDS, it's life in prison, where you'll probably get AIDS. If you're a normal person and you know someone who is gay, but you don't tell anyone, that's a jail sentence. It's absolutely ridiculous what they're trying to do.

I told one of the gay flight attendants to introduce himself to the President so that the President would then be guilty of knowing a gay person. The entire crew is getting upset over this guy's presence. It's like someone kicked the hornets' nest.

Okay, so the new rumor around the plane is that the President doesn't support this insane legislation, so that's good. He earned some brownie points there. Both he and his wife donated to UNICEF when we came around with our blue donation bags; that was cool too.

I said we should just cut out the middleman and give all the money we collected straight to the President to take back to his country.

Most people when faced with the opportunity to become immortal take it without question. I wasn't thinking about that when I walked right past the sleeping ex-president of Brazil, world power and the fifth most populous country in the world, as well as home to the best soccer players ever. I didn't think anything of it when we boarded the plane and heard he was going to be in first class. A couple of the Brazilian flight attendants seemed really excited about it. The rest of us didn't care too much. I guess I'd think it'd be pretty cool if Bill Clinton was on the plane, so I kinda got on board with the hysteria. I made a pass by the guy as he sat in first class before takeoff. He didn't seem regal or anything; he looked like a normal passenger. I asked the Brazilian stews if he was ever on their money. Somehow that offended them.

So three and a half hours later we're done with the service and the entire plane is dark and asleep since it's like 2 a.m. I didn't feel like sleeping in the bunks when it was my break, so I sat in the last row of first class with another one of the flight attendants on break. She slept; I just watched a movie. The ex-president was just across the aisle from me, only three feet away. He lay asleep, just looking like anyone else in the world. I stared at him and tried to make him seem important. I squinted my eyes and tilted my head to different angles but it just wasn't working. It was at that moment I realized that I was the closest person to this once, and maybe still, great man. Some people would pay a lot of money to have the access that I have, for good or bad agendas. All I have to do is reach out and I could touch him.

That's when the urge hit me. I've never had a seriously violent thought in my life, but in that instant I wanted to strangle him. I don't even know why I thought that, but it gave me butterflies. There was just something so wonderfully eerie about killing a world leader on a full, but sleeping plane over the middle of the Caribbean.

I felt like I would be doing him a service. I mean he looked so devastatingly ordinary lying there, like a shaved lion. Getting murdered in cold blood would probably elevate him to god-like status for the rest of time. In less than a week there'd be statues devoted to him in every major city in Brazil. I could make him immortal. It wasn't until later I realized that my immortality would be ensured as well, but likely that wasn't anything I was interested in, and certainly not for that. I guess it was just that I was in the right place at the right time to drastically alter the world and I totally knew it.

Knowing that I was living in that moment was what was so incredible and empowering. Very few people are presented with such a moment in their lives and if they are, they probably don't realize the full importance of it while it's happening.

The random thought has crossed my mind about what would happen if during one of my cockpit babysitting missions I just played around with every important-looking dial, control, and lever. I'd kill a plane full of people and everyone might remember that flight 651 went down on May 19, 2006, but in 100 years it'd just be a side note, not even worth mentioning in the annals of time and history. Certainly no one would remember that I was the one that brought the plane down. It's very likely that no one would even know that a person intentionally brought down the plane. It'd probably be chalked up as just one of those things that never have a reason or explanation, engine failure or something.

Chapter 48

So before you think about yourself and how cool you'll think you seem when you come back to your friends with a story or lame souvenir from a celebrity who tolerated you for a few hours, just put yourself in their shoes for a few minutes. Think about what Johnny Depp must go through every single day of his existence. He goes out for a cup of coffee and half the people he passes along the way stop and point, or, god forbid, try to talk to him. The person who takes his order will want to say something. The person that serves him that coffee will want some sort of interaction. He gets in a cab and the driver will want a piece. He goes into a store to buy a gift and the salespeople are fighting themselves to help him. The other people who just so happen to be in the store are all taking out their phones and taking pictures which will be on Facebook in 2.3 seconds. He goes into a bar to have a beer and random people feel the need to tell him why he's fantastic or horrible. It just goes on and on and on all day long and I don't see how they don't all turn into assholes who make you talk to their assistants or avoid eye contact. I can't imagine being bothered every single time you're in a room with at least three other strangers. Please don't let that continue on the plane. You have a job to do.

You'll always have some people from main cabin who will want to go up and say hello or ask for an autograph, and even though you sound like a dick, say absolutely not. What happens in the terminal area or at baggage claim is not your concern, but protect them when you have them in your plane. Protect them from the other crew members as well. We all have one or two people we will go gaga over so it's understandable. Most celebrities I could not care less about, but I don't think I'd be able to keep myself from saying something to David Lynch, Jack Nicholson, Morrissey, or Bret Easton Ellis. Some of your colleagues have a list longer than mine and it will include anyone that's been on anything ever.

We all have our ones, so help your fellow crew members from being that annoying crew member. We all have the potential to be the whacked-out freak—it's inside all of us—so we have to be there for each other to help quell the beast.

Part 11: Final Descent & Ride to the Hotel

Buh bye!

Chapter 49

Now that the service is complete and you're done messing with the famous people, you'll hear those five magical words we all long to hear from the second we take off: "Flight attendants, prepare for landing." If there are any passengers you want to wrestle a number from or pick a fight with, do it now. It'll be your last chance.

It's also a good time to pre-scan the cabin for potential magazines that might be left behind. Leftover magazines are like gold in the flight attendant world, and as soon as the passengers deplane the Great Magazine Hunt begins. You'll be fighting the other flight attendants for them, the pilots as well. The pilots get bored as hell up in the cockpit so they're always on the lookout for the latest magazine or newspaper. God forbid they buy one in the terminal before boarding the plane.

The more proactive flight attendants will make a PA before landing asking the passengers to give up all their trash, including reading materials that won't be taken off the plane with them. You know, in order to "make it easier on the cleaners after landing" or to "help turn around the aircraft faster." Of course, this is all bullshit. We just want the papers and magazines without having to pay for them. Flight attendants are just as cheap as the pilots.

The girls will go straight for the gossip rags and fashion publications. The gay boys will fight over Men's Health. Maxim and Stuff usually go untouched until the pilots make it back to coach. If you have a real team player on your crew, they'll snatch the Maxim for you. If you notice a stewardess swiping one of those semi-porn magazines for herself, do everything you can to hang out with that girl on the layover! That's someone you want to party with.

Right before landing, some airlines will collect money from the passengers for various charities, such as UNICEF. UNICEF calls their program "Change for Good" and they help children in need.

Some flight attendants call this the "Change for Car Tolls" service. I'd say there are only a few stews evil enough to steal from a charity organization that helps feed and immunize children, but there are a few out there. There's a special place in hell for those people.

The passengers seem to love it when you announce the statistics after you collect the money. It's also a good way to make the premium cabins feel guilty when it's revealed that coach donated $150 and first class only $.75. If it's an international flight, you may get currency from many different countries. You can announce how many dollars, pounds, euros, reis, kronen, pesos, shekels, yen, and rubles you get. The passengers love hearing about that and it makes them feel like they really are making a difference, which they are. The change that annoys us can save lives thousands of miles away.

All the passengers are seated and buckled in with their seat backs in the upright and most uncomfortable position, or at least they should be. If someone refuses to buckle their seat belt, don't make it your big battle for the day. It will only drive you crazy. You're required to tell them to do it, but you don't have to put a gun to their head. If they chose to be unsafe, so be it. You've done your FAA-mandated duties and it's on them if they get hurt when the captain stops short.

Now it's time to do some shopping for the layover. If you need milk for your morning coffee, soft drinks, alcohol, snacks, or silverware, now is the time to secure those items. Grab a water bottle and fill it with vodka. Some flight attendants will collect the unused bread from all the cabins and bring it with them on their layover. What would someone do with a garbage bag full of stale bread, you may ask? To feed the birds, of course. The birds in London know to hang around Kensington Palace in Hyde Park. You see a lot of fat birds around Kensington Palace. It's a cheap way to spend the layover, at least.

Once you're set for your layover, take your jump seat and pray for a safe landing. Go over what you'll do in case something goes wrong and you have to start an evacuation. Pray that there isn't livestock on the runway if you're in the Dominican Republic or a flock of geese anywhere else. If you get a super smooth landing, smirk to yourself, remembering the story about the pilot having the landing of his life an hour after joining the Mile High Club.

Double and triple check that you remembered to disarm your doors, especially after a very long flight. It's a horrible feeling when you're just closing your eyes to sleep in your bed and all of a sudden you can't remember if you left the doors in the armed mode. If you did, a caterer or cabin service guy could get seriously injured or even killed if they went to open your door and the slide inflates in their face.

On certain flights the flight attendants will have to clean the aircraft on the ground. Those flights are annoying, and the most disgusting aspects of the job are usually revealed during this time. Be very careful of any balled-up blanket on the floor. You have no idea if it was just tossed down or was placed down because something evil and vile is inside. Wear gloves.

The same is true with the seat back pockets. For as long as there's been air travel, passengers, flight attendants, and cleaning crews alike have been fascinated by the contents of the seat back pockets.

They always remind me of that game on The Price Is Right when the contestant had to blindly stick their hand in the big bag and pull out a chip. Sometimes the chip would help them win a wonderful prize. Sometimes the chip would get them closer to the booby prize. Sometimes the chip would be a strike and they were one step closer to leaving the show with only whatever shitty thing they had won to get them out of Contestants' Row and on to the stage.

Almost everyone I talk to has a story of leaving something behind on the plane, usually in the seat back pocket. I myself left my little Canon Elph digital camera in seat 19C on JetStar flight 912 from Sydney to Townsville on Saturday, February 21, 2004, not that I really remember or am still incredibly bitter. No, it's not like I had the entire Australian/New Zealand holiday on that camera or anything!

Most flight attendants have a story about finding a wedding ring, iPod, or wallet in there. They say they get returned to the rightful owner, but I'm really not sure. This never happens to me, in any case. I only find chewed-up gum and wet tissues.

Still, though, we all think that there's something magical in there, like there is in the cartoons when someone sticks their hand into a kangaroo's pouch. You can't just go in with your guns blazing, though; there could be a million things in there and only five are good: iPod, iPad, camera, PSP, or wallet. You need to treat that seat back pocket with the utmost respect and with a poet's tenderness. Pretend the entire thing is a Fabergé egg. I know someone who got stuck by a used needle! Now he's addicted to heroin.

Chapter 50

Other than the unknown surprises, there are some things you know will be in the seat back pocket: the inflight magazine, online shopping catalogue, and that staple of the ages, the barf bag. Yes, they're still there and yes, people still often use them. Which reminds me, be careful when you handle yours; sometimes people like to use them and just put them back in the seat back pocket. Neither the flight attendants nor the aircraft cleaners will notice this, so it will remain in there, stewing, festering, and morphing into something quite alien and disgusting.

The worst thing about the barf bag is that it's single-use and the size for a toddler's needs. Unfortunately, the sick person isn't always a tiny child and they're not just throwing up once. That little baggie gets filled up pretty quickly and then we have a problem. They can either go to bag number two or make a run for the bathroom.

Personally, when I hear that someone is getting sick, I fetch one of the large "market bags" we use to collect rubbish. Those things are massive and don't leak. An entire row could use it as a hurling trough and there'd still be plenty of room for others that get sick from the sight and smell of the original pukers. It's always best to expect the worst when it comes to passenger regurgitation.

Surprisingly enough, we do use those barf bags for other purposes, really useful things. Sometimes passengers have medications that need to be kept cold so we'll fill the bags with ice and put their meds on top, then return everything to the passenger. Sometimes people get injured or feel feverish so we can turn the bags into little ice packs (always checking to make sure they're clean inside first, of course.)

Whenever we have a super cool and/or smoking hot passenger whom the crew wants to bestow a gift to, those little bags are the perfect size to stash a handful of vodka minis. It's kinda like we're packing their lunch for them as they run out the door and off to school, except they're running out of the plane and off to have a smoke instead of to elementary school to learn the three Rs.

The point is, those seat back pockets are the scariest thing on an airplane. If you have to clean the aircraft, go through those things with the utmost care. Yeah, you may find a little treasure left behind by someone in a rush, but more time than not, whatever you come across is going to give you nightmares or an opiate addiction.

Chapter 51

Now you're off the plane and out of the airport. Only airline people will get out of a plane, step onto a dirty tarmac that reeks of jet fuel, and vocalize their enjoyment of this breath of "fresh" air. It's true, though. Standing under a Boeing 777 at Chicago O'Hare feels refreshing after being inside that same aircraft with recirculated air for the past ten hours.

When your chariot arrives to drive you to the hotel, you immediately donate a dollar to the tip envelope for the driver. It's really just hush money, telling the driver that he didn't see nothing that's going on in his van and will keep his trap shut if he knows what's good for him.

When I got hired in the late 1990s it was still kosher to "buddy buck." That's when you find a buddy on your crew and one of you pays the driver going to the hotel and the other one pays on the return ride. That way you only have to depart with one precious dollar rather than two. I thought the concept of buddy bucking was gone like the dinosaurs, but a few months ago I got called out to work a flight with another base, one of the very senior bases that does everything old school. On the drive to the hotel one of the gray-haired lasses asked me if I'd found a buddy yet for the tip. I thought she was kidding so I laughed and made a sarcastic comment about being cheap. When I noticed all eleven of the other flight attendants were looking at me with rage in their eyes, I realized that she wasn't joking. It was a bit awkward. I gave a full dollar anyway and the other lady that didn't have a partner grumbled about having to do the same.

Much like drunken sex, the drive to the hotel can be as short as three minutes or as long as two and a half hours, so know your destination and plan accordingly. If it's a long drive, make sure you hit the Little Boys' room before you get off the plane, and have plenty of crew juice to pass the time.

The process of getting on the bus and to the hotel seems

simple enough, but of course crew members can find ways to make it annoying and painful. First of all, some crew members think that certain seats belong to them and will pout if they don't get it. Some want shotgun, others want the last row of the bus. Most everyone will throw down their bags on their seat next to them in hopes of not having to sit by anyone else, but on most buses at least two people will have to sit next to someone. It's a battle of wills to which people have to double up. In those cases it's good when a pilot is sleeping with a flight attendant on the crew; they always sit next to each other.

One of the pilots will always try to take shotgun, even if he's 5'4" and one of the stewards is 6'4". It's usually the first officer. I guess he's just used to sitting to the right of the one in charge of the vessel. Those habits are hard to break.

In some iffy countries you may get guards with machine guns accompanying you to the hotel. In the sketchiest of places the crew gets in an unmarked van, followed closely by a police van. Once you get to the hotel you notice there are more armed guards on the roof overlooking the perimeter. Yeah, it gets very real in places like Guayaquil. It's not shocking to see bullet holes in the crew vans in Brazil as well. There are way too many stories floating around about crews getting pulled over and robbed in South America.

Once everyone is settled in, you start the journey to the hotel for the layover, the best part of the job. In some places, like Santo Domingo, you only drive for a couple of minutes and then you stop at the local bar for a beer run. The captain will collect a buck or two from everyone and return with a sack full of ice-cold Presidentes. It tastes so good because you've earned it after dealing with so many cases of DDS.

If you're not in a place where you can make a stop, hopefully someone has thought ahead and made a gallon of crew juice. I'm sure your instructors didn't mention crew juice in your work training, but it's as important as anything else you learned at the Charm Farm.

Crew juice is an umbrella term referring to anything

alcoholic made on the plane with ingredients found onboard solely for consumption on the van ride to the hotel or at the hotel itself. If you take minis off the plane and sneak them into a Yankees game to mix with your $8 Pepsi, that's not crew juice, that's just stealing. The airline version of Top Chef's "Restaurant Wars" is Crew Juice Battles.

Crew juice is usually made in gallon jugs and comes in a variety of colors and strengths. Common concoctions are fruity rum/vodka drinks, champagne-infused, the mudslide variety, and my favorite... red wine sangria.

Some flight attendants make their name by making jello shots, which are always a crowd pleaser. We've tried every flavor out there and everyone has their favorites. I like classic lemon with vodka, but watermelon with vodka has been making a resurgence lately, as has tropical punch with rum. It's not unusual for flight attendants to tell passengers we don't have any more champagne when really it's all been used in crew drinks that are chilling on ice. The nice thing to do would be for us to use the crappy pre-departure champagne and save the good stuff for the paying passengers, but no, we're a group with refined taste and high standards. Only the best go into our mimosas.

It's usually the galley's responsibility to make the crew juice, since they have the best access to the goods and the most free time on their hands once we get into the air. If there are three cabins on the plane you might get three jugs of different drinks. Some people take it very seriously and guard their recipe with their lives. They won't even give you a hint of what's in it. These are the same people who see it as a victory when their gallon is gone first. They'll push theirs on the crew like a used-car salesman and then talk shit about yours. "Oh no, sorry, my super secret wonderful drink is gone, but there's still plenty of Andy's sangria left if you want some of that." It really gets under their skin if you tell them you don't really care for whatever they made.

Everyone has their favorite drink and there are lengthy discussions on who does what the best. I like to call my friend Andy's sangria recipe "the babymaker." I'm not sure if that's a misnomer or not. It's my drink of choice for a long van ride after a longer flight. I'd love it if more flight attendants would make it, so here's the formula for anyone wanting to try; I'm sure Andy won't mind:

- One carton Minute Maid OJ
- Two cans of Minute Maid Cranberry Apple Juice
- Grapes from the Business Class Dessert Service
- Fresh fruit from the First Class Breakfast Service
- Berries from the Ice Cream Sundae Service in First Class
- Two bottles of the lighter red wine
- 4 to 8 minis of vodka to give it kick
- 2 minis of Amaretto to cut the harshness
- 1 can of Ginger Ale as the passengers are deplaning to give it some refreshing sparkle

Put the juices in as soon as you have an empty gallon jug and put it on dry ice. Add the rest of the ingredients as they become available throughout the flight. By the time you land it's very cold and maybe a little slushy. Some people like the slush, but I prefer it to be just short of slushy, just very cold, but totally a liquid. The fruit that has been marinating in the drink for hours can really pack a punch.

When trying to decide if you have enough crew juice or if you should make one more batch, the answer is always yes, make more. It's better to have too much than not enough. You never know when you'll be stuck in traffic for an hour. It's not unusual to stumble off the van in some places like Paris, where even on good days the drive is well over an hour. It's a sad sight to see exhausted, trashed crew members with their uniforms untucked and half unbuttoned. For some reason hotels give us our rooms much quicker when we're drinking crew juice in their lobby in front of the other guests.

In some cities, like Rome or Paris, the van ride to the hotel will seem like you're on a tour bus because of all the sights you'll see. Make sure you have a window seat for those cities, especially Rome, since you never know when an earthquake is going to take out the Coliseum.

Part 12: Layover Hotels

Your home away from home.

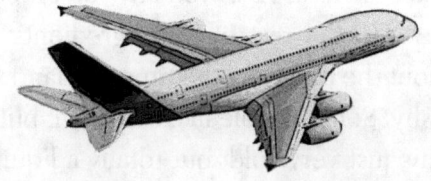

Chapter 52

A layover is like an alien abduction. Someone reaches down from above, plucks you out of your home, takes you up into the heavens, sends you to some strange city you've never been to before where you spend a night in isolation, and then drops you off at home again a day or two later.

Everything in your city goes on without you and doesn't even notice your departure or return. It's like the city didn't miss a beat, but for the flash that you're gone, for you, at least, it was lived in super slow motion, seemingly lasting days, weeks, months. Inside your cubicle with the big comfy bed, desk, and clean, functioning bath/shower, time doesn't exist and people don't exist. It's just a couple of cocktails, a book, a walk, some food, you, and of course, a hotel room.

When airline crews complain about waiting "forever" for a room, that means different things depending on where you are. If you're in the United States you start to get antsy and bitchy after ten minutes of standing around in the lobby. In places like Rome, sometimes you wait nearly two hours for your room to be ready, and you don't even think of the word "forever" until you pass the hour mark. That's when you leave your stuff at the front desk and go do your shopping at the grocery store or have a beer, still in uniform, of course.

Hotel rooms are your home away from home and a little slice of space just for you. If you're a full-time flyer then you may spend between sixty and a hundred nights a year in a hotel room, depending on the type of trip you fly. If you have seven two-day trips each month, then that ends up being around eighty-four nights at a hotel each year. If you only do five three-day Europe trips, then you'll start at the sixty mark. That's before you pick up a single extra trip, and everyone starting out picks up at least one extra trip a month. So you'll spend roughly a fourth of your year/life in hotel rooms. Learn to love them.

Make sure you get a reward card for every chain of hotels out there. Some hotels won't give airline crews credit for their stay for some reason, but if you kiss ass to an employee, then they'll usually do it for you on the sly. If you make friends with that employee, they may even add a few nights to your card, especially if you shower him with airline goodies (i.e., free drinks). Having free nights at a hotel is the best thing you could ask for once you start traveling for fun. Your flights will be next to nothing, so if you can keep the accommodation spending to a minimum, you're looking at an incredibly cheap vacation.

The airlines have promised you certain things when it comes to accommodation on the job. You're not supposed to be on the bottom floor for safety reasons. The hotel should have food available 24/7, or at least food very near to the hotel. You're always given the option of a non-smoking room, which, however, may be on a floor that allows smoking. Those rooms are annoying—like the smoke knows to stop at your door and not go in.

That's about it as far as the hotel's responsibility to the airline crewmember goes. As long as the hotel meets those criteria, then they're an option for the Hotel Board to decide on. The range of hotels is staggering. For the most part it's an inverse relationship. The nicer the country, the more meager the hotel. The shittier the country, the more luxurious the hotel. Tokyo is a closet. Port-au-Prince is a palace.

Don't put it past the company to put you up at a hotel that's known to be haunted. We stay at several places where many people have sworn to have seen some sort of apparition. The most famous hotels for that are the Grant in San Diego and the Omni Parker House in Boston, where Harvey Parker and others still hang out in rooms and in the halls. Other notorious haunted spots are in El Paso, Vail, Caracas, and Rochester, Minnesota. Sometimes these ghosts will just be hanging out in the hall or in your room, minding their own business, but sometimes they like to turn on the television and sit on your bed, I'm told. I believe the stories that come from the era before Ambien more so than the ones nowadays.

You'll find that some of your crew members are way too particular when they request their room. It's ridiculous and it's embarrassing. I feel so sorry for anyone that has to deal with pilots and flight attendants, especially van drivers and hotel staff. You must really be a masochist to voluntarily put up with that hell. I don't feel as bad for airport security; we give them a hard time, but they usually deserve it.

There are a million reasons and excuses why a crew member might not want a particular room. Some crew members don't want to be on a floor too high up because there's no water pressure. The low floors have too much street noise. The rooms near ice machines and elevators are too noisy. The rooms near the microwave room are also too noisy with people coming in and out at all hours. In fact, they don't want to even be on the same floor that has a communal microwave because the entire floor smells like weird food, especially if Asian airlines stay at the hotel. It's like these finicky people have a particular room in mind and won't quit until they get it. Airline people get a little too comfortable and start taking things for granted. It's the unbearable lightness of being.

When the crew are all stumbling to their rooms, bleary-eyed and ready to pass out, be a gentleman and go with the ladies to check their room out. The new hires of today may find that creepy, but the ladies that have been flying for years will appreciate it. It used to happen all the time without question but lately it's a rarity. You're going to hear so many messed-up stories about stewardesses going into their rooms where some weirdo is waiting in the closet or under the bed. I've never known anyone to experience that, but we've all heard the stories and you're conscious of the potential danger. By sticking your head into their room when they first get in, you're not being creepy, you're being a good guy. Just make a quick scan of the place and check behind the curtains along with under the bed and in the shower. It takes thirty seconds, but you can prove that chivalry is not dead.

Chapter 53

Even though all rooms are different, you'll try to keep a basic setup and routine. We crave structure and are all creatures of habit. You'll keep your suitcase in the same place in every single room. Some people utilize the closet and the drawers. I don't bother with the drawers because it's just too much work to unpack and then repack a few hours later. It's easier living out of the suitcase.

First things first—check the room clock and make sure the time is correct. I'd say one out of four rooms will have incorrect time, sometimes by many hours. If you're going to use that clock as your alarm, it's going to need to be right. Nothing is worse than being woken up by a phone call from the captain saying the crew is on the bus waiting for you! If you're in a country where the power goes out often, make sure you have a backup alarm somewhere.

Next order of business is to rearrange the furniture so that you can get to an outlet. Sometimes just finding a usable outlet takes an hour; they may be behind the heavy bed or immovable armoire. The ones in the bathroom are always an option. In places like Rio they may have several outlets with different voltage. One may give 220 volts while another is only for 110. It might be a good idea to see what your electronic device requires before you fry a $3,000 toy.

After that, set up the bathroom how you want it. Put out the toiletries just so, and hang your uniform neatly in the closet. Check to see what the hotel gives you as far as bathroom amenities. Some have some amazing products. Tokyo gives you some random white thing that looks like it's either a scrunchie or cockring. None of us have figured that one out yet so we use it as both.

Pray to God that you don't have a bathroom that has that annoying half door in the shower. I have never understood the appeal of that thing. It just causes the entire bathroom to get sopping wet and dangerously slippery. Plus it's hard to adjust the water temperature without getting completely into the shower with that damn half door.

The best bathrooms have a bowed shower rod that creates the illusion of more space. The less you have to touch that shower curtain, the better.

Some people have a room-cleaning ritual that includes putting on their own sheets and pillowcases brought from home. The hotel sheets get washed, so I'm okay with those, but the comforters or duvets are ignored, so those are pretty nasty and my naked body will never touch them. It's hard to be a successful germaphobe and a flight attendant at the same time; there just aren't enough hours in the day. Something has got to give.

Ignorance really is bliss. Don't think too deeply on what may or may not be in your room or look too closely to the refilled body wash/shampoo bottles. At least the little bottle of mouthwash is factory sealed. Ignore that undercover news report you saw online about how the glasses get cleaned in hotel rooms—sometimes with the same rag that was just used to wipe off the toilet. And God forbid, never look under the bed!

Some people use the shower cap as a condom for the remote control and phone receiver. To test for bedbugs put the bar of soap on the bed and check back with it later. Apparently bedbugs head right for that. I'm not sure if that's true; it may be one of those tricks you use to fool yourself into thinking everything is just fine. That's okay, though, because perception is reality. I've yet to see a bedbug running for my bar of cheap soap.

One of my favorite layover games is Find The Maid's Hair. Obviously, you have to check for the one maid hair that's always found in a hotel shower. It's like playing Where's Waldo. It may take you half an hour, but that hair is always in there somewhere, sometimes on the ceiling—don't forget to check the ceiling!

A word to the wise: some people use the coffee makers to clean their panty hose. Gross. I sometimes use it to reheat food or warm a can of soup. It can also be used to cook gnocchi, edamame, and corn on the cob. I've also found that if your room has one of those fancy pant-pressers you can use that to make a pseudo grilled cheese sandwich. It's a step up from using the iron like you did in college. The iron is also an option for toasting and melting things. In a pinch you can use the shoe horn as a spoon, as MacGyver would do.

You'll do all your dirty stuff in a hotel room, the messy things you don't want to do at home, like dyeing your hair or having menstrual sex. I used to try to keep the room as clean as possible, as a favor to the maid. I tried to be a team player. I put a liner in the trash can, which I'm sure helps a lot. I tried to leave the room cleaner than I found it, but then I heard that rooms left like that don't really get cleaned that well by the maids. Now I'll trash their room on purpose just so it HAS to be cleaned.

You usually get a little fridge in your room, but if you're staying somewhere cold you can use the ledge outside the window as a fridge extension. It really frees up some space, especially if your fridge is crammed full of useless minibar items that cost way too much and you'll never touch.

In some places, such as Caracas, you can sometimes get free porn if you clip your ID to the cable going into the TV. Most hotels are onto that one because some idiot flight attendant left his ID behind when he checked out and then had to call the hotel for someone to get it. How do you explain why your ID is clipped to the back of a TV unless something is up? Every now and then your porn channel will come in unscrambled. If that happens, watch it for as long as you can because once you turn the channel, it's gone forever. When you turn back it'll be scrambled again and the free porn will be nothing but a distant memory. So call your crew to come over for the free show and make sure everyone gets their fill before you change the channel.

Some hotels have secret hiding places that crew members will use to leave goodies for each other. The Los Angeles Bonaventure was famous for that. The hotel is circular and the far wall of the hotel rooms is curved and made entirely of windows. Because the ceiling doesn't exactly fit flush to the curved wall, there are little gaps where you can reach up into the ceiling if you stand on the desk. People would leave all sorts of things up there: porn, minis of liquor, wine,

People magazine, Polaroid pics, or just little silly notes to "whomever it concerns." I wanted to write a novel that way, a collaboration of the three hundred people who stayed in room 212 during a particular year. It'd be like Mad Libs on steroids.

You'll find that spending so much time in hotels will eliminate certain chores you have to do at home, like shopping for toilet paper, shampoo, hand lotion, towels, stationery, pens (DoubleTree's are the best), hangers, and shower curtains. If you tell the maid that your significant other LOVES the way you smell in their lotion, she's likely to hook you up with dozens of bottles. She doesn't care, it doesn't come out of her paycheck. Score! Don't go for the duvet on the Heavenly Bed because the hotel will have corporate security meet you before you even step onto the plane. You will lose your job over that one.

The worst feeling is checking out of the hotel and realizing you left food in the fridge (or on the ledge outside the window.) That precious food has probably been all around the world with you and you were so looking forward to having that on the flight back home. You might need to leave a Post-it note on the door to remind yourself. On the rare occasions I have food in my fridge, I'll leave my tie on the knob of the front door to remind me.

So make your room your own and learn to love living out of a suitcase. It may be one of the few things you really have control over when you're on the job. Try to see a layover as a much-needed break from reality rather than being stuck away from all that are near and dear to you. It really can be a fantastic sanctuary if you look at it the right way.

Chapter 54

If your crew hasn't finished all the crew juice on the van ride to the hotel, that's a perfect reason to have a "debrief session" in someone's room immediately upon arrival. Debriefing is a little celebration airline crews have from time to time. We celebrate not dying in a plane crash or killing any passengers en route. If the alcohol makes it through the van ride and then through the duration of the debrief, it may be seen later at the "pre-departure drinking session" that occurs after everyone naps, but before we meet at the hotel bar or go out for food. The debriefing session is never held in the room of someone who smokes or is known to take nasty craps as soon as they get to their room.

If the layover is long enough you might get the dreaded Two-Hangover-Layover. The stars have to be aligned just so to make a 2HL a possibility. First, you need a long layover. It helps if you land in the morning after an all-night flight. The crew will have crew juice on the van, then debrief until everyone is properly wasted and delirious. That's when you take a nap and wake up a few hours later with your first hangover.

You rally through that nastiness and have dinner with the crew and start in on more drinks. That might last until the wee hours of the night. The next morning you get Part Two of the hangover. Those mornings are the worst, and being on the airplane makes it a thousand times worse. That's when you think about your college days and see how old you've really become. You'll glare with disdain at the new hires that look fresh-as-a-daisy.

If you fly international trips all around the world, then you'll see The Simpsons in every language. Portuguese is the best. Everyone goes a good job dubbing Homer and all the other major characters, but the Portuguese take the time to give the proper respect to the lesser characters like Smithers and Troy McClure. That is what's impressive about the Portuguese dubbing, the attention to detail and the way they go above and beyond. Everyone else does the second- and third-tier characters half-assed. They think by simply making Homer sound dumb and Marge screechy, their job is done. For shame.

You'll find yourself ecstatic to find anything in English in some cities. You'll watch things in Central America that you'd never watch in a million years at home. Monk seems like torture in my living room, but it's a blessing in Honduras. I'm a huge fan of Murder, She Wrote, but only in England. In China you may only get one English-speaking channel and it's sure as shit a news station, usually BBC or CNN. That's when you catch up on your international finance trends.

You do get exposed to the local flavor of these places you fly to if you watch their local programming. You can learn all about the intricacies of cockfighting by watching Dominican television at 4 a.m. In Japan you'll learn that almost anything found in the ocean can be used in a salad by watching their cooking shows. Whether you like it or not, you'll become a soccer fan because it's on television in every country in the world.

If you're in a country where you don't understand the exchange rate, don't assume "it can't be that bad." Next thing you know you'll be spending $200 on a bottle of Coke, Pringles, Toblerone, and a five-minute phone call just because you have no idea how much a Swiss franc is worth.

Helpful tidbit: text-sex is a horrible idea when you're overseas and your honey is back in the States. It costs a fortune and is too slow moving to be enjoyable for either person. You're better off to pay the hotel's Internet charge and just Skype. Some of your coworkers will fly to certain cities solely because the hotel has free wireless Internet in the rooms. Others will avoid those cities just so they can be unreachable.

Most flight personnel are medicated and most self-medicate because we all think we're smarter than the drug's instructions. You need to know what you're taking and how it's going to affect you. Some people can take prescription sleeping pills and fall right asleep as they are intended to do. If you're one of those people, consider yourself very lucky.

For others, it has the opposite effect and they may get hungry, or adventuresome, or in need to chat with someone on the phone for great lengths. If you're a sleep snacker, don't keep food in your room. If you're prone to calling random people and talking for an hour to each one, lock your phone. If you tend to wander the halls in your underwear, put something in front of the door to block yourself. Even the simple task of getting up to go pee can go horribly wrong. You open the wrong door and the next thing you know, you're locked out of your room, naked. You'd be shocked how many pilots and flight attendants end up naked in the halls for boring reasons.

I know quite a few people that have wandered out into the halls, naked, and locked themselves out. Apparently the staff's response time in Japan is the best for when you pop out of the elevator into the lobby buck naked at 3 a.m. Someone will hurdle the front desk and run at you with a coat or towel before you have time to blink. In Italy they wait for you to go up to them at the front desk and then think about maybe talking to you. I guess they don't really think there's a problem until you go up to them and tell them that you didn't mean to be naked in their lobby and would like to be let back in your room.

I've never been locked out of a room without any clothes on, but I think before I resort to going down to the lobby, I'd first try to go by the elevators to see if there were any curtains to rip down. If that didn't work, I'd find the floor's laundry room and look for a stray towel or sheet to cover up with. Getting into the elevator would be a last resort; I've seen way too many movies where nakedness and elevators have gone horribly wrong.

My last trip was with my dear friend Natasha. We went to San Juan the first night and Santiago, Dominican Republic, the next. Natasha's friend Vera was also flying with us. In San Juan the three of us got together to play cards and drink. The purser lived in San Juan so he didn't stay at the hotel. We took his key and used his hotel room as the party room. We toyed with the idea of ordering room service and porn, but ultimately decided against it. After about six games of the card game "Asshole" we were all pretty drunk. I only brought a small bottle of alcohol to drink, but they kept making me drink after mine was gone. I couldn't say anything about it; I was always the asshole.

Next night we get to the Dominican Republic an hour late so it's almost 3:30 a.m. by the time we get into our rooms. This time we brought plenty of alcohol and snacks to the party. Even the pilots showed up. Alex the purser came out for once too. We haven't really liked him that much because he told Natasha she was stupid on our first trip of the month. He's been kissing her ass since then, but still isn't in our good graces. Natasha can hold a grudge and if my friend wants to be mad, I'll be mad with her.

Alex and the pilots don't know how to play the drinking game of Asshole, even after we explain the game and play a practice hand. So of course they play poorly and are drinking regularly. Drunk and increasingly belligerent, Vera gets mad that Natasha and I pick on Alex and make him drink all the time, but he has it coming. I'm President from the first game and hold my position the entire two hours we play. I'm a fair Prez, though, and don't really abuse my power. Natasha is usually the Vice President so she makes Alex drink until he can't drink anymore. He just starts laughing uncontrollably every time she says "Drink." That, of course, earns him another drink. Natasha is really taking her revenge on our purser and I don't blame her at all. Vera is getting pissed at her, though. She says he doesn't understand the game because English isn't his first language.

The pilots are learning the game quickly so we stop feeling sorry for them for losing. They take the commands very well. Pilots aren't usually in positions where they have to take orders, especially not from people half their age, especially not the captain who used to be a Marine. He rolls his eyes a couple times and only once did I make him drink for the eye rolling. They were extremely good sports, I gotta say.

The casino closed at 5 a.m., but we had just gotten into the groove of the game at 5 a.m. so we stay in Vera's room and keep playing cards. My super-charged Mudslides are gone, as are the beers. I still have a thing of sangria going around, but soon that will be out. Natasha had a liter of rum, and there's half of that left. At around 6 a.m. everyone is too drunk to continue with Asshole. Vera is passed out in her bed, but gets up briefly to puke in the toilet. The pilots are slurry and barely have their eyes open. Somehow Alex is still as coherent as he was when he started the game, which wasn't very, but he's not getting any worse.

We play a few hands of poker for chocolate chip cookies but end up eating all of our betting chips. When Alex stands up to go to the bathroom we see how drunk he really is. I look at Natasha and she looks at me. I think we've settled the score for the "stupid" remark he made two weeks ago.

At 6:30 a.m. we decide it's time for the free breakfast downstairs, but only Natasha and I make it down. The first officer tried to follow us, but he was way too drunk. He bounced off the walls all the way down the hall and ended up just going back to his room. It's a scary thing to see people puke, pass out, and stumble around oblivious while you feel only slightly buzzed. Even heavy-drinking Natasha was visibly drunk, and I know I had just as much to drink as everyone else. Even though I was dispensing the drinks in the game, I drank along with whoever I made drink and I wasn't drinking pussy drinks like Bailey's on the rocks the say Alex was.

Natasha and I are the only ones in the breakfast room except for the four employees. There was a guy at the omelet station, a couple of guys by the coffee and tea, and then another guy that seats you. We were complete embarrassments. I got an obscene heap of bacon (which I don't usually eat) while Natasha spills the coffee all over the floor. While we're eating, I drop Fruit Loops everywhere and Natasha drools out watermelon seeds and spits them down onto her plate. One gets stuck on her chin and stays there until the waiter gives her a napkin. When we left, the waiter and his twin brother gave me the worst go-to-hell looks I've ever seen. As we walked out they continued the glare until we were at the elevator. Oh well, I thought, we could have been much worse.

We went back to her room to watch television. Natasha fell asleep immediately. I flipped around the channels for the next half hour until I found cockfighting at 7:30 a.m., right about the time when little kids would be waking up and turning on cartoons.

I was morbidly fascinated by it. I knew I didn't want to watch and I certainly didn't want to see how it ended, but I couldn't seem to turn the channel. I was hypnotized. The roosters didn't have razors on their feet like I thought they were supposed to, they just pecked and scratched. I joined in mid-fight and I have no idea how long it had been going on. Five minutes later one rooster started wobbling and after another minute finally just flopped over. There was no blood and not much suffering from what I could tell.

What got me was that the commentator was going wild on it. He called the action so fast, like it was table tennis and he was describing each and every shot as they occurred. Of course it was in Spanish so I have no idea what he was saying, but I couldn't imagine it being much more than, "The fluffier cock jumps and pecks and then is pecked in return. Now he pecks some more into the head and gets scratched in the chest." The same three things happened over and over until one lay there dead, but the announcer managed to be very colorful and rarely used the same phrase twice as far as I could tell. I guess it's like how the Eskimos have more than thirty words for snow. The Dominicans have more than thirty phrases for the way a rooster can peck another rooster on top of the head.

Chapter 55

Now that brings us to the rules of the room party. First of all, never host the room party. It's always better to be able to walk away from the madness when you want to go to sleep. You also don't have to clean everything up, even though a good guest always does their part. Lastly, if room service is ordered, it won't be charged to you. The only benefit to hosting the room party is that you can be in complete control of the music and you're in a good position to hook up with a crew member, at least in a better position than if you're in the pilot's room. There won't be that awkward moment when it's a battle of who can hang the longest and end up with the trashed stewardess at the end of the night. If the party is in your room then of course you'll be there for the duration.

If you're coming up from the hotel bar or a room party and want to make a move on one of your crew members, do it before you get on the elevator, unless you know her room number. Nothing is more awkward than when you realize you and your target are on different floors and you have to get something going while other people on the elevator watch you. If you know her room then you can always make the completely transparent call to her room a few minutes after you get off the elevator, asking her if she wants to watch TV. It doesn't matter that the television invitation seems like complete bullshit, it's all part of the game. You both know that it means "Do you want to hook up?" The television ruse gives the girl a chance to not seem too easy. After all, she's just saying yes to watching a movie, not having sex, right? Yeah. Right. It's always a good idea to have some sort of drink in your fridge in case the after-party goes into extra innings. It could at least be the bait to get someone into your room.

As proud as you are of the rock star trashing you've given your hotel room, do your best to clean it up. If you're that desperate to have it documented for the ages, take a photo or video and then get to work. Those maids get paid shit and the last thing they need is to clean up after your debauchery. I see that now.

    I'm looking around at the decadence of this Tampa hotel room and I realize how I've sorely missed times like these. There are empty glasses scattered about, still reeking of wine, screwdrivers, mudslides, beer, and champagne. There are stains in the carpet from where drinks were kicked over. There's a book of matches behind the bed as well as cigarette butts. The stains on the bed penetrated not only the sheet and liner, but made it all the way down to the mattress. A soaked deck of naked-lady playing cards is scattered about the end table and down on the floor below. My camera, which captured most of that strip poker game, is sitting on the other bed where AJ passed out halfway through the night.

    There are empty minis of Crown and vodka littering the desk, looking every bit the part of ten pins just bowled over by a sixteen-pound ball. The bottle of champagne, which wasn't even opened until the sun came up, is now hollow and sitting in the ice bucket, which holds stale, lukewarm water. A used condom and the blue wrapper adorn the top of the trashcan, which is very nearly overflowing with rubbish. The mattress is half off the bed.

    I feel sorry for the maid, but at the same time I'm damn proud of the scene. Motley Crüe or the Gallaghers couldn't have done it better. The Gideons would be appalled if they knew what their Bible was witness to last night. And the whole time I was on the clock. I can't remember when the job was this fun. Finally, some of the classic sex, drugs, rock 'n' roll, and adventure that drew me to the profession in the first place. I didn't see last night coming at all. That's what makes it so memorable, the randomness of it.

    I start to get all the dirty glasses together: four from my room and eight more from other people's rooms. It's the least I can do. I throw all the empties away, which fills up both the living room trashcan and the bathroom one. I hide the condom under some tissues. I take the linens and ball them up by the door. What do they do with those sheets that are soiled beyond belief anyways?

I take the underwear pieces and try to guess what belongs to whom. You can never mistake the smell of a good layover; it's a mix of hotel comforter, stale alcohol, and sex, with a touch of shame and regret. Every single night some flight attendant is having a layover like this one. I'm just glad it found me this time.

Chapter 56

Sometimes you get woken up before your alarm clock goes off, which is one of the worst things to happen to a person. Occasionally it's a maid who ignores your Do Not Disturb sign, but more often than not, it's a hotel staff member sliding a single piece of paper under your door. No matter how sleepy you were, as soon as you hear that slight sound, you'll be wide awake.

What that piece of paper says could be anything. Think of yourself as a spy and you're being sent top secret amendments to your assignment. Honestly, that's exactly what it is. Sometimes the piece of paper that gets put under your crews' doors is just to inform you that your inbound plane is a little late so your pickup from the hotel will be delayed an hour. No big deal. Sometimes you find out about a volcano erupting in Iceland and you will be told to remain at the hotel until further notice. Seven days later you get another piece of paper telling you that it's finally time to work a flight back home.

Occasionally, a situation will arise where a plane will be needed somewhere but no passengers are going to be on it. That's called ferrying a flight. It's just pilots and flight attendants and that's it. Crews make the most of ferried flights. Sometimes there will be pajama parties. If you're on a big plane with more than one cabin, you may turn one cabin into a party area and first class into the sleeping area. This is when you can finally surf on trays during takeoff. You've no doubt heard about flight attendants doing that, and this is when you get to do it. If you're on a dual aisle aircraft, you can have two people go at once and race. For those obsessed with joining the Mile High Club, ferried flights are a great time to tick that off of your Bucket List.

Part 13: Out and About on Layovers

Bring a camera and a credit card.

Chapter 57

When you first start flying, you'll get pissed when the other flight attendants don't want to go out and explore the city you're in, or at least meet at the hotel bar for a nightcap. They just check in to the hotel, go into their room, and you don't see them until the next day at pickup. There's a term for those people: "slam-clickers." Their door slams, their lock clicks, and that's all you hear from them. They're the fun-burglars of the airline industry and are against everything new-hire flight attendants stand for.

I didn't understand the slam-clicking at first. I thought they were cheating themselves out of the main reason they got the job in the first place. How are you going to be an international man of mystery if you don't leave your hotel room? After a while, though, you'll understand that the isolation and peace and quiet is one of the main draws of the job. You can leave all the noise of home life: the spouse, the kids, the obligations, or whatever, and just have some time to yourself without any interruption. I've got to admit, sometimes I love a good slam-click and you will too, but that's years down the road for you. For all practical purposes, unless you have a family at home, there are no good reasons that warrant slam-clickery from a young single guy new to the job! There's a big world out there to explore, so let's get on with it!

Here is one of the problems of being an outgoing person and hanging out with your crew on every layover, especially if you live in New York City, crammed into a tiny apartment with many roommates. You go on a work trip, so the crew is like, "Sweet, we're in Los Angeles or Austin or Athens or Fill in Name of City, let's go out!!" Then you come home and your roommates or building mates are like, "Hey, Brian's back in town, let's go out!!"

Before you know it, it's a nonstop party and there is just no rest for the wicked. Staying in at home is just impossible because there are way too many fun people pulling you out. The only opportunity to even have a chance at rest is on the layovers, but if you've never been to that layover city, you're not going to want to just stay in and watch TV. And forget about it if you are laying over in a city where you know people and make the mistake of actually telling them you're coming in town. If you do that, plans are made and your hands are tied. You have to be very disciplined not to run yourself into exhaustion. You also have to be able to stand up to the bullies and say, "No! I'm staying in this time!"

As soon as you get your monthly schedule, get online and see what's going on in those cities. Always check for concerts, performances, and sporting events. Ask the hotel's concierge about the local bars and do whatever it takes to make at least one friend in every city you fly to. The civilians think that we crave a piece of ass in every city, but for the most part, we just want someone to hang out with and show us around a bit.

Some flight attendants will get online and use social media to find friends in these new cities, while others will find a bar or coffee shop they like and stay loyal to it until they meet the others that call it an extension of their house as well. After you connect with just one person, the whole city will open up to you. You'll get to know their friends and they'll show you the places the locals like to go to, the places that make the city unique. Before long you'll be a local in about fifty cities all over the world. That's one of the best things about this job—you really will be a part of any city you want be a part of.

If you're in a country with a funny language, cling to that speaker for the entire layover if they'll let you. Even if they stand for everything you hate and they annoy you to no end, suck it up and do whatever they're doing for just that first layover. They can give you an overview of the city, country, culture, and at the very least, help you order food at the restaurant. Use that bastard for all they're worth. Eat 'em up and spit 'em out!

If God is really smiling down on you, the speaker will be cool and introduce you to some of their friends in town. Most speakers fly to the same cities over and over again for years on end. That's all they know. They know those cities better than they know their own. Our Italian speakers only fly to Milan and Rome and so they know both places like the back of their hands. I bet I could blindfold one of those Italian speakers, drop them off in a random Roman neighborhood, and they'd make it back to the hotel with no problem at all. All you need is that one connection and then things can open up as quickly as you want them to. Do whatever it takes to get your foot in the door.

One of the best parts about flying abroad, especially to random places like Auckland, New Zealand, or Istanbul, Turkey, is that your boring ol' American accent will actually work for you. The stronger the accent, the better, so really lay it on thick! It doesn't matter if you don't really have an accent because people that aren't used to hearing Americans in person will think you sound like a movie star. Make sure you know how that particular country feels about America first, though. If you're in Paris you may want to pretend to be Canadian. Bring a backpack with a big annoying maple leaf patch on it just in case you need to have something on you to back up your "I'm from Toronto, eh" story.

If there is no Speaker to take you out and you're flying with a bunch of slam-clickers, get out anyways if it's a city you've never been to before. You never know when you'll be there again. Your airline may pull out of that market in two weeks so don't assume that you can just do something next time. Being tired isn't a good enough reason to stay in and sleep the day away. Even if you're exhausted when you land in Amsterdam at 9 a.m. and the Bed Sirens are calling you, take a shot of espresso and hit the ground running. You'll be amazed how long you can stay awake if you just keep going. The second you stop and put your feet up you'll fall asleep for hours, but if you keep on the go, you can go forever.

Even if you don't know the city at all, just walk around and explore. The front desk will have a map of the area. If the city has a mass transit system, the front desk will most likely have a map for that as well, along with detailed instructions on how to use it. I spent my first layover in London just riding around on the Underground and popping my head up in various neighborhoods that sounded interesting. It was one of the greatest days of my life. Those red double-decker bus tours that most major cities offer are fantastic. They give you a great overview of the city as well as take you to the major must-see spots. I've even done the New York City one after I'd lived in the city for over ten years, and it was amazing. Quick tip: if you're standing in front of the duomo in Milan (or any landmark in a crowded city) and want someone to take your photo of you standing in front of it with your own camera, find the fattest person you can find. That way if they try to run off with it, you can easily chase them down. Don't pick the fit fourteen-year-old local boy wearing running shoes. Better than a fat person, find a girl in stilettos, or anyone with a nicer camera than yours.

One of my coworkers was wandering around New Delhi and stumbled upon a Bollywood movie being filmed. I guess they needed some pasty white people to fill in the background because they asked her to be in the production. That started what could turn out to be a lucrative acting career. You just never know what you'll run into.

On one layover in Rome I was wandering around the Trastevere area after dinner and came across a special Mass for Saint Egidio, the patron saint for the area. The church was packed and everything was in Italian, but it was one of the coolest things I've ever seen. It was the most I've ever felt from a religious ceremony and I didn't understand a word. It was probably better that way.

If you're in Milan and you've heard that you need to get tickets weeks in advance to see the Last Supper, don't listen. I showed up without a ticket and waited until a large tour group showed up, one where they had more tickets than people. I was able to buy one of the extras for face value and take the tour. True, it was in Japanese, but I still got to see the damn thing. It's crumbling, you know?

If you know there's something going on and you don't have a ticket, go anyway and see what happens. Sometimes there are scalpers and sometimes people have extra tickets for whatever reason. Sometimes you can even tell them that you're from New York and if they're impressed by that, they may let you in for free. One night we stood outside a music venue in Zurich for an hour trying to find an extra ticket to the show. In complete desperation we offered the door guy some cash to let us slip in. My friend had undone a button or two on her shirt before we asked, but whatever, two minutes later we were right in front of the stage. Another option is to bring the liquor minis with you wherever you go for bartering purposes. You'd be surprised where those things can get you. They open as many doors as cleavage does.

Chapter 58

Because straight male flight attendants are as rare as unicorns, there will be many layovers where the rest of your crew will want to go to a gay bar. Don't be afraid of the gay bars! They're usually a lot of fun. There are always girls there with far less male competition and you might even get a drink bought for you if you play your cards right. How often does that happen in a normal bar?

More important than the prospect of a free drink, you'll earn a ton of brownie points from your gay coworkers. It's one thing if you are thought to tolerate homosexuality—that's the bare minimum to get by in this world and certainly in this profession. It's a completely different thing if you're known to be able to hang with the gay boys on their turf without bitching and moaning. If you can acclimate and assimilate then you will truly earn their respect, and that's a very good thing. A great side effect of the gay boys respecting you is that the girls you work with will notice that you're not a homophobic asshole. That goes a long way. Just notice how much tail the pilots get if they're brave and secure enough to enter a gay club. Most won't.

Worst case scenario, you're at a gay bar in Athens during a strip show when a random Russian guy pumped up with Viagra and dressed as a cowboy comes out and dances for you. Then, when he's naked, the emcee asks the crowd for a volunteer to rub him down with lotion. I'm not sure what the best response is, but slowly backing your way into the crowd so that it engulfs you doesn't work that well, at least not when your gay friend and coworker Mikey is yelling for you to be the guy because it's your birthday. Just a little FYI.

Even if you're flying with a lame crew, be prepared for anything. You never know what other crews will be staying at your hotel or what locals you'll meet out and about. There may even be some crews from a different airline staying at your hotel. It's always ideal to go interline and keep your shenanigans out of the gossip mill of your airline. The more you can do under the radar, the better.

The smartest guys are better prepared than Boy Scouts and always have some sort of game to play in case of boredom while sitting around a room drinking and watching foreign television. Dice, a deck of cards, or Mad Libs can go a long way if you're having drinks with crew members in a hotel room. It sounds boring, but nothing is a bad idea if it distracts you while you're getting drunk. Always have some music ready to go as well, and be mindful that people like different kinds of music. Invest in the largest iPod you can and put as much music on it as you can, even if it's music you hate. I never listen to Gwen Stefani, but I sure as hell have her on my iPod in case I'm hanging out with a group of stewardesses who love her. Give the people what they want! Rihanna 'til dawn!

If you don't have any game to play or any music and have to resort to staring at the television, I've found that watching figuring skating is the great compromise for airline crews. It's pretty much the only thing everyone can tolerate. The girls like the pageantry, the gay boys like the outfits, and the straight guys like the cut-throat competition. It's a win-win-win.

Meeting up with the entire crew for a big family dinner sounds like a wonderful bonding experience. The concept makes you feel all warm and fuzzy inside. People will think your entire crew of pilots and flight attendants have united to transport a planeful of passengers to their destination in a friendly and professional manner, and now everyone involved is getting together to share in a meal, some drinks, and some laughs. It sounds lovely, doesn't it? Don't be fooled by this! It's a trap!

> It was my first Paris layover and since I don't speak a lick of French, I decided to stick with my crew. Usually I like to venture out on my own in a new city, but I knew dinner was going to be a massive problem if left to my own devices.
>
> In addition to being a vegetarian, I'm by far the pickiest

eater I know and I could see myself accidentally ordering all kinds of horrible things without outside guidance. Even the most popular items on the menu could be something disgusting and I wouldn't even realize it.

For some reason I'm incredibly shy about trying to order food in strange countries. I've heard horror stories about Parisians giving major attitude and scorn to Americans who don't at least try to speak the language. I'd love to try, but I just can't. I really don't know the language whatsoever. That bluff would be a miserable fail.

The pilots and five of the other flight attendants (including our French speaker from the flight) agree to meet under the Eiffel Tower at 8 p.m. I spend most of the day running around with my camera, trying to capture as much as of the city as I could on film in the hours given. I made sure I was at the Eiffel Tower at 8:00 though. In fact, I was there at 7:00, just in time to get yelled at in French for stepping on some grass where apparently there's a "Keep Off Grass" sign.

We find an Italian place in a not-so-touristy area just across the Seine. If I'd been smart enough to think of Italian food I wouldn't need to be with the crew. I can read the names of Italian dishes no problem. Oh well, I'm here now so let's roll with it.

I'm a pretty light eater and I like to save money when I go out. I think it's ridiculous to spend 12 euro on a single glass of wine, especially if you're just going to have the one glass and not catch a buzz. What's the point? I don't do appetizers or salad unless that's going to be my entire meal. I never take dessert or an after-dinner drink. All of that is just a waste of money for me. I can have some drinks at a bar before dinner for much cheaper. I can eat an ice cream from a street vendor after we leave the restaurant at a fraction of the cost.

So the crew orders and I watch it happen. A couple of people want this appetizer and a couple more want this other one. It's decided that the table will order three apps and everyone will just share them. I don't object. I let it happen. I like the way everyone is cooperating.

I'm drinking soda, but everyone else gets wine with sparkling water chasers. Again, it's decided that three bottles of each is good for everyone to share. I think that's a smart decision on their part and fail to recognize how and why I'm being a complete idiot.

I have one basic pasta dish while everyone else gets some soup, salad, antipasti, and second course. I marvel at the appetites these people have, even those of the skinny girls and waif-thin gay boys I'm flying with. The wine runs dry and the flight attendants order more. I wonder if I'm getting paid the same amount as they are; the tab is really adding up in a hurry!

If I knew the pilots were going to be paying for the meal I might partake in some of the extras, but I know that's not going to happen. There are two gay boys with us and the pilots very rarely treat guys to dinner, especially the gay ones. I'm not willing to bank on the possibility that my dinner will be free. I order sensibly and thriftily.

Everyone finishes and they ask us if we want desserts, cordials, or coffee. All three are ordered. I think about it, but look at the prices and decide against it. I can get a latte for a third of that price at the coffee shop just around the corner from the hotel. Again, I think I'm being so responsible and smart. I'm minutes away from seeing the error of my ways.

The moment arrives when the bill comes. It never occurred to me that paying for what you ordered wouldn't be an option. My crew, now wasted on wine and sambuca, insist that if we just divide by eight then we'll be set. Everyone is okay with that. It's at that point that I realize why the flight attendants were ordering more than the pilots.

They knew this was going to happen. If the pilots are going to order all these extras and then make the crew split the bill, the only way to come out ahead is to top them and order more yourself. Well played, flight attendants, well played.

There's nothing I could do but pull out sixty euros and think about the fifteen euros' worth of Coke and penne alla arrabiata I had. I grab the last bottle of wine still standing and empty it into my pristine, virginal glass. If I'm paying for this I may as well get as much out of it as I can. I grab a fork and shovel the rest of the tiramisu into my mouth. Lesson learned, but at a price.

Now I avoid eating with the crews as much as I can, at least in that large of a group. Smaller groups will let you get away with paying for what you order, but never a group of eight. Never after that much alcohol. The only way to "win" is to order the appetizer, and the soup, and the salad, and the wine, and the third bottle, and the fifth bottle, and the dessert with Cognac, and anything else you could possibly want. Hell, get a souvenir shirt and hat thrown on the tab too while you're at it! As long as you're eating and drinking more than everyone else, you come out ahead since the bill is getting split evenly. If you don't play the game like that, it's going to be a dinner from hell. Lesson learned. Once bitten, twice shy, babe.

Chapter 59

No matter what city you're in, know when the last train or bus departs from the area you're hanging out in to where your hotel is, or at least know how much a cab home will be. It can be downright terrifying looking at your watch in Camden Town just to see that the last train back to Kensington left three minutes ago. That's a crazy expensive cab ride home or a super slow night bus filled with degenerates and freaks. Basically, you're fucked.

If you're in Amsterdam and want to catch a late-night train back to the airport hotel from Central Station, when the attendant tells you to go to Track 1, make sure you know if you're to get on the train already sitting on Track 1 or if you should wait until the next one arriving. I didn't ask that question and jumped on the train already at the platform and an hour later I ended up in Utrecht. At daybreak I finally made it back to my room just in time to shower, change, and get down for pickup. Knowledge is power.

Don't be surprised if you see your airline's blankets out in the real world. I've gone to baseball games in San Francisco, music festivals in Belgium, and beaches in Coney Island where I've seen our blankets from main cabin wrapped around a former passenger. You're not in uniform and you haven't identified yourself as an employee, so go ahead and mess with them. Pretend like they're in trouble. If you can't scare them, at least embarrass them for being so cheap or laugh to yourself knowing how incredibly filthy those things are.

Chapter 60

The "Layover Love Laws" are complex and ever-changing. It's hard to figure out exactly what's appropriate or required after you hook up with a crewmember on a layover. There are a myriad of factors that come into play when you decide how to handle the situation the moments after you hook up, the next morning, back on the plane, when you see each other again on the next trip, and so on. It's no different than anyone else out there hooking up with a coworker, except you don't really know when you'll see that person again. It could be in a few days, it could be in a few years. There will be some flight attendants at your base you see all the time and others that you only hear stories about and you'll wonder if they really exist, like Kaiser Soze.

It can be awkward if you hook up with a coworker on the first trip of the month and then have to fly with her again six more times during the month. Will it be an ongoing thing for October or a one-off? The best thing to do is be an adult and have a chat so you know where you stand. Even if you may never see that girl after the month, your legacy will live on because flight attendants love to gossip. Your base may seem massive, but after a while everyone does get to know each other and you need to have a good reputation. Don't screw over your coworkers and be an asshole. Don't use the stewardesses and throw them out like trash. It will come back to haunt you. You can slut around and do your thing, but be respectful and make sure everyone knows what the score is. Honesty is the best policy.

We've already gone over the pros and cons of dating flight attendants. If you date a civilian there's another set of pros and cons. Obviously a plus is that they stay in one place and you get to spend the night with them every time you're at home. They probably make more money than you too. The worst part is that they have these crazy preconceived notions about what goes on during a layover, and trust is a massive issue. Once I thought I was doing a good thing by bringing my non-airline girlfriend on a layover, just to show her what it's really like. I expected it to be very typical: the crew meets downstairs for a drink, we have dinner, we have another drink, and then that's that.

My layovers are just like that 99 percent of the time. I even told my crew to be on their best behavior, that the future of my life was dependent on her thinking that all of my layovers are tame and subdued. What happens? My good friend and fellow straight guy is making out with some sexy Latina chick he just met, my good girlfriend is trashed and giving a lap dance to an older gay man while he's photographing them making out, telling everyone that he's going to send the pictures to his mother because "she'll be so proud." Then the pilots roll in and start buying shots, and normal shots become body shots. A stewardess from another base took a liking to my girlfriend and suggested a threesome. It was the exact opposite of what I wanted my girlfriend to see and very different from a normal layover. The relationship kind of fell apart after that, though it's hard to say if that peek into my layover world had anything to do with it. She swears it didn't, but I'm not too sure.

One of the hardest parts of the job is witnessing the infidelity. At first it seems like it's just a young naive stewardess messing around with a pilot because his wife "just doesn't get him anymore." Then you start to notice that even the happily married people are screwing around and don't think anything about it. Some of the ballsier pilots will bring their girlfriends with them on the trips and sit there with the crew at the pub and tell stories about his wife and kids while the girl-on-the-side is stroking his penis under the table.

You will become so desensitized to it and after a while it won't even shock you. Even if you don't cheat, you'll still be way too comfortable and accepting of it and you won't even bat an eye. It just becomes commonplace. I didn't realize how bad the airlines were until I heard a civilian friend talk about the drama in her office because an executive made out with his secretary at the office

Christmas party under the mistletoe. I thought, "Yeah? And? Did she and the bi-curious temp go down on him behind the Christmas tree while an elf filmed it?" It was at that point I realized that maybe my morality bar has been set a little low.

If you are going to cheat on your girlfriend or wife, just make sure you do it with someone else who has something to lose. Don't go for the young hot girl who could become attached and actually call you at home. Go for the married one that understands the situation and is discreet. It's hard living in a world where oftentimes there are no consequences for one's actions.

The theory is that flight attendants are away from home and can get away with God-knows-what without anyone finding out. The truth is, their spouses are at home alone with more familiar people and can get away with just as much if not more. There has to be unwavering trust on both sides.

I know of one lady that made the mistake of just flying weekends. She did this for years because she thought she was doing the right thing. She'd be around to help with the household chores during the week and would do her flying on the weekends when the husband would be around to take over. One day she shows up to the airport to see that her flight had cancelled. Excited about being off, she returns home to be with her husband only to find him in bed with another woman. Apparently this affair had been going on for years, but only on the weekends. She got rid of that guy and has since remarried. Now she intentionally flies a sporadic, inconsistent schedule, just to keep him guessing.

Chapter 61

The FAA says that you cannot have an alcoholic drink within eight hours of being on the plane for work. Some crews will joke that the rule is not to have a drink within eight feet of the plane. Hardy har.

This isn't a rule to mess around with, though. It's very serious and any number of people can bust you on it. It could be another crew member, or the van driver, or the people at security. For a while in London the security people seemed really interested in our layovers and were always asking us what we did. Of course, we'd happily tell them all about it. It wasn't until a few people got fired that we realized that they didn't give a shit about the great finds at Harrods, they were just smelling our breath for alcohol. If you still reek like moonshine when you go through security and they try this on you, try to talk as you breathe in. Better yet, always carry mints.

I don't know anyone who hasn't broken the eight-hour rule. Sometimes your layover is only eight hours and if you've had a hellish day, damn straight you're going to have a couple of drinks to unwind. Right from the first sip you've already violated the eight-hour rule. You'll usually get away with nights like that, because you don't smell like a strip club. It's those long nights out when you have an early pickup that will get you.

Most flight attendants and pilots alike have had at least one night where you get back to the hotel just ten minutes before pickup time. It's especially awkward if you stagger by the pilots in the lobby as you come in wearing your dirty, smelly, going-out clothes from the night before, and then see them again ten minutes later in your uniform, pretending to be sober and ready to work.

It's terrifying if the roles are reversed. You're down for pickup like a good boy and then you see a wasted old man with a tie around his head and lipstick on his collar come stumbling into the hotel and head toward the elevator. By the time you're done laughing at that jackass you notice that he's back and wearing a white uniform with four stripes, signifying that he's the captain of your plane. That's when you pray that someone has the guts to say something. It's one thing if we're still drunk; we can't really do much to bring down the plane. It's more of an annoyance than anything, a customer service glitch. Drunk pilots (who will never admit they're drunk) can cause a catastrophe.

One final bit of layover advice is to always keep your room number with you when you're away from the hotel. In one month you may have fourteen different rooms in fourteen different cities and it's very easy to get confused. Also, keep the name and address of your hotel on you in case you get wasted out on the town or beaten to a pulp and left for dead.

It's a good idea to have that information on you at all times, especially if you're in a country where you don't speak the language. Most hotels will give you a paper key holder that has the hotel information, but some don't. If you don't have that info provided for you, write it down yourself and keep it with you. If at all possible have it written in English and whatever other language they speak there. You can always point to the address and the driver will know where to take you.

If you're getting wasted in Las Vegas you may want to leave a trail of breadcrumbs so that you can find your way out of the labyrinth that is the casinos. Those things are built to keep people in, and being trashed doesn't make it any easier to find your way out. You might turn up again three hours later, totally broke, but somehow married.

Part 14: What I've Learned from Gay Coworkers

From docking to donkey punches.

Chapter 62

Working alongside gay men will open your eyes and minds in ways you cannot yet imagine. I've learned more about gay sex and the gay lifestyle than most normal, everyday gay men will ever know if they live to be one hundred. If this is something you don't want to know or hear about, get out of the business now.

First and foremost, to paint a realistic picture, you will have to come to terms with the fact that the hotel bed you're sleeping in has been the scene of gay sex, perhaps as recently as an hour before you got the key. Again, if that sort of image will keep you up at night, you don't stand a chance in this industry. Get over yourself and have fun at your new job at Denny's.

Once you've been accepted by the homosexuals and they stop editing themselves in front of you, your world will take a very interesting turn. Your vocabulary will expand exponentially. You'll hear so many nicknames for gay men and they'll have no problem calling themselves these terms in normal conversation between themselves, even if some don't make any sense. We're still trying to figure out exactly why "shirt-lifter" is a derogatory term. Even my best gay friends don't get it. Whoever came up with that one wasn't on their A-game. It's like that dickhead guy in Roxanne who called Steve Martin's character "big nose," and then Steve Martin abruptly thought of twenty more creative things he could have said in his wasted opportunity.

You'll have this new kick-ass vocabulary to use under their supervision, but you'd never hear a self-respecting human utter these same words behind their backs. Remember that. Once you're down with the gays you can use these terms in their presence as well, but just remember your green light to use these nicknames ends the second they're not around. Don't think you can use them with the general public or with gay men you don't know personally—especially with the ones you don't know personally. Just because your crew lets you join in the fun doesn't mean that every gay man in the world is going to know that you've been granted that liberty.

It's the same as how even though your three black friends let you make certain jokes around them and they know it's not coming from a bad place, it doesn't mean that the memo has gotten out to every black man in the world that you've been pre-approved to make racist remarks whenever you want. Be respectful.

You're going to be very jealous when you're hanging around the gay members of your crew and they check in with the geosocial networking application called Grindr. To watch them in action on that thing is so entertaining. To see how easy it is for two guys to meet and hook up is mind-blowing. It's how every straight guy wishes it could be for them and how we imagine it really is for Colin Farrell or Tommy Lee. Just last night in Rio I made my friend whip out his phone and check the Grindr situation. From somewhere on the resort grounds there were a couple of potentials and several more up in the favelas behind us. I made him send out a message or two and within seconds someone had responded, asking if he was a top. Unfortunately, my friend was not a top so everything fizzled out. Had he been a top I very well could've been ditched as soon as our drink was over. It was just that easy. Yeah, there's a straight version but do you really want to hook up with a girl that would be on it?

Whether you like it or not, you're going to know when every major city across the world celebrates Gay Pride and when and where all the circuit parties are. I didn't even know what a circuit party was until I put on that uniform. If you know what they are already, there's a chance you'll be one of the "straights" who will be coming out of the closet before you've completed Year One.

Most everyone knows the general terms used in the gay male world. There are such things as a top, bottom, and bear. Now I know that there are also subsets to all of these. There are bossy bottoms, power bottoms, a bear code, and bear cubs. Twink is still one of my favorite terms for a waif-thin, hairless boy who looks twelve. The best part about twinks is that they like being called twinks, according to my twink friends. Likewise it's more of a compliment to call a bear a big ol' bear than a borderline bear.

You'll also learn terms like Strawberry Shortcake, docking, and Torah-chasers. Very soon you'll know that guys that are into eating feces describe it as if you were to eat whatever the person ate the day before, only burned. I know, I know, you didn't need to know that and you wish you could go back in time by ten seconds and never have read that sentence. But you know what, you're going to hear a lot worse, so start building up your tolerance now. When your coworker tells you that the Indian guy he went out with the night before had semen that tasted like curry, you won't even bat an eye.

If you don't know the difference between a Shower and a Grower, you will. You'll also hear what the most popular and effective lubricant is at the time. Last I heard it's Eros. If you have never seen Steel Magnolias or Mommie Dearest, within a year you'll be able to quote them from start to finish, same with any song by Cher, Madonna, or Lady Gaga. I guess it'll also be true of any Pam Ann bit. Touch trolley... Touch galley. Don't worry, it won't be painful when you get inundated with this stuff. It's fun to be in on the jokes.

You will get the low-down on all the erectile dysfunction medication out there. Apparently, it does make a difference what you take. According to my sources, Viagra is no longer the money pill. It's good for a night of constant sex, but make sure you're in a safe place because your erection won't be going down, even when you're not turned on. Viagra and Levitra both take about thirty minutes to come on and last up to six hours. Cialis was what they called "The Weekender," good for a whole weekend of sex, and you have complete control on when it works and when it doesn't. I guess I don't understand what that means and how exactly you control it. The gay men at my airline prefer Cialis these days. It comes on twice as quick and lasts way longer.

A word to the wise: know how these pills affect you before you try to take one on a short layover. You may find yourself in a very embarrassing situation that you can't do anything about. The only time I ever wore my company-issued apron was for exactly that reason.

Chapter 63

Being around gay men all the time will hone your gaydar. I can tell within seconds if a stranger is straight or gay. I'm just as good at telling a closet case as any gay man I know. I used to be shocked when I'd find out someone was gay when they really didn't seem it. Now I'm shocked when I get it wrong, and I'm not altogether sure that I did get it wrong. I think maybe the person I'm skeptical of just hasn't come to terms with it yet.

This was probably the most endearing lesson I learned about gay men—that they're exactly like straight men in almost every way.

> No matter how hard you try, no matter how many times you tell your brain that she repeatedly said, "I just want to sleep," your penis won't let you get tired.
> Oh, she turned over! What does that mean? I'll stick out my leg a little in their direction and see if they're coming my way! You always leave some part of your body about a centimeter away from the other person. You don't want to initiate anything just in case they were being serious when they said they just wanted to sleep, but still you're right there just in case and it's not your fault if they move and rub against you. You can't be blamed for that, now can you?
> In that situation I can't even start to get drowsy until I hear snoring. Even then, if I hear repositioning, I'm like a coyote in the desert. My head will pop up, my ears will stand up straight, and all senses are on full alert. For some reason it was very warming to hear that Trey was exactly the same way.
> I figured it'd be too easy for gay men. I guess that's my naivety, but I figured if they're comfortable enough with each other to be in the same bed, then why not mess around? I know how guys are and if there are two guys alone in a bed, then it should be

a given, right? I didn't know that there was still uncertainty and nervousness. Of course it was naïve of me; people are people.

Just as I know of some girls that swear they don't want anything to happen, but then get pissed off at you the next day for not trying anything the night before, there are gay men that say and do exactly the same thing.

Thus, the thoughts racing in our heads continue when the lights are out and everything is dead silent. If we as men could harness the brain activity and emotional exercise we use in those dark hours of the night, we could move mountains. If we utilized our minds as hard and diligently as we do then all the time, then it would be absolutely spectacular. I think that's what the other 90 percent of our brain is for: thinking about all the different possibilities that may come from lying in a bed next to someone you somewhat fancy, how to achieve all of those outcomes, what would the result be of those outcomes tomorrow morning and further down the road, and if we really care about the long-term stuff at all.

All those thoughts, in addition to paying attention to every move, breath, stir, sound, and smell of the object of your momentary obsession, exercises your brain to its absolute capacity. As much as we think about it, we all know that it isn't as complex as all that. All the person has to do is put their arm around you and the millions of possibilities are narrowed down to one, and that's such a great moment when it happens.   I'm so happy to know that my brothers in the same-sex oriented world deal with the same struggles as I do. It truly is a universal phenomenon and something I wish to discuss immediately with my lesbian friends.

In today's society most of us are exposed to homosexuals and it's no big deal at all. We're really all the same when it comes to 99 percent of what makes us... us. If anything, we should be happy that the most stylish, well-manicured, fit, sensitive specimens of male human beings want to sleep with each other. It gives normal straight slobs like ourselves a good chance to date girls who are way out of our league. If it were up to me everyone in the world would be gay besides me.

Part 14: Non-Revving & Commuting

Marry me, fly standby!

Chapter 64

The most alluring and fantastic benefit of this job is the next-to-nothing flying we get to do on our days off. That is the main perk and the sole reason most of us took the job. I don't want to know the flight attendants who take this job because they like to serve people food and drinks, or actually think that they're here for safety reasons. If you're not seeing the world, then work at Bennigan's and give your job to someone who'll utilize it to its fullest. Otherwise, you're just like those lucky people who get on Survivor, and then quit halfway through. I hate those people. The flight benefits are what it's all about, but they come with a price.

The most beautiful combination of any two words in the English language may be "cellar door," but the most horrific combination has got to be "standby." That's what you are as a non-revenue passenger, non-rev for short.

Yes, you have these amazingly cheap tickets to fly anywhere in the world, as long as there is space available. Sometimes you get on the first flight you have your eye on, sometimes you get on one a week later, and there's nothing you can do about it. Flying standby, as with everything else in life, requires you to be like a palm tree…flexible.

Whether you're non-revving somewhere fun or just commuting back to base for work, the gate agents are the gatekeepers to the plane you want to ride on. Although bribing them won't get you on a full plane, it certainly won't hurt your cause. You want as many agents as friends as possible, not as enemies. If you piss one off they can make your life hell by adding comments to your PNR. Always bring a little something for the agents, whether it be a gift certificate to Starbucks or a box of chocolates. A little gesture like that could go a long way.

Same holds true with the working flight attendants on the plane you're riding on. Bring something for them as well. They are in a position to hook you up and will do so 99 percent of the time.

If they can't upgrade you, then they'll at least bring you free drinks and maybe a fancy first class amenity kit. Most flight attendants are looking for any reason to be nice to passengers and shower them with gifts.

One bad thing about standby is that even if you get on a flight, you'll be the last one on and by that time the overhead bins will be full. If you know there's room on the plane for you, ask the agent if you can get on first and stash your bags. If you're in uniform then they'll usually let you. They can only say yes or no so you might as well ask; another reason to be buds with the agents.

Always wear your uniform when you're non-revving, at least until you get onto the plane. That way you can get through security faster and be allowed to pre-board with the working crew. Once you get onboard, slip into something more comfortable and have a cocktail.

Go out of your way to get on a flight where you know the crew. Having a buddy from the get-go saves you a lot of hassle and money. You won't waste your money non-revving in first class if your bestie is purser and will secretly upgrade you for free. It's a great idea to be friends with as many coworkers as possible on the most popular social network. Even if you're not super close with them you can shoot them a message and let them know you plan on being on their flight. It can't hurt.

Even though the crew will be obligated to treat you like a normal passenger, they really will hate you if you're as high maintenance as the rest of the group. When you're flying for free it's best to be as self-sufficient as possible, at least until you feel out the crew. Bring your own bottle of water. Get something to eat before the flight. Don't try every single wine they have to offer and make them open up the port, Tokaji, or sherry. Don't ask for things out of the "sequence of service." When they're making salads, don't ask for ice cream.

Sometimes when you're flying standby, the crew won't know you're an airline employee. It's on their paperwork, but no one really checks the paperwork. If you want the crew to know you're a flight attendant and deserve to be treated like royalty, there are several subtle ways to let them know. The easiest way is not to be subtle at all. When you get onboard thank the crew for the ride and tell them that you work for so-and-so airline. But most of us aren't that forward so you have to go to plan B or C.

Wearing your ID around your neck is kind of a dick move, but it gets the job done. Same with rolling up with luggage that has tags that read "crew" all over it. Having a company-issued bidsheet out on your tray table listing all the trips your base flies is a kinder, gentler way to let the crew know that you're one of them. Paying for your drinks with your airline's credit union's card is also effective and not as obvious.

That's pretty much all you need to know as far as how to act as a non-rev. It's simple, really—smile and nod at all times. If someone asks you to change seats or take the chicken when you want beef, just do it.

Chapter 65

Dealing with the general public can get to anyone after a while so you're going to need to have a special place to get away. Everyone needs a little sanctuary where they can recharge and reload. It needs to be easy to get to (one leg away preferably), cheap, and fun. Mine is Barbados. I have a specific place I like to stay at and several good places where I like to dine. I even have a special beach I like to frequent. That's my idea of heaven and I know it's always there waiting for me. If life starts getting a little too crazy, four hours and $300 will give a friend and me a kickass four-day holiday in the sun surrounded by turquoise water.

If a flight is full and there are seventy standbys on the list, that doesn't always mean that you won't get on the flight. Oftentimes the standbys are people riding on employees' passes and not real crew members. There are usually extra jump seats that only flight attendants can sit in. Even the pilots aren't allowed to sit there if it's open. Make sure you know what kind of plane you'll be flying on and how many flight attendants work it. Knowing if there's one or three empty jump seats makes a world of difference. You may be seventy-one on the standby list but only the second that's jump seat qualified.

Another hot tip is to have your watch set exactly to your company's time. You're allowed to check in as a standby twenty-four hours before departure and oftentimes you'll be fighting with several other flight attendants to get that coveted first spot on the list, the one that guarantees you the first open seat, or at the very least, the jump seat.

It's not unusual for several flight attendants to be working a flight and then running to catch a commuting flight back to the same city. You're really not supposed to check in for your commuting flight until after your inbound plane gets to the gate but in reality, as soon as someone can catch a phone signal, they're in the process of checking in. This sometimes even happens while you're still in the air or taxiing in. It can get awkward if you manage to get the last seat on the plane, right from under the nose of the lady sitting next to you on the jump seat as you're landing. People have gotten into fist fights. Some bitter losers will turn around and tell the company that you broke the rules and checked in too early, even though they were trying to do the same thing. It's cut-throat out there in non-rev land, man!

A sneaky tactic is to train your significant other how to check in for you. That way they can do it while you're halfway over the Atlantic and it won't even matter who calls in first when the wheels hit the ground. If you get busted doing that you can get in serious trouble, though. You can even lose your flying benefits for a few months. A flight attendant without flying benefits is no flight attendant at all.

Always have a Plan B, C, and D when non-revving. Even if your direct flight to wherever looks wide open, you never know what can happen. A cancellation earlier in the day can cause everything else that day to fill up immediately. Have alternate routes in mind. You don't want to be spending the night in the Amman airport, ranked as one of the nastiest major airports in the world.

It's 1:07 a.m. right now. I've been at the Amman airport for six hours and the next flight I MAY catch is in another 9:37 hours. It was an amazing ten days in the Middle East but now the pendulum has swung.

I never thought I'd be sitting in an employee cafeteria in an airport in Jordan, chilling with the baggage handlers and watching handball in Arabic, but here I am. A young man has already offered me some of whatever he was eating. I said no thank you but I'm curious what it was. I really am hungry.

I have a diet 7UP and paprika-flavored Mr. Chips with me at my table. I'm already starting to go a bit dizzy from sleep deprivation but I can't think about that. I have a long night ahead of me. I just hope this place stays open all night. They have departures all night so I may be in luck. No way I'm spending another fucking

$100 on a hotel after everything else I spent on this trip. I can handle this. It'll build character.

At around 11:15 p.m. I knew I wasn't going to get on the Delta flight straight to New York. No non-revenue passengers did. They had seats open, but elected to take cargo rather than people and so the plane was too heavy for both.

All the Delta employees and pass riders had options. They immediately listed for their partner Air France's flight to Paris leaving at 1:45 a.m. Since I don't work for Delta they weren't able to help me. They said the next flight would be in two days, maybe.

I didn't have anything to do so I just hung out with this retired Delta wife and a family of five from North Carolina. Their kids were about 8, 12, and 17, I imagine. The father patiently explained that they may be at this for a couple of days before they got out of Amman. Since I didn't have anything to do, they were my entertainment and I told them so. I was the comic relief in their non-rev misadventure. I made jokes and told them that if they just filmed this whole ordeal and sent it to Amazing Race, they'd get on for sure. They loved me.

For two hours I followed them around, living vicariously through them since I couldn't get on that flight even if I wanted to, even if I bought a last-second full fare ticket. I asked the family how they were going to split the family up if they only had three seats available. They hadn't come up with an answer and I said they'd better do it now, in case it comes to that, and they force an answer immediately.

The mom and the seventeen-year-old would go first, then who knows. The retired lady didn't seem bothered by any of it. She didn't care what happened and knew it wasn't in her control. None of us had any control.

If I had Internet access then I could come up with various plans and even buy a ticket if need be, but Internet was not to be found. That made us completely useless in all of this. That was the most frustrating part. It's stressful enough when you have to scramble for exit strategies and you have a computer at your disposal; it's quite another not having that, or a list of flights, or a departure board. I'm trying not to think about it and neither was my retired friend, who was spending a week visiting the Holy Land. She must have found peace. I must've too.

At the last second the Air France people ran over and took away all my friends. I should be happy because now they aren't competition for the Royal Jordanian flight to New York tomorrow morning, but I liked their company. We felt like we were in it together. We were just starting to get to know each other and laugh at our predicament when they were whisked away and taken to Paris. They started to run off but then stopped in their tracks to look back at me. No one left behind! I heroically waved them on. "Forget about me, I'll be all right! Save yourselves!"

I never really considered Royal Jordanian as a heavy hitter in my airline's global alliance. We tolerated them, but never took them seriously. I mean what does Royal Jordanian really bring to the table? Today, however, I don't give a shit about any other airline in the world. It's all about Royal Jordanian and I'll sing their praises for all time if I get on that flight tomorrow.

I had nothing left to do in Terminal 2 except to say bon voyage and watch Turkish Airlines check in so I came over to this local café nestled between the two terminals. My cab driver had told me there was Internet here, but he lied. I don't even have a signal. At least in the other terminal I had a signal that didn't do anything. I have a Vicodin and I'm debating on taking it. I'd like to have an outlet so I can charge my computer. At the very least I can watch movies or write in my journal some more. I'm at 54 percent right now.

This airport is in the middle of nowhere. It's all barren land and bedouins for half an hour in any direction. The employees hanging out in the airport employee cafeteria (all male) briefly put the TV on what I'm assuming is the closest they get to porn in Jordan. A guy was lying in bed with a naked girl but the sheets were pulled up so you couldn't see anything. The men staring at the TV were giggling like school girls and kept looking over at me. One raised his eyebrows and nodded up to the TV, making sure I saw what was on. I nodded back and pretended to be into it. I raised my eyebrows and smiled like a pervert. I gave two thumbs up.

From there they moved on to American wrestling. It's in English but with Arabic subtitles. I wonder if they can understand what they're saying or if they're just watching the action. I'm getting a great peek at what happens with Muslim Jordanian men at 2 a.m. at a desolate airport in the middle of a desert.

There are now fourteen men watching RAW and a couple more watching from the open window outside. They are into this shit. All eyes are glued to the screen. Everyone is chain-smoking and laughing uncontrollably at the most exciting moments. I've never enjoyed watching wrestling more than this moment. This is unreal. I feel so far removed from everything I know and I could not be happier.

4:10 a.m. I'm halfway through the movie Highway. I don't want the sun to come up, but I realize it's a necessary step in getting to my 10:45 a.m. flight. I have to pee but I don't want to pack up all my stuff and drag it to the bathroom. I left the café and am now in Terminal I arrivals. No one is here, not a soul in the entire terminal.

I'm charging my computer at the World News café but sitting in the black seats that aren't comfortable at all. I could easily fall asleep and think that maybe I should. I also think that maybe I should take the bus to the Tulip Hotel to try to catch an Internet signal. I need to tell my mom not to pick me up at the airport in Dallas tomorrow. I'll be boarding a flight (hopefully) right when I should've been landing in New York. This weekend is kind of screwed now, but I'm not really that upset about it. I'm completely alone in an empty terminal in an empty airport 30 km away from Amman, Jordan. This may very well go down as one of the strangest nights of my life and I'm totally appreciating that fact.

    5:10 a.m. People are starting to filter in. The sky is still dark. My movie is over and the battery is 94 percent charged. I'm listening to the playlist I made specifically for the next time I'm in bed with someone and I need music on in the background. My shirt smells and I need to change it. I also still need to pee but still don't want to pack up everything and move on. I'm not sure what it'll take for me to break down. My breath smells pretty bad, I think. I don't know how I'm going to talk to agents and explain my situation, especially if they don't talk English good like me. It's going to be a fucking nightmare. Even if I was awake and alert it'd be a nightmare. Even if they spoke English as a first language it'd be a nightmare. I don't see how this will all play out with me getting a ticket and a seat on a Royal Jordanian flight to New York City. It's insane to think that it's even an option for me.

    Who does that? One minute I'm on Delta but now I can just jump on a completely different airline and still get home, at no additional cost, just like that? I don't care. I'm really trying to stay emotionally distant from all of it. I hope I can glide through these hours like a dream and somehow end up in America, not really sure how or why it all happened. It really is the only way it can happen at this point. I'm so tired and disoriented, I might as well be tripping on acid. I'm just going to go limp and let nature do its thing and put me where I need to be.

    The alternative is to miss this flight and then miss the next one to London at noon. If that happens I'm getting a hotel room and sleeping forever. I'll regroup and check things out online. The only thing I feel I need to do is tell my mom not to bother going to Dallas at all but I think she's already there. I feel bad about that and I feel bad that I may not be able to tell her to forget about me and go on to Rochester, Texas, where my family is having a reunion. I mean how long will she wait before she goes?

    My Super Sexy Playlist is now the soundtrack to my plight, and that's a good thing. I'm coming up with a great idea for a screenplay. It'll take place between 1 a.m. and 6 a.m. in a deserted Middle Eastern airport. The story is only part about getting out of the Middle East. It's mainly about what's going on through the guy's head and the memories he entertains as the night drags on and on and on. What those memories are going to be in the movie are still unclear, but I love having this airport as a backdrop. I'll also need to find a way to convey the levels of crazy the guy goes through as the ordeal continues. I'll get Hermann Hesse on it.

People, real people, are starting to come in and order coffee. They're trying to wake up. They've been asleep and are starting their day. I'm not there. I'm fighting to stay awake. Joy Division, Surfer Blood, Slowdive, Raveonettes, MGMT, and Vampire Weekend are keeping it interesting. I still don't see any signs of the sky lightening. Killing time alone in the airport or with the employees at the Twin Peaks-esque cafe was tolerable and inspiring, but now normal people are going to be around and all over the place. These last few hours are going to be fucking torture.

I should take my Vicodin but I already feel like I'm heavily fucked on opiates. I have two Advil gel caps and one Vicodin in my right pants pocket and an Ambien in my left pants pocket. I've gone past the time for the painkiller. The sleep deprivation will certainly cause a headache sooner or later, so I probably should go ahead and take the gel caps. Once I have a seat on a plane, any plane, and we push back and take flight, I'll take the Ambien. I hope to God the flight is a long one and takes me most of the way to Texas.

I feel like a kid. I feel like a wide-eyed twenty-year-old on his own in a foreign country for the first time. It's not really a great feeling when I catch a reflection and see that I'm not that kid anymore.

7:19 a.m. I'm now through security and waiting to talk to an agent. This is where I was about eleven hours ago. They said in thirty minutes New York will be open and I can try to check in. I'm not that optimistic. It doesn't seem like anything good will come of this. I think I'm destined to live in this airport for the rest of my life.

I'm already thinking about how to spruce up the place.

Terminal 1 looks identical to Terminal 2. The layout is exactly the same and has all the same shops in precisely the same locations. I had to triple check to make sure I didn't go in a big circle and end up where I started. Amman has a tendency to do that to a person.

I noticed one slight difference between the terminals, though. One has a pharmacy. That's the only difference. Now that I'm on the other side of the X-ray machines, I can see that the similarities still hold up, except that instead of sixteen seats for non-revs, over here they have thirty-two.

I have no idea what's beyond the big wall behind me. That's where I hope to go soon. I know Immigration is back there and then an escalator. After that I have no clue. I imagine the day when I can ascend that escalator. I bet it will be like ascending to heaven. I have no idea what's on the other side, but I'm sure it's good. I'm positive I want to be on that side. I bet there's food, at least.

I was passing out in the lobby when the sun started to come out. I kept nodding off in an embarrassing way. I think I've caught my fourth wind because now I'm wide awake. I've been in this airport for over twelve hours now.

9:46 a.m. It's just getting silly how tired and disoriented I am. I feel like I'm in a college psych experiment. When I got into line to check in the guy said "Good Morning" to me. I thought he was very mistaken since it wasn't even close to morning but upon reflection, it was 9:15 a.m. I have a seat so it looks like I'm on my way. You can find me in 22F!!

I think this flight will get into New York at around 5 p.m. so I guess it's possible for me to make it all the way to Rochester by tonight. Of course, if I had Internet I'd know exactly what time the flights leave JFK and LGA and when they land in Dallas. I could make a plan of attack. I'd love to think that I have a shot at catching the JFK flight to Dallas but I have no idea when that leaves. I'd also like to know when the last flight to Abilene is tonight. There are so many productive things I could be doing right now, but I can't do any of them. Someone needs to make an app with every flight in the world on it.

It's going to be a major rush trying to ascertain all this information in the moments right when I land. Maybe while I'm waiting for my luggage to come around I can list for a Dallas flight. And an Abilene flight. And get in touch with my mom. I'm just glad to be one step closer. I really don't know how I'd react if I didn't get on. At first I'm sure I'd be okay because I'd just get a cheap hotel room and sleep for twelve hours but after I was rested and coherent again, I'd realize that I was still stuck in fucking Amman with no real way home. No matter. I'll sleep for twelve hours in 22J.

Yeah, not so much! I think my exhaustion ran full circle because I only slept for a couple of hours on the plane. I even took my sleeping pill and couldn't sleep properly. Sitting in between two infants didn't help. A third one was behind me. They didn't cry much but I was constantly grabbed and kicked and it smelled like formula and dirty diapers. The bulkhead and no leg room was in front of me. It was a pretty miserable flight all around. The entertainment system was sub par; it was just a single movie that everyone had to watch. There was nothing royal about Royal Jordanian but they got me out of Amman and into New York, that's all I can ask for.

Chapter 66

What could be better than being able to fly around the country for free or round trip to any other continent for less than the price of a pair of designer jeans? Answer… to be able to do it with someone else. If you're married, your spouse will get the same flight benefits as you, which is massive. If you're not married, every airline has some sort of buddy pass system set up. Some airlines allow you to give your passes to anyone for a very discounted set price regardless of destination or distance.

Every airline is different. With mine, I can treat ten of my nearest and dearest to somewhat reduced tickets. The price is right but the catch is that it's all standby, a very low priority standby. The silver lining is that I can assign one lucky person as my "Registered Companion" and they have the exact privileges as I do. Whatever I can do, so can they. The Registered Companion goes away when I get married. My spouse will in essence become the Registered Companion, whether I want her to be or not. Being someone's Registered Companion is like winning the lottery.

Because so many flight attendants are gay and we all live in a messed-up time when they can't get married in every state, we have a loophole to allow life partners of flight attendants to have the same travel benefits; thus, the Registered Companion.

Be very selective when you choose your buddy, you'll be stuck with them for a while. My airline makes you commit to one for an entire year so we make sure we don't give that gift to someone we've just started dating the week before. It's Murphy's Law that six days after you fill out the forms and make them your Registered Companion, you decide that you're really not that into her and move on to the next girl.

It's better to give it to a good friend, but not just any good friend. Don't give it to anyone that can only use the benefits during the busiest times of the year. School teachers are horrible Registered

Companions because the only time they're free to travel is exactly when the flights are at their most full. You need to find someone that can take time off in October, April, February, or May. October and May are my favorite times to go to northern hemisphere spots. The weather is decent, but it's not high season. June through September and the time between Thanksgiving and New Year's is just stupid. You're setting yourself up for heartache. Not only is it a high-traffic season, the weather is sometimes bad and can wreak havoc. Good friendships can be lost by trying to non-rev together during those months.

Some people will tell you that you should always make sure you're getting sex out of your Registered Companion; otherwise, you're not properly using it. That's just silly and pretty pathetic. If that's the bait you need to get some lovin', there's something wrong with you. There's shame in your game.

Again, date interline. Your honey bunny will have her own travel benefits and you can then make your unemployed best guy friend your Registered Companion. That way you can have kick-ass holidays in Australia and Amsterdam with him, as well as help him carry on his long-distance relationship with his amazing girlfriend in Sweden. The girlfriend in Sweden will be so happy that you're making it all happen for them that she'll let you spend a week at her praise-life flat in Stockholm and show you one of the best weeks of your life.

Chapter 67

The low point of most vacations abroad is getting out of the airport when you land. I'm not talking about Customs and Immigration, I just mean literally leaving the airport property, provided that they don't have a decent public transit system. Thank you, Amsterdam, for taking care of that in epic fashion! Sometimes worse things happen to you during your trip, but those things are unexpected. On every trip you take you're going to have to deal with exiting the airport, unless you're some kind of weirdo that just likes visiting airports.

You will be hustled and get the run-around and there isn't anything you can do about it. You think going to an official taxi stand is the way to go, well, not always. You think taking a ride from someone dressed really well is a smart move, well, not always. Last time I was somewhere dodgy was when I was in Buenos Aires.

I checked out the ride situation when I exited the terminal. There were several people trying to get me into their cars but I didn't commit at first. I noticed that well over half of the cars out there were black and yellow Radio Taxis. I figured they were probably the most honest ones out there, so I took them. They probably were the most honest but they still ripped me off shamelessly. The lesson I learned from them: always have small denominations to avoid relying on them to give you change. They never have change. Even if you see the exact change in their hand, they'll lie and tell you that's not really money, it's lottery tickets or Kleenex or some shit like that.

Don't be fooled by any driver with a crucifix or rosary beads hanging from the rearview mirror. It's doesn't mean they won't financially rape you. Don't buy it if there's a plastic Jesus or Virgin Mary on the dashboard. Those saint cards that look like baseball cards on the visor don't mean that the driver is a Christian and won't break any of the Ten Commandments just to get a few extra pesos out of you. There is no God in a Third World taxi.

First and foremost when getting into a cab in a country where you don't speak the language is to not let the cabbie know that you don't know the language or where you're trying to get to. Know the destination of where you want to go and how to pronounce it correctly. Even if you don't know any other words in that language, know how to say, "Take me to so-and-so please." The first time I went to Australia I told the driver I needed to get to Clovelly beach. I pronounced it "Claw Velly" instead of "Cloe Velly" and forty minutes later I was where I needed to go. It wasn't until days later when I took a cab back to the airport that I realized how close those two places are to each other and how horribly the driver had ripped me off by taking the most scenic route possible. I think we were somewhere near Ayers Rock for a while. So say the destination correctly and hopefully your bluff will work. A good follow-up step is to take out your cell phone and pretend like you're talking to someone the entire time you're in the cab. That keeps the driver from asking you questions and accidentally discovering that you're completely full of crap. If you don't want to keep up that charade then put headphones on and ignore the driver if he tries to talk to you.

If there are tolls to pay en route pay them yourself as you go through them. Oftentimes the driver will tell you that he'll take care of it and you can just add it to the fare at the end. "Wow, that's was nice of him," you'll think! Bullshit! Keep your eye on the sign on what they charge. You will be charged at least ten times that when it comes time to pay the guy. He'll explain it by making up some crazy excuse like the "Driving an Aries shorter than six feet tall on a Thursday following a New Moon" surcharge.

When you finally get to your destination he'll try to get you one last time, or take it upon himself to tip himself. Put up some resistance to keep at least some of your money but don't create a bad scene that could turn dangerous. The old trick of showing him your empty wallet works. Turn those pockets inside out and translate the phrase, "You can't get blood from a stone." It's frustrating and infuriating, and you'll feel completely useless/helpless, but at least you're where you need to be and the nightmare is over.

When getting back to the airport you can play it just right and not be screwed over too badly. You want to tell the driver that you're in a hurry but not too much of a hurry. If he thinks you have plenty of time then he'll go down random streets and purposely get stuck in traffic, or worse, fill up with gas while the meter runs. That's when all of a sudden all four tires need to be filled with air and the oil needs to be changed. He'll drag that drive out as long as possible and take you for as much as he can. If you tell him that you're in a big hurry, however, he'll try to charge you for some sort of expediting fee that doesn't exist at all. He'll say he can get you to the airport in time for your flight but he'll need extra money because he'll be breaking all sorts of speeding and traffic laws. It's a fine line and you need to know how to walk it. To avoid the gas station detour, check his tank before you get in; that way you know and he knows that you're not a complete schmuck. Go ahead and take out your air pressure gauge and check the tire pressure as well. At least give the tires a kick.

If you must talk to the driver, tell him that his city is your favorite city you've ever been to. Tell him the food is wonderful, their local sports team is the best, and the girls are beautiful. This might make him happy but it won't stop him from doing that thing he can do to the meter to make it charge faster. I thought that was an urban legend until I saw a guy do it, again in Argentina. He did something weird with some wires under the hood and I didn't think anything of it. By the time we got to the airport it read 340 pesos on the meter when it was only 150 going the other direction from the same spot. Only 8 of those 340 pesos were wasted at the gas station as he let the gas slowly drip into the tank. Some cabbies rig their meters so that they flip for an eighth of a mile every time they perform a certain operation, like flipping on a turn signal or flashing their brights. I know, pretty brilliant! Now I know why my guy kept running the windshield wipers!

Forget all about the NYC Taxi Customer Bill of Rights. Those don't exist anywhere but New York. And don't get your hopes up of stumbling into Cash Cab Bogotá, it doesn't exist. Ben Bailey won't be giving you money as you get taken around town. There will be no Red Light Challenge. Street Shout Outs would probably be a bad idea anyways.

So 99 percent of the cab drivers you come across, especially in poorer countries, will try to take you for all that you have. It's going to happen so just don't let it ruin your holiday. It's inevitable. It will suck and even though you know it'll suck, you'll still complain while it's happening exactly how you knew it was going to happen. Just suck it up, get through it, and get on with your holiday. It's smooth sailing after that, until the cab ride back to the airport.

Part 16: Ill Effects

What the small print says.

Chapter 68

I'm not going to lie to you and tell you that being a flight attendant is the best thing you could do with your life. It's not. Far from it. It offers you a great many opportunities and a fairly stress-free existence, but it certainly lacks some things that many find important.

I used to love being in airports. I could people watch for hours. I loved thinking about where they were going and what kind of adventures they were getting themselves into. The simple act of being on a plane used to be incredible before I got this job. I was perfectly content to just stare out a window and get taken away to somewhere for away. That's gone for the most part. The romance is gone.

It's not just the flying that's lost its luster. I also don't like people as much anymore. After fourteen years of working in customer service with so many people, it wears on you. I used to be such a nice guy, but now I'm jaded at best. I'm not sure if it's that I'm simply getting older, the job, or the fact that I lived in New York City for too long, but my love for the general public is rapidly depleting.

I think those certain foreign carriers have it right about making their inflight crew quit at thirty. Keep the work force young and pretty. Once you hit thirty, you're done. Game over. It seems unfair at first, but if you know that you have an expiration date the day you get hired, then it isn't a big deal. You know exactly when your job will end and you can make plans for what to do next. Those flight attendants don't dread going to work and they're actually pleasant and helpful to the passengers. By forcing everyone to quit at thirty (or whatever age you want, it's arbitrary) they are really making the employees happier and therefore providing a better service. The flight attendants appreciate their time at the job and don't feel chained to it like a lot of my colleagues do. There is a specific day it will all come to an end and that must be comforting.

I would love to try my hand at something else, but honestly

it's just way too easy to keep on being a flight attendant. You get used to the ease and flexibility of the job and no other job seems good enough to give it all up. Therefore, you're stuck on the hamster wheel until you realize you're an old man with very little in savings.

If I knew that I had to quit six years ago when I turned thirty, I would've come up with a plan. I would have no choice but to evolve. As it is, though, this is just a merry-go-round and I can't seem to get off. I'll never quit because it's too good to quit. So I just keep going around and around and around. I wish someone would put a gun to my head and tell me that on some specific day in the future, I had to quit. That would do me, and many other flight attendants in America, a world of good. Way too many flight attendants go down to sleep for their inflight rest and never wake up. I can't think of a more depressing way to go.

One of the hardest things for me to give up was time with my family during holidays. That can be very depressing. As a new-hire flight attendant you will be working every single holiday known to man—don't think you won't. Hopefully, you work for an airline that gives you double time for working holidays. The best you can hope for is that you're somewhere fun for a holiday.

Honestly, being somewhere random for Christmas or Thanksgiving isn't that bad. The crews really come together for those situations when we're all working and we don't want to be. We'll go out of our way to make it special. People will bring traditional foods and we'll decorate the plane to create the festive atmosphere. The hotels will often do that for us as well. Even the hotel in London will give us a feast for Thanksgiving and a party for July 4th, which is fantastic since they don't celebrate either day. In fact, Independence Day is us celebrating the fact that we're not British! I guess they're kind of glad that we're not a part of the British Empire anymore as well.

Another ill effect of this job, besides the threat of terrorists and plane malfunction, is the radiation we're exposed to. Passengers and crew are most exposed on long-haul flights at more northerly latitudes. That's because the earth's atmosphere is thickest over the equator and thinnest over the poles. During a flight from New York to London, travelers receive about the same dose of radiation as a chest X-ray; from New York to Tokyo, two chest X-rays. Some of us flew to London seventy-five times last year. I'm just thinking about it from a guy's standpoint here. Think about if you were a woman and were considering having children. That adds a whole new level of concern for the job and their health.

You may work at a small base where everyone knows each other by first name, but most likely your airline is a large, heartless corporation. To anyone that matters, you will just be a number. When cuts need to be made they will do what it takes without any regard to your personal situation. They don't care about it at all. This could be a blessing or a curse. Some people like to be anonymous and fly under the radar. Other people like to matter and be acknowledged for a job well done. If you need someone to look you in the eye and tell you that you're doing a good job and pat you on the back, this isn't the job for you. You are just a warm body and easily replaced, and sometimes the CEO will say as much in public to the media. Dealing with corporate bullshit and their evil practices is not fun. Just remember at the end of the day they want to make a profit—that's all they care about. That ultimately benefits you. You'll like the ruthless way they treat the market and the competition, just not the way they treat you in the same manner.

Not many jobs out there are perfect. Even if they were perfect, most people would come up with a way to find fault in it. That's just the way we are. We take things for granted way too easily and that goes for everything: our loved ones, our health, our job, and even our appliances and electronics.

I would be remiss not to point out the downsides to the job to give you something to think about. Your company won't level with you so someone should. For most people who take the job, the positives outweigh the negatives by far. BY FAR! For others, though, they can't get past one or more of the negatives. Being away from your loved ones for every holiday is certainly a massive roadblock in life. If you're lucky, you have a family that won't mind celebrating Christmas a little early or late, just to fit it around your schedule. That makes a huge difference. It's not really the date that matters, it's the time you get to spend with your loved ones, and being deprived of that really makes you appreciate it when you have it.

Part 17: Call to Duty

Get out there and make us proud,

"Straight" boy!

Chapter 69

That's about it as far as an overview for what to expect with the flight attendant profession. It's a wonderful way to go through life and you were very lucky to be hired into it. Don't take it for granted, and never get down on the passengers for making you do what you're paid to do. You have it very easy and don't you forget it. What more could you ask for in a profession that doesn't require a college diploma? Honestly.

This is a once in a lifetime opportunity and it shouldn't be squandered. Ask any former flight attendant who's quit the job if they regretted it later on and most will say yes. My old roommate quit and even after five years she didn't regret it one bit. After another five years she tells me that she applied to become a new-hire flight attendant for another airline, starting at square one, for far less pay, and she didn't get the job. She was devastated.

Never quit, just drop your trips. Technically, you can be a flight attendant and never fly. There are always other flight attendants looking to make a little extra money and will gladly pick up your trips if you're over it. If a trip isn't dropping, dangle a little bit of money out and someone will take it. It doesn't take much.

Time will fly by and every month you'll notice your seniority getting a little better every time you receive your schedule. That more than anything will keep you going. As more and more new hires come under you, it only gets better. You are going to places you can't yet imagine and will meet more interesting people than you thought existed on this planet.

Yeah, every couple of years we all hit that wall where we hate everything about the job. When that happens, drop a couple of trips to free up a block of days off, use your kick-ass flight benefits, and jet off to somewhere amazing to get your head straight. While you're hiking through Petra, skiing in Austria, or scuba diving in the Great Barrier Reef it might hit home that you're getting to do that once in a lifetime trip because of your job. You can have a once in a lifetime trip three times a year if you wanted to!

It's a huge world and you can start ticking off countries and experiences one at a time. The only catch in being able to have these opportunities is that you have to go up in a plane with like-minded individuals and sling some drinks and food at some passengers who are most likely happy to be traveling as well. Oh, and when you land, you're in some other city or country that's just waiting to be explored. It's not that bad of a gig. It's insane to think that some people much smarter than you are slaving over deadlines and projects and driving themselves to an early heart attack all in the name of a buck. Maybe they're not that smart after all.

www.ingramcontent.com/pod-product-compliance
Lightning Source LLC
LaVergne TN
LVHW051514070426
835507LV00023B/3113